502

Nationalism: Myth and Reality

Boyd C. Shafer

NATIONALISM
MYTH AND REALITY

ɔ | c

Harcourt, Brace and Company
NEW YORK

To K. and A. in the hope that their
world will be more peaceful than mine

PREFACE

This is an inquiry based on twenty years of reading and reflection into the meaning of nationalism, how and why it arose, illusions concerning its origins and delusions concerning its nature, and finally its relation to some fundamental similarities among men and nations. Because the subject is vast and the literature too voluminous for a lifetime of research, attention is devoted chiefly to France, Great Britain, and the United States, though, as the text will reveal, reference is made to other nationalisms where such comparisons will be helpful. Unlike most other historical studies of the subject, this one endeavors to study the interplay of idea and institution in the molding of nationalism. The assumption is that these cannot be separated if the sentiment is to be fully comprehended. The volume does not pretend to be a definitive work on nationalism. If it focuses the attention of his fellow citizens upon the chief problem of our time, that is as much as the author may hope.

"Political nationalism," Norman Angell remarked in 1932, "has become for the European of our age, the most important thing in the world, more important than civilization, humanity, decency, kindness, piety; more important than life itself." With this evaluation the present writer disagrees in only two respects. Nationalism has become "the most important thing in the world" not only for Europeans but for Americans, Asians, and Africans, in fact for nearly all modern men. Moreover, nationalism embraces not only the political but all phases of life—men

vii

have come to work and produce and live not only for themselves but for the nation; even their truths and their Gods have often become national.

The writer is a historian. More than is perhaps customary for a historian he has found it not only enlightening but imperative to draw upon the findings of other social sciences, of psychology, anthropology, and biology. He has no illusions concerning his amateur status outside the field of history, but he believes that historical work may be enriched by the findings of other disciplines. While only the author is responsible for opinions expressed, he owes much to the pioneer works and to the advice of Carlton J. H. Hayes. His debt to the monumental researches of Hans Kohn will be apparent to any student. Without the pioneer studies of other scholars like Johannet, Meinecke, Mitscherlich, Hertz, Delaisi, Klineberg, and Weill, the book could not have been written. His graduate students, slaving over seminar papers, have supplied many facts and modified many an a priori judgment. The University of Arkansas provided research and clerical assistance. The libraries of the Universities of Iowa, Arkansas, Minnesota, Chicago, Wisconsin, Missouri, of Cornell, Columbia, Harvard, and Western Reserve Universities, the Library of Congress, the New York Public Library, and the Bibliothèque Nationale have all opened their doors to him. Guy Stanton Ford, Roderic Davison, and Catharine Seybold read the volume in manuscript and Joseph Strayer read chapter five, and all four offered wise suggestions. Whatever qualities of readability this book possesses come in large part from his wife, Carol L. Shafer. Only because it is customary for an author's name to appear on a title page, does his appear on this one, for the work, whatever it is worth, is his only in the sense that he put together the work of other scholars and his friends. But at the same time only he is responsible for the views expressed.

BOYD C. SHAFER

January, 1955

CONTENTS

Section V
Delusions about Man and His Groupings   213

Section I

DEFINITIONS

Chapter I

TOWARD A DEFINITION OF NATIONALISM

ɔ|ɕ

A century of study of the group loyalty that has most powerfully motivated men in our time, nationalism, has produced no precise and acceptable definition.[1] Many French, British, German, Italian, Russian, and American students have tried their hand with varying but never complete success.[2] Other students have found flaws and omissions, and for the purposes of their own studies or influenced by their own political philosophies have proceeded to form their own definitions. Clarity has seldom been achieved, scientific study has thus been hindered.

A short, scholarly definition of a sentence or two, a precise definition which includes everything nationalism contains and excludes all that is irrelevant, may be impossible. Yet if nationalism is to be understood, clearer general understanding of what the word means must be achieved. Here an attempt is made to identify some of the elements commonly embodied in the idea, and to eliminate some of the semantic confusion that has grown up around it.

The confusion in meaning has not been unnatural. While the period between 1789 and 1955 saw intensification, especially in wartime, of the sentiment everywhere, different historical factors have been involved in the mak-

1 The notes begin on p. 241.

ing of each nation, nationality, and nationalism. Differing
political, economic, social, and geographic conditions have
influenced their development. The etymology of the basic
word, nation, helps little, for it comes from the Latin *natio*
which has the same stem as *natus,* and both come from
nascor, meaning simply, "I am born." [3] The nationalism
of each people has hence expressed itself differently and
altered with time. The American nationalisms, lacking deep
roots in history and evolving under different material conditions, are/not exactly synonymous with those of Europe
and Asia. The lateness of German and Italian unification,
as well as their different earlier histories, has made their
nationalisms somewhat dissimilar to those of older Britain
and France. A moat of twenty miles has helped to differentiate British nationalism from that of the French, who have
been little protected by river and mountain. The revolutionary national patriotism of France in 1789-1790, influenced by eighteenth-century rationalism, was more humanitarian than that of the French in a year of war and terror,
1793, while the nationalism of Bismarck's Germany of
1871 was mild compared to that of Hitler's totalitarian
Reich in 1939. The national spirit of rich, industrial, liberal
nineteenth-century Britain was not the same as that of
poor, agricultural, autocratic Tsarist Russia, though both
experienced a messianic zeal toward imperial expansion.
The nationalism of contemporary China with its masses
of illiterate people, its poverty, its communism, differs in
many ways from that of the richer and better educated
Western nations. Consequently, because the thing itself has
differed and changed, the meaning given the word has
varied with each language, each nationalist, and with each
period of time. Quite understandably, students, looking at
it from different nations, at different times, and for different reasons, have defined it differently.[4]

This understandable confusion does not excuse anachronistic and faulty usage of the word nor does it preclude
description of common elements in contemporary national-

isms. An often committed error of students of ideas is to tear generic words like nation and nationalism from their historical context, to read their contemporary substance back into the past, and thus to see in the past the generalities and universals evident actually and only in contemporary life.[5] The result is not only false history but further misunderstanding.

Any use of the word nationalism to describe historical happenings before the eighteenth century is probably anachronistic. Loyalty to family and tribe appeared in prehistoric societies. Patriotism toward city-state and empire existed in ancient Greece and Rome. Consciousness of nationality and some forms of national patriotism can be traced back to the late medieval period in France and England.[6] That patriotism identifiable with devotion to the nation spread widely and became popular in western Europe only toward the end of the eighteenth century during the era of the French Revolution.[7] It is with reference to this era that the term nationalism can accurately be used for the first time. Not until the first half of the twentieth century did this patriotism become for most (not all) men so intense and active a devotion to the national group and to the nation-state that it can rightly be called nationalism in the fullest modern sense.[8] The careful scholar must be aware not only of the danger of this fairly obvious anachronism; it is equally erroneous to say that the sentiment was always incipient and to trace it in contrived chronological sequence from origins in primitive and early historical societies.[9] Loyalty, patriotism, and national consciousness are ingredients in nationalism and preceded it in time. Out of them as well as other ideas and conditions the sentiment developed, but when *only they* existed, modern nationalism did not. Unless one assumes an unjustifiable historical determinism they might never have combined and developed into nationalism.[10]

If nationalism has been falsely seen long before it came into being, the word has also been used much too narrowly.

Scholars like to categorize and nationalists are eager to make a case for their own brand of nationalism. By nationalism today may be meant (1) the love of a common soil, race, language, or historical culture, (2) a desire for the political independence, security, and prestige of the nation, (3) a mystical devotion to a vague, sometimes even supernatural, social organism which, known as the nation or *Volk,* is more than the sum of its parts, (4) the dogma that the individual lives exclusively for the nation with the corollary that the nation is an end in itself, or (5) the doctrine that the nation (the nationalist's own) is or should be dominant if not supreme among other nations and should take aggressive action to this end.[11]

None of these definitions is wrong, but all are too narrow, too exclusive. Taken alone each describes only one aspect of nationalism. Modern nationalism is compounded of all of them and more.

A discussion of two extreme conceptions of what constitutes a nation will illustrate the inadequacy of any narrow definition. To some nationalists, otherwise of widely different views, like Renan, Treitschke, Barrès, and Zangwill, the nation was a kind of Hegelian organism, a soul or a spiritual principle arising out of the history and the nature of man.[12] To a modern social scientist this may seem either nonsense or pure mysticism, in any case a myth to be ignored or refuted.[13] Yet the historical and contemporary significance of this "myth" cannot be denied. Nationalists everywhere have worshiped the nation, if not as supernatural creation, then as something beyond the individuals and institutions which compose it. As this worship is part of the substance of contemporary nationalism it must, whatever the basis of fact behind it, be included in descriptions of it, and yet it is only part of it. Likewise the more realistic though too clever definition of Huxley and Haddon cannot be cavalierly dismissed. To them a nation was a "society united by a common error as to its origins and a common aversion to its neighbors."[14] It may be rightly objected that nation and nationalism are more than compounded error and aversion, that as institution and idea they have developed historically into concrete realities quite apart from their origins. It is true, owing to the almost exclusive study of perverted national history, that nations are misinformed about their own origins and development, and that they are often partly united, particularly in times of crisis and war, by hostility to their neighbors. But false history and aversion are by no means all of nationalism. They are two reasons for it but they remain only part of it.

Nationalism is what the nationalists have made it; it is not a neat, fixed concept but a varying combination of beliefs and conditions. It may be in part founded on myth but myths like other errors have a way of perpetuating themselves and of becoming not true but real. The fact is that myth and actuality and truth and error are inextricably intermixed in modern nationalism. The only reasonable way to get at the nature of nationalism is to determine what beliefs—however true or false—and what conditions—however misinterpreted—are commonly— present.[15] The following ten are here hypothetically advanced. No claim is laid for their infallibility or finality.

1. A certain defined (often vaguely) unit of territory (whether possessed or coveted).

2. Some common cultural characteristics such as language (or widely understood languages), customs, manners, and literature (folk tales and lore are a beginning). If an individual believes he shares these, and wishes to continue sharing them, he is usually said to be a member of the nationality.

3. Some common dominant social (as Christian) and economic (as capitalistic or recently communistic) institutions.

4. A common independent or sovereign government (type does not matter) or the desire for one. The "principle"

that each nationality should be separate and independent
is involved here.

5. A belief in a common history (it can be invented)
and in a common origin (often mistakenly conceived to be
racial in nature).[16]

6. A love or esteem for fellow nationals (not necessarily
as individuals).

7. A devotion to the entity (however little comprehended) called the nation, which embodies the common
territory, culture, social and economic institutions, government, and the fellow nationals, and which is at the same
time (whether organism or not) more than their sum.

8. A common pride in the achievements (often the military more than the cultural) of this nation and a common
sorrow in its tragedies (particularly its defeats).

9. A disregard for or hostility to other (not necessarily
all) like groups, especially if these prevent or seem to
threaten the separate national existence.

10. A hope that the nation will have a great and glorious
future (usually in territorial expansion) and become supreme in some way (in world power if the nation is already
large).

To almost any generalization about nationalism, and
obviously to the above ten, exceptions can be raised. Few
nationals know intimately their own "rocks and rills" and
the national states' desire for territory often seems to have
no real bounds. As everyone knows, the Swiss use four languages. In the United States the dominant group is white
and of western European origin but over 10 per cent are
colored, chiefly from Africa. These exceptions do not in-
validate the generalizations as these are qualified above. It
is not necessary to know a territory to love it or want it.
The Swiss have overcome their language barriers by being
able to speak and understand more than one of their
languages. A common race is not essential but rather a
belief in a common history of the dominant group or a
willingness to assimilate (or crush) the minority groups for

national actions. Further, all of the beliefs and conditions need not always be present in the same degree and combination. The Swiss may stress their common history and their common defense so much that they do not need the fiction of a common race or the tie of one language. Nationalism, however, is developed and strong in proportion as these beliefs and conditions are present, and the presence of all of them in some degree is essential before nationalism fully materializes.

A weightier objection may be that most of these ten beliefs and conditions could be and often have been the basis of unity and devotion in other human institutions such as church or empire. The answer is not that they could not apply to other institutions but that today for historical reasons they do apply peculiarly to the nation, that group of like-minded people living together (or hoping to) within the same political boundaries.

The historical factors in the formation of the nation and nationalism are numerous and extremely complex. They are described in Chapters II to XI. Disraeli approximated part of the truth when he, following Montesquieu and Burke, wrote in 1836 that nations were "gradually created by a variety of influences—the influence of original organization, of climate, soil, religion, laws, customs, manners, extraordinary accidents and incidents in their history, and the individual character of their illustrious citizens." [17] But Disraeli made the process too simple. A conservative politician, he here overlooked, for example, the politico-economic influences in the formation of the nation, those forces which led to the nation-state rather than to a city-state or empire and which in turn helped shape the nation. What he ignored is of as much import as what he mentioned.

The nation-state, or the political organization of the nation, came into being and became dominant in part because that form of institution fitted the economic organization [18] and the state of transportation and communication of modern times. Nation-states did not develop earlier because feudal, agricultural Europe did not need or foster them. The middle and working classes were not strong enough to demand them or did not desire them. The local nature and low level of industry, the trickle of trade and the bad roads did not demand or permit them. And the slow communication of ideas and the illiteracy of the bulk of the people prevented the rise of that national consciousness essential to their rise and growth.[19] Conversely the nation-state and nationalism are possibly beginning to decline today because modern technology, the volume of industrial production and commerce, the speed of communication, and perhaps the enlightenment of many people are making national boundaries obsolete.[20]

This is to say nothing more than that as a result of a multitude of historical, political, economic, and social forces a sentiment of unity grew within groups of people which expressed itself in devotion to what was called the nation. Nationalism, then, becomes a concept so complex and changing that it defies short, logical definition. At present by the word may be denoted that sentiment unifying a group of people who have a real or imagined common historical experience and a common aspiration to live together as a separate group in the future. This unifying sentiment expresses itself in loyalty to the nation-state whatever the government, in love of native land however little known, in pride in common culture and economic and social institutions though these may not be understood, in preference for fellow nationals in contrast to disregard for members of other groups, and in zeal not only for group security but for glory and expansion. In its most modern form it requires, as Rousseau advocated as early as the eighteenth century, almost absolute devotion to and conformity with the will of the nation-state as this is expressed by the ruler or rulers (autocratic or democratic), and it demands the supremacy (in watchmaking or military might) of the nation to which the nationalist belongs.

⌊Nationalism may not yet have reached its final stage. Even Hitler's totalitarian Germany did not completely submerge all individuals and all other loyalties. Nationalism may be transformed into some larger sentiment by the creation of world institutions and consciousness. It may disappear through the destructive conquests of a super nation or in class warfare. One thing is certain. It is complex and dynamic. Like all human phenomena it has several dimensions, its structure constantly varies, and it moves with time. As it changes so must scholarly descriptions of it. Tidy formulas do not fit a sentiment which is itself in the process of becoming.⌉

ILLUSIONS CONCERNING THE BASIS OF NATIONS AND NATIONALISM

Chapter II

SOME METAPHYSICAL MYTHS

ͻ|ͼ

Nations have been declared to be the result of every human physical and mental variation and of every environmental difference as well as the handiwork of God, destiny, and nature. No one has yet adduced sunspots, but regardless of fact or logic little else has been missed. That nationalities, national consciousness, and the national state arise out of something and from somewhere seems fairly obvious. That they arise out of the cultures and civilizations of men is a truism except to patriotic fanatics who see them as divinely inspired or as created by nature. But most explanations—metaphysical, environmental, human—are a bit less than proved, and, considered alone, are less than complete. Many of them are little more than a priori guesses which cannot bear the test of fact or reason. Some of them reveal chiefly the nationality, the rationalizations, or the wish-fancies of their authors. A few are downright ridiculous.

If we set aside metaphysical fantasies as incapable of proof, most other attempts at explanation have too little factual support or leave out too much. Little is known of the genesis of man's social groupings that would permit definitive conclusions concerning the formation of nations and nationalism. There has been much conjecture and argument. There are many myths, little that is certain. This chapter and the two following discuss some of the illusions concerning ways nations and national feeling began and developed.

In our present state of knowledge only broad hypotheses can be formulated concerning the rise of nations. These must take much into account and much for granted. They are far from universal, timeless laws. Even the most obvious generalizations, common ancestry and common environment, cannot stand careful examination. The inhabitants of every modern nation are of mixed ancestry and many nations have similar environments while what are termed common ancestries and common environments came into being long before modern nations came into existence. Facts are available, almost too many facts. They must all be collected, scrutinized, all the valid ones catalogued. But even when catalogued their multiple relationships are not clear. The difficulty is, What do they mean?

Illusions concerning the beginnings of the nation as institution and idea arise from faulty thinking, from the desire of some groups to prove themselves superior or from attempts to make a few facts or guesses explain too much. They appear most often in the oversimplification which fanatics employ because they are fanatics, which propagandists use to win converts, and to which social scientists and historians succumb in their laudable desire to be scientific. In all three cases the aim is a simple generalization which will explain everything in a one-two-three categorical fashion. The result is the same, another illusion. This erroneous thinking is often associated with false or partial history. Since, for example, nations now exhibit similar characteristics they are all imagined to have similar origins, and so *the* reason for the rise of nations becomes, for instance, the desire of the middle classes for markets, or a group's right to natural boundaries, conclusions which can stem only from real or willful ignorance of history and are demonstrably false. Or since, in general, peoples of different nationalities use different languages, language is thought to be a or *the* "cause" of nationality while all the other forces leading to it are ignored. Or since men are gregarious the nation is thought to be *the* inevitable result, when, in fact, their gregariousness may lead and has led to many other kinds of groupings.

To have a simple explanation is satisfying to the soul. But simple explanations of human institutions and actions are nearly always wrong, revealing only the naïveté or the interest of their authors. Nations and nationalisms have had a multitude of origins; these have varied with every people and with time. American, English, and French nationalisms appear to be very much alike today. They vary in genesis and history. Eastern nationalisms, the Russian, Chinese, and Indian, are now much like the Western but in origin and development the differences are many. This is not to say that there are no common denominators; it is to say only that the simple formula is an illusion!

The illusions are manifold into which scholars and zealous patriots have fallen when they have sought sweeping, all-inclusive answers where few facts are available and these explain much less than is asked of them. For convenience of discussion the most obvious illusions will be here analyzed under eight headings.

1. The supernatural
   The nation as creation of God, nature,
   mystical forces
2. Physical environmental conditions
   The nation determined by soil, climate,
   natural boundaries
3. Physical and spiritual nature of man
   The nation rooted in race, tribe, blood,
   instinct
4. Economic institutions and needs
   The nation as the product of the bourgeoisie
   and their demand for markets and status

5. Political security and prestige
    The nation as the result of the struggle
    for existence and the desire for power
6. Language
    The nation unified within and separated
    from other nations by speech
7. Social need
    The nation as an outcome of the human need for
    social life
8. History
    The nations as the products of their respective
    common pasts

   Most of the reasons for nation and nationalism that fall
under these headings may and often do afford insight,
especially if they are not considered separately and are
combined with some of the others. The intention is to examine what is illusory in them.

   When men have not been able to find a factual or material explanation of human institutions they have fallen
back upon God and miracle or some vague mystical force
like destiny, fate, and natural law. These being inexplicable seem to explain everything. When physics or ethics
supply no answers or are hesitant, metaphysics and the
supernatural are called upon. A nation thus comes into
existence because of the divine voices heard by Jeanne
d'Arc or is assumed to be the natural state of man in society. The nation thus begins and develops because its
members obey the "voices of angels," because they hear
divine national heroes who can no longer speak, or because
of some world force of which it is only the instrument.
Here is myth, exciting myth, illusion so strongly held that
for the believers it may become reality. With God as his
bulwark the good nationalist may feel anointed like Clovis,
who was baptized by Saint Remi with holy oil carried by
a dove sent from Heaven. Or he may feel himself in tune
with the wonderful forces of nature as did Rousseau or the

vital forces of humanity as did Mazzini. Thus, at any rate, he can avoid thought and find first cause explained without disquieting question.

That God created individual nations is no longer strongly held except in patriotic sermons or political speeches of the 4th or 14th of July variety. The contemporary world has few Bossuets to draw a scheme of political life from the Scriptures. But that God consciously created his particular nation has been and is a belief of many a patriot. Scanty documentation has made little difference.

The proposition is stated in different ways at different times by different men. The substance is the same. As early as the fifteenth century Jan Hus (1369?-1415) believed that divine will as well as natural feeling commanded that the Bohemians should be first in Bohemia.[1] In the first half of the eighteenth century the English statesman and philosopher Bolingbroke (1678-1751) thought it clear that God had constituted groups of mankind "very differently,"[2] and a half-century later the German philosophers Herder (1744-1803) and Fichte (1762-1814) were maintaining that God had created the nations as part of His divine plan.[3] To Fichte the nation was a true manifestation of divinity: "Only when each people, left to itself, develops and forms itself in accordance with its own peculiar quality, and only when in every people each individual develops himself in accordance with that common quality, as well as in accordance with his own peculiar quality,— then, and then only, does the manifestation of divinity appear in its true mirror as it ought to be."[4] The English divine, F. D. Maurice (1805-1872), in his sermon on the death of Wellington in 1852, started with the Old Testament and the Jews to show that the nation was the "most perfect condition of society."[5] In America a few years earlier John Quincy Adams (1767-1848) wrote to his famous father, "The whole continent of North America appears to be destined by *Divine Providence* to be peopled by *one nation*."[6] During the same period Mazzini (1805-

1872), writing of his beloved and disunited Italy, also fathomed the will of divine providence: God gave Italians their country and had thus provided their means of acting. God had, he imagined, divided humanity into groups or nuclei and had so created the germ of nationality.[7]

God, then, in creating the different peoples and in guiding their destinies, really formed the nation as means and end for man.[8] Often the patriots believed as well that God had especially chosen their own nation, just as, in Moses' words, the children of Israel were a "holy people" chosen "above all the nations that are on earth." [9] Like the "chosen people" of the Old Testament, many Englishmen, Russians, and Americans, for example, have each believed He had in modern times chosen them.[10] In England in the nineteenth century an Anglo-Israel Identity Society went so far as to declare that the English people descended from the Lost Tribes. Around 1848, in fact, every one of the great European groups was being told by its intellectuals that it had "the right to consider itself as the chosen people." [11]

In the late nineteenth and in the twentieth century patriots invoked divine providence less sincerely and more often to win votes, and scholars were wont to find other rationalizations for the nation. But the idea that God created the nations to be worshiped by the faithful patriots remained—as political speeches and military communiqués and religious sermons, especially in wartime, abundantly revealed. As late as 1930 a good internationalist, Herbert Adams Gibbons, wrote, "The good Lord put us in a certain country in the same way he put us in a certain family." [12] The only difficulty was fact. But, of course, the true believer did not need fact and the hostile critic could be silenced by the labels of "unpatriotic" or "red." There was, to be sure, no way to prove or disprove the belief. There were no facts.

There is no intention here to wrestle with the monumental questions of divine intervention in human history, of God's role in the political and social affairs of men. These are questions for the theologians. But that God willed the creation of the modern nations is at least doubtful. Nations did not appear until modern times. Most men in earlier history lived within other kinds of social groupings, tribe, city-state, empire, feudal principality, theocracy. If the Jews set a precedent they were not until recent times a nation but a people with a traditional religious faith and culture. Finally, it cannot be overlooked that through no other form of social organization have men so often broken the commandment, "Thou shalt not kill."

Under the pressure of Newtonian physics, the scientific method, and the eighteenth-century stress on rationalism and nature, the explanation of history as divine revelation slowly declined. Another illusion arose. As the late American historian Robert Binkley remarked of the nineteenth-century intellectuals, the most advanced eighteenth-century thinkers could not attribute an "anthropomorphic quality" to the nation so "they made it resemble rather those great synthetic generalizations of natural science" such as gravitation, and conservation of energy "which prevailed with majestic omnipotence in the world of nature." [13]

As early as 1651 Hobbes (1588-1679) found the justification for strong, absolute national government in the "poor nasty, brutish and short" nature of man, and in the natural laws which governed society.[14] In Hobbes, it is true, the idea of nationality as such is not present but his sovereign whose authority stemmed from nature was the monarch of a national state. Most Western political philosophers who came after Hobbes in the seventeenth and eighteenth centuries likewise assumed laws of nature, and they went on to project backward a contract something like a national constitution between the national sovereign and the national subjects or citizens. Cosmopolitans often, they seldom stressed nationality; but the imagined or idealized governments for which they found origins in the obscurity of a dim past were, nevertheless, national governments. Locke's (1632-1704) essays on civil government were discourses on the government of England as he imagined it had been and thought it ought to be. Locke, like Hobbes, was not directly concerned with the nation; he even thought separate and independent states evil. But the human nature he postulated for his philosophical structure in *The Essay on Human Understanding* was a *tabula rasa* written upon by national institutions, and his citizens of the commonwealth were propertied stockholders in the joint enterprise or commonwealth which would later more often be called the nation.

As the eighteenth century rebelled against divine support for the Old Regime, it substituted nature as first cause and motivator of society. As it did so the nation became the "natural" social group for man, and devotion to it was considered natural, good, and incipient from the beginning. To the romanticists of the Enlightenment like Rousseau (1712-1778) this was vividly clear. At some imagined beginning of time each man gave his liberties and powers to the natural association (or the nation) and thenceforth governed and was governed by the general (or national) will through a common (or national) government to which he owed absolute devotion (patriotism) and obedience (patriotic duty). Rousseau's good men, born of nature and shaped by a happy, patriotic education, formed a "constant, unalterable and pure" general will,[15] which was another name for an inviolate national will. Though he would perhaps have preferred a city-state like his revered Geneva, Rousseau gave primacy to the community, and beginning with him the "natural" community was increasingly conceived to be the nation.

To the romantic fanatic, facts mattered no more than to the religious zealot. When Rousseau descended from the foggy heights of his natural utopia to concrete proposals for government, he was less certain of nature's power. In order that the ideal "ancient customs" might be re-estab-

lished he advised the king of Poland never to leave his
subjects alone, to see always that through education they
again learned to love their country and reacquired their
"natural repugnance" to strangers. The king was to emu-
late Moses and Lycurgus, who by constant care excited
the natural love of country among the Jews and Spartans.[16]

Evidently, since Rousseau had to teach kings their duties, nature's design concerning the nation and national
patriotism was not revealed either to kings or ordinary
men. Or perhaps natural laws did not exist. That did not
perturb the romantic apostles of nature. Nor did it make
any difference to more sober eighteenth-century rational-
ists like the Scotsman Adam Smith (1723-1790), who could
deduce much from thinner assumptions about nature. To
Smith the state or sovereignty into which men were "born
and educated and under the protection of which" they
lived was "by nature most strongly recommended" to them.
Since it contained "all the objects" of their "kindest affections," their children, parents, relations, and friends, their
prosperity and their safety, it was "by nature, therefore, en-
deared" to them. "That wisdom," he declared, "which contrived the system of human affections, as well as that of
every part of nature, seems to have judged that the interest
of the great society of mankind would be best promoted
by directing the principal attention of each individual to
that particular portion of it which was most within the
sphere both of his abilities and understanding." [17]

With Smith the rational man, as with Rousseau the
romantic, that which was not understood became postulated. Through the dawn of the modern democratic era
the belief in a natural basis for the nations retained great
strength. To the pamphleteers and politicians of the early
French Revolution,[18] to Carnot and his fellow Jacobins of
'93, and to the German patriots fighting Napoleon like
Fichte and Görres, *"la loi naturelle"* and *"Naturtrieb"*
were the basic philosophic justifications for national patriotism.[19] In the United States to this day the fundamental

documents of independence and nationhood are those which appeal to natural law as fundamental justification for the nation. Everywhere people still believe that "it's just natural" for men to live in nations, and that it is "unnatural" for them to be "unpatriotic" or "disloyal."

The illusion continues despite the fact that later utilitarian and pragmatist philosophers and modern anthropologists and social scientists have found few or no natural laws that govern the origin and formation of societies and determine what kind will develop. In one limited sense the illusion has, it is true, a basis in history. Most modern peoples have established nations and developed nationalism and hence the institution and the sentiment have become quite universal.

But that an idea is universal at one period in history does not prove it is natural. There is no more proof of the natural origin of nations than there is that Germans decended from Mannus, the son of the god Tuisco who was born from the Earth, or that the Franks were the progeny of Francion by Hector. No one knows what if anything nature intended. A religious group, an economic class, might be just as natural or unnatural, and probably cultural development, not nature, determined their form as well as that of the nation.

Patriots for whom God and nature have not sufficed have often fallen back on mystical forces in the universe. These they have dragged up out of nowhere—often with brilliant rhetoric which impresses all but the most skeptical. Usually these amount to explaining the nation by the national spirit which, as the late Professor Binkley also remarked, is like saying corn grows because of the corn spirit.[20] Thus, for example, the Danish Bishop Grundtvig (1783-1872), best known for his establishment of the folk schools, accounted for the inexplicable but unbreakable fellowship of the nation by a "hidden but active life-force" which he called the *"Folkaanden"* (national spirit).[21] Thus the German romanticists like Herder saw the nation as an end product of the eternal *Volksgeist*.[22] Thus the Swiss political philosopher Bluntschli (1808-1881) spoke of a "national spirit (*Volksgeist*) and a national will (*Volkeswille*) which [are] something more than the mere sum of the spirit and will of the individuals composing the nation." [23] And a twentieth-century English student, Hanbury Hankin, was able to divine the "communal mind" of the nation from the mentality of the *Nibelungenlied* story of the fifth-century battle against the Huns.[24]

The mysticism went deeper than this in the minds of a statesman like Edmund Burke (1729-1797), a historian like Ernest Renan (1823-1892), a philosopher like Hegel (1770-1831), a patriotic zealot like Maurice Barrès (1862-1923). Upholder of British traditions as he supported the American Revolution and attacked the French, Burke conceived the nation to be a historically evolved, continuous company of people, institutions, customs, which extended in time, numbers, and space. It was a divinely inspired union of the historical, the present, and the unborn generations,[25] an entity apart from and above the individuals composing it. It was not merely a momentary aggregation of individuals nor was it the result of natural laws as the French Revolutionists thought. The nation was a historical, organic personality that embodied the "moral essences," the experience and wisdom of the ages.[26]

While Hegel may not have been a nationalist in the strictest sense, he worshiped the state and with his dialectic laid a mystical foundation for the nation-state on a high philosophical plane where God, the world-spirit, reason, nature, and history intermingled and became one. In the profound and seldom clear introductions to his *Philosophy of Right* [27] and *Philosophy of History* he proclaimed that each people was imbued with a world force endowing it with a peculiar spirit and special purpose, and that the state was the final "embodiment of dialectic evolution" flowing out of the historical experience and genius of a people. The state was the "march of God in the world," "the power of reason realizing itself as will." The nation as a state was the "spirit substantively realized and directly real." The constitution of the nation-state was "above and beyond what is made"; it was "divine and perpetual." Thus the state was a historical, a "spiritual organism," a manifestation of the world intellect above any concrete fact or puny ethical judgment of the individual.[28] Stressing what he called his historical method, Hegel paid little attention to historical fact in his grand dialectic, here taking from history only what he needed for the philosophic glorification of the state. While Hegel would, of course, have denied that he was a mystic in his view of the nation-state, he was little else. If his ponderous preachments on the state possessed any validity, it was beyond the comprehension of reasonable men, unless among these are to be included the fascist totalitarians of the twentieth century.[29]

Though Renan started with history he, too, arrived at an explanation of the nation that went beyond historical fact to some deeper metaphysical force.[30] Men were not the slaves of race, language, religion, the course of their rivers, or the direction of their mountain ranges. The nation was "a soul, a spiritual principle" arising not only out of common "memories, sacrifices, glories, afflictions and regrets," but also out of the historically determined will (*volonté*) to live together and carry out the heritage. Out of the common heritage each aggregation of men which was "healthy in spirit and warm in heart" created a "moral conscience," a "spiritual family," the nation. Hence the nation was two things which were really one, the legacy of ancestors and a common will: "to have done great things together, to wish to do more of them, here is the essential condition to be a people." So strongly did Renan feel that ancestors made "us what we are" that he thought the "cult of ancestors the most legitimate of all cults." The skeptical, critical scholar dismissed the divine and put historical mysticism in its place. Bowing down before the past he never perceived that while he made the past explain the present he had not explained the past: what made the memories, the ancestors, common. What seemed plausible analysis was partly based upon another illusion.

Auguste Maurice Barrès, one of the last of the French reactionary royalists, carried the cult of the ancestral dead to an absurd extreme, especially during the patriotic bloodletting of World War I. So ecstatic and involved was his nationalism as expressed in numerous novels and essays that it is almost impossible to reach the sense of it. What he seemed in his mysticism to reiterate was this: National feeling was a sentiment or sensibility based on the soil and the relation of the living to the dead, the dead of whom the living were only a prolongation. Nationalism was therefore but the "acceptance of a determinism." A Frenchman was only one who "became conscious of his formation," of the fact that all history had made him what he was, and knew that his ancestors in "terrible wrath" looked down upon him and watched him. The purpose of all history, all thought, all effort was to create the nation and nationalism, particularly the French nation and nationalism.[31] Further than this in affirmation without substance no nationalist has ever gone.

A nation is not a metaphysical or a psychological soul above and beyond men.[32] Individuals comprise a nation. They possess traditions and historically evolved institutions in common. This does not transform them into a living entity, a collective organism. A nation is not a being like an individual man nor is it a supernatural being.[33] It is not a collective personality, a collective mind, a collective soul. Such things are absurdities, contradictions in terms. A nation cannot think, remember, create, only the individuals in it can, and all of them *because* they are individuals, think, remember, create in a different fashion. Their thoughts, their memories, their creations may be alike or similar but they cannot be transformed into something more than their sum. Since each individual is different in personality and culture, it may even be unlikely that their characteristics can be totaled into some completely different product, any more than can houses, horses, and hoptoads. In any case to explain the nation as a mystical organism is not to explain it at all, for the explanation but substitutes an unknowable for thought.

Chapter III

SOME "PHYSICAL" MYTHS

ℑ|ℭ

There are other descriptions of the rise of the nation that have been less fantastic and have found support in something more than active imagination or false history. That physical environmental conditions, particularly the climate and the land, have helped shape human groups and the differences among them is easily observable and has long been recognized. Aristotle, who knew everything that the Greeks knew, discussed the relationship of environment and societies, and the Roman word *patria* reveals the close connection between soil and group loyalty known to the Romans.

In the early fourteenth century John of Paris, the Domincian monk who opposed the pope for the French King Philip the Fair, advocated a French national state on the ground of differences in climate and character.[1] In the early seventeenth century a little-known French-Scottish poet, John Barclay (1582-1621), after living in Europe spoke of a spirit proper to every region "which doth in a manner shape the studies and manners of the inhabitants according to itself." [2] Later in the same century the French Bishop Bossuet deduced from the Scriptures that "human society requires men to love the land which they occupy together, regarding it as a mother and a nurse, attaching themselves to it and finding in it a bond of union. Men in reality feel themselves strongly bound together when they comprehend that the same soil which supported and nourished them while alive will receive them in its bosom when they die." [3]

The eighteenth and nineteenth centuries also saw land, climate, and geography as major conditioning factors. Montesquieu's stress upon the physical environment in forming "the Spirit of the Laws" of each nation is well known. Rousseau was less vague than usual when, commenting on the Abbé de Saint Pierre's *Project for a Treaty of Perpetual Peace,* he wrote that the political order of Europe was in some respects the work of physical nature and urged the establishment of natural national boundaries such as rivers.[4] Herder, the early romantic philosopher, thought the physical environment, particularly the climate, chiefly responsible for the branching out of nationalities from the common stem of humanity.[5]

In mid-nineteenth-century England, Henry Thomas Buckle (1821-1862) tried to show scientifically how climate, food, and soil rather than race "originated" the "large and conspicuous differences between nations." [6] While the Victorian scholar of early institutions in England, Ireland, and India, Sir Henry Maine (1822-1888), believed kinship the original basis of societies, he thought that "For all groups of men larger than the Family, the Land on which they live tends to become the bond of union between them. . . ." [7]

When the scientific method began to be applied more thoroughly to geography toward the end of the nineteenth century and during the twentieth, more significant studies on the relation of environment to human societies appeared. Scholars such as Friedrich Ratzel, Ellen Semple, Jean Brunhes, and Ellsworth Huntington [8] tried to isolate specific ways environment conditioned men. While the geographers were not especially concerned with the origins of nations and nationality, their studies often lent weight to what before had only been conjecture. Nations began and differed, the argument ran, because of soil, climate, resources, and natural obstacles.

That these have influenced men in their views and loyalties, their institutions and groupings, their customs and habits, is clear. Men apparently tend to love the localities of their birth, the surroundings in which they grow up and with which they become familiar. They, in their lesser ways, usually regard them as Shakespeare did England—other Edens, demi-paradises, blessed plots. And as Scott sang, few men have had souls so dead that they have never said, "This is my own, my native land." Men tend also to be uncomfortable in strange surroundings; these often upset them physiologically as well as psychologically. Soils and climates do differ and certainly people cannot live without being affected by them. A temperate climate and a rich soil may not only enable greater economic production but a greater flowering of the arts than an arctic climate and an infertile soil where men must constantly fight the elements in order to eat and sleep. A tropical climate may permit easier acquisition of food and bring a higher incidence of certain diseases such as malaria than a temperate climate. Men can scarcely live at all at the most extreme temperatures or at the lowest or highest altitudes the Earth affords. Living habits at high altitudes usually must be simpler than those at sea level or a little above. On desert sands or arctic wastes social life can only be nomadic as the group searches for sustenance; in lush jungle it can be sedentary but hardly urban. A river, a sea, or a mountain chain may divide peoples and may make communication between them difficult. Where transportation and communication are easy, peoples have usually congregated and often unified.

All this and more is true. But however obvious the influences of physical environment there is no proved connection between it and the rise of nations. Nations and nationalism first appeared in temperate zones, in territories with comparatively rich soils and resources, and usually

where natural obstacles were few. But does this prove anything except coexistence of these geographic factors? Possibly, though the relationship is tenuous, anything but
direct, and the old logical error of *post hoc, ergo propter
hoc* may be involved. Nations and nationalism have also
appeared in nearly every climate, in rich and poor lands
and where the natural barriers are many. The only generalization possible is this: *At the least* physical environment
permits and sets limits to human groupings and development; *at the most* it may exercise some positive influence
upon the direction of that development and hence upon
the variation among nations. Probably it wielded a strong
influence in the early historical evolution of all historical
groups including the nation. What its precise influence
upon later societal development has been, cannot, for want
of scientific controls, be determined. That geography has
been but one of many influences is as much as can be
stated.

Each of the major nations today possesses a variety of
soils and climates. In Russia and the United States the
range of climates and physical conditions is extreme. On
the other hand, the climates of many different nations,
France and Germany, Italy and Spain, do not widely differ. Weather maps, like maps of the world's resources, do
not resemble those that mark political boundaries. Nor
are there in nature lines of demarcation which can be
called naturally national. Boundaries have been established
chiefly by diplomacy and war. If there now exist what are
called natural national boundaries, the nations, like France
and the United States, have pushed out to them. They
did not exist as boundaries until long after the nations
started, and have never been constant. Many natural obstacles, like the Rockies and the Urals, the Mississippi,
the Elbe, and the Volga, do not divide, and some do, like
the Pyrenees and the Rhine. The difference between those
that divide and those that do not is political not physical.
The sacred "natural" boundaries of France—the Rhine,

the Alps, the Pyrenees—were established not by nature but by Louis XIV, his predecessors and successors, authoritarian rulers like Richelieu and republican patriots like Carnot.

Finally, the most cherished belief of all, that love of the native land creates the nation, possesses slight foundation.[9] Men may naturally love the locality of their birth and childhood but scarcely the whole territory of their nation. They cannot intimately know, even in the modern day of swift transportation and mass production photography, more than a small area. The bit of soil upon which they were born, matured, and died may be forever theirs. It may be, as in the case of the Alpine region in France and the lake region in England, much unlike most of the rest of the nation. Or it may be more like some bit of foreign land: the Rockies resemble the Alps more than the Mississippi basin, and long stretches along the Hudson could be mistaken for the Rhine country.

In one unusual psychological sense love of soil and a belief in natural boundaries may perhaps have contributed to national feeling. Old conceptions of inviolable private ownership of a certain fixed area could have been transferred to political life. Francis Delaisi called this an "agrarian myth." [10] The sovereign family on its land then became the sovereign nation upon its territory. But this is analogy and not explanation. While the idea is plausible, the step between family and nation is large, and the nation would not arise out of family and land any more than would other types of political organization. The homeland affords something to be respected or loved, the climate and resources permit types of loyalties to arise and perhaps stimulate *these* rather than *those* types of thought and activity. But why national loyalty rather than loyalty to empire or just the place of birth and maturation?

Exactly when "race" became entangled with nationality cannot be determined.[11] So much ambiguity has grown up about both terms that it is impossible to tell when race was first thought to be a major factor. We can be certain, however, that this was in recent times, for race did not become a significant way of classifying men into groups until the eighteenth century. Not until the second half of the nineteenth century did it become a convenient catchall explanation for any and all diversities in human characteristics and activities as well as the alleged superiority or inferiority of human groups.[12]

In the eighteenth century scientists like Linnaeus, Buffon, Dauberton, and Blumenbach made the word "race" more than a vague way of naming any differing group by using it as a classification of men based upon physical characteristics, especially the degree of skin pigmentation and the shape of the skull.[13] During the nineteenth century the term began to be associated not only with physical differences but mental and spiritual character. Until the second quarter of the twentieth century few students, even among the most respectable of scholars, were able to escape the virus of what might be called race thinking. A defender of the peculiar institution of the American South would go as far as to declare that "the deepest thing about any man—except his humanity itself—is his race,"[14] and extremists like the German Nazis might even deny the common humanity. Thus arose insistence upon a common familial or racial background as a basis for nationhood.[15]

The early nineteenth-century German nationalists—Arndt, Jahn, Görres, and Fichte—were not racists in the strict sense but in the words of Arndt they claimed the Germans had not been "bastardized by a foreign people," that the "fortunate Germans were an original people."[16] Friedrich Schlegel generalized this kind of notion in his philosophic lectures of 1804-1806 when he asserted, "The concept of the nation implies that all of its members shall form only one individual. In order that this may be brought about, all the members must be at least descended from the same source."[17]

The argument varied as the nineteenth century wore on.

One race or a fusion of races made the nation. Michelet (1798-1874), the poet-historian of France, believed that "all the races of the world contributed to the endowment of France." While the base was the "mobile Gael," the Iberians gave "hardness and cunning," the Semites supplied "commercial-mindedness," and all the others contributed something vital.[18] In England Bishop Stubbs (1825-1901), the Oxford historian, traced England to "the blood in our veins that came from German ancestors," [19] and Sir Henry Maine pontificated, "The history of political ideas begins, in fact, with the assumption that kinship in blood is the sole possible ground of community in political functions." Throughout the Western world similar beliefs were propagated.[20] In the United States the historians Fiske and Hosmer less vehemently echoed the German historians Niebuhr and Mommsen in their view that race was a chief agent in history.

Racialism grew steadily, especially after Count Gobineau (1816-1882) published his *Essai sur l'inégalité des races humaines* in 1854 and Darwin (1809-1882) his *On the Origin of Species by Means of Natural Selection* in 1859. After these volumes it became increasingly important for the nationalist to show the distinctive racial composition of his nation in order to prove its fitness and superiority in the competitive struggle of evolution.

Houston Stewart Chamberlain (1855-1927), the Englishman who was more German than the Germans, carried this thinking to hysterical extremes in 1899 with the brilliant rhetoric and factual emptiness of his *Foundations of the Nineteenth Century*. To him—and he had many followers —all of modern civilization since the year 1200 was the creation of the genius of "Teutonic blood." "At the fall of the Roman empire in the place of the nations of former history that had disappeared there now sprang up a race of men, the Germanic peoples, just as creative and individualistic (and consequently with the natural inclination for forming States) as the Hellenes and Romans. . . ."

The universal divine monarchy fell before "the naturally inevitable formation of nations demanded by the instinct of the German people. . . ." [21]

Race thus became one of the stock explanations of nationhood. To convey the idea of common blood Heinrich Treitschke (1834-1896), the nationalist German historian, believed that the word "nationality" had to be used.[22] Charles Maurras (1868-1952), the patriotic French royalist, perceived France before the Franks, claiming it descended from the "Gallo-Roman type" of man.[23] The French psychologist of groups and mobs, Gustave Le Bon (1841-1931), detected behind the character of every nation the "unchangeable soul of race weaving itself its own destiny." [24] Sir Arthur Keith (1866-   ), the eminent English anthropologist, discovered somehow that the feeling of nationality developed out of "tribal instinct," fostered in "nature's cradles" in early man. Nature had separated "mankind into herds and tribes and kept them isolated and pure for an endless period . . . by real and most effective barriers in the human heart." [25] According to the English-American psychologist William MacDougall (1871-1938), nations in part arose out of a homogeneity of innate qualities of moral disposition and intellectual capacities which were racial in character.[26] A modern Jewish student, Bernard Joseph, was certain that nationality was a "force beyond the control of man and a sentiment . . . deeply rooted in human nature." [27] The outstanding German historian, Friedrich Meinecke (1862-1954), admitting that all nations were racially mixed, maintained that without exception there had to be a "natural nucleus which remained through blood intermixture." [28] And, of course, Adolf Hitler and the Nazis shouted that race was the beginning of everything, including the German nation.[29]

Whether termed "blood," "instinct," "natural character," or "inborn qualities," the explanation of nationality as a manifestation of race is arrant nonsense. What the English historian Buckle wrote a hundred years ago still holds true, "inherent natural differences [among nations] may or may not exist but most assuredly have never been proven." [30] No one knows just what a race is. Anthropologists, sociologists, zoologists, authorities of all kinds differ widely upon the meaning of the word as well as the facts behind it.[31] Since the definitions and the "facts" differ, any careful student finds it almost impossible to draw any implications or conclusions other than that in "averages" the physical characteristics of human groups vary slightly from each other.[32]

Little is known, except for a few bones, of earliest man. In historical time, races, whatever they are, have ceaselessly mixed and all modern nationalities are probably as heterogeneous as Defoe asserted Englishmen were. In the biological sense all European populations, for example, are mixtures of at least two or more races, of Nordics, Baltics, Alpines, Dinarii, Armenoids, Mediterraneans, Atlanto-Mediterraneans, Orientals, Iran-Afghans, East Africans, and probably a good many others.[33] In modern history boundary lines of nationality and language so overlap the lines of so-called races, and the racial lines are so confused and indefinite that nothing in the way of relationships can be established. Probably as the anthropologist Ralph Linton declared, only a race with women too hideous to attract men of other tribes and men too cowardly to steal women of other tribes could be "pure." [34] None, of whom we have any record, have been thus exclusively composed. In historical time every variety of man has not only been a variety but has wandered, undergone local modifications, and crossed with other varieties whenever the opportunity arose.

As races, tribes, groups have crossed, the genes of their individuals have mixed (*not* blended) with those of other groups. The result has been as many combinations and recombinations of genes as there are men and possible combinations, and in historical time these mount into astronomical numbers. What this has meant for the concept of race was concisely put by Professor William Boyd, a fine geneticist: "Since so many variable gene and chromosome structures exist and since these different gene and chromosome structures can form a large variety of combinations, we should be certain to find individuals [in any group] classified as belonging to one race in so far as some gene, say F, was concerned, but who would belong to a different race in regard to gene G, and a still different race in regard to gene H." [35]

Again, all that is possible is to classify peoples by the statistical averages of some of their measurable *physical* features. Even with these measurements the answers as to race will depend upon which features are measured, skulls or genes, bones or blood types. Further, while such measurements usually reveal small graduated differences, none affords ground for generalizations beyond the fact that in a specific characteristic these or those differences occur among groups. In Europe we know that skulls can be divided into the broadheads (brachycephalic) and the longheads (dolichocephalic). This tells us only that some Europeans possess broader heads than others and some longer heads than others.[36] We know further that the broadheads seem to be becoming more and more widespread, and that the length of the longheads in Europe seems to have been exaggerated—that "the average of no [so-called] Nordic European nationality succeeds in falling within the technical limits of dolichocephaly. . . ." [37] Certain other differences, in blood types, for instance, have been determined but none that can always be associated with other types of differences. Hence no exclusive racial characteristics that clearly divide peoples can be established beyond a shadow of doubt or, for that matter, bright, sunlit doubt.

If the differentiating physical characteristics could be pinned down once and for all, still little would be revealed about the formation of nations. No demonstrable relationship between physical and mental characteristics, except in abnormalities, has ever been discovered.[38] Skull and blood type tell us nothing about a man except about his skull and blood type. Brilliance, energy, strength may or may not occur in a group with broad heads, dark hair, and medium stature. But the second group of characteristics are not the cause of the first. Probably no relationship between them exists, except that both may happen to be characteristics of some individuals within the group.

If the relation between race and mental characteristics is impossible to determine, then we have little evidence that race is a basic factor in nationality. Empirical evidence directly confirms this conclusion. Racial backgrounds, in fact, have "nothing to do with the modern political nationalities. . . . Northern Germany is prevailingly Nordic, southern Germany Alpine. Northern Italy is Alpine, the rest . . . Mediterranean. All three are definitely represented in France." [39]

In our present state of knowledge, then, we know in point of fact little or nothing about racial mental characteristics. We do not know that they even exist. Further, we cannot at present disentangle genetic from environmental factors in the development not only of the group but the individual as well. No scientific way of controlling either the genes or the environment so that one or the other can be isolated and examined has yet been found.

Chapter IV

SOME CULTURAL MYTHS

ꙮ|ꙮ

At this point in our knowledge it would appear that national characteristics in so far as they exist are largely
shaped not by nature but by culture, the government, economic institutions and conditions, the family and social
relationships, by childhood training, education, propaganda, diet, health, the general environment [1]—by everything and anything that is human and peculiar to a time
and place.[2] Such characteristics are not shared in the same
degree and combination by all the individuals comprising
the nation. They constantly change as the culture changes.
Probably, then, human culture and not the physical nature
of man "must be considered the dominant factor in establishing the basic personality types [if any exist] for various
societies"[3] just as it is for the individuals in the societies,
for the societies are the individuals which comprise them.
The concept of race is itself a cultural invention. At best
it is only one attempt at scientific classification of men for
the purpose of facilitating further study. At worst it is a
way of exploiting a prejudice to gain a personal or group
advantage.

If the total culture, not nature alone, is for the most part
responsible for nations and nationalism, it does not follow
that the cultural explanations are all valid. Illusions have
likewise crept into the cultural explanations. These usually
are the result of overemphasis upon one or two causal fac-

tors. Simple answers are sought where the phenomena are complex and changing. Economic conditions, the power of the state, the struggle for existence, language, social need, and even nonexistent common histories have each been authoritatively stated to be *the most basic* or *the basic reason* for the rise of the nation. There is substance in each of these explanations; error lies in exclusive or perhaps dominant concern with one of them.

The best known of the oversimplifications is the Marxian: The national state is the logical outcome of the bourgeoisie's attempt to capture the market; or to put it another way, the nation is one stage of social organization in the historical evolution of the world toward communism—the phase in which the middle class and their economic order, capitalism, dominate. The government of the modern national state, according to Karl Marx (1818-1883), was "nothing more than a committee for the administration of the consolidated affairs of the bourgeois class as a whole." [4] Nicolai Lenin (1870-1924), Marx's greatest disciple, explained clearly what the committee did. "In order to achieve complete victory for commodity production, the bourgeoisie must capture the home market, must have politically united territories with a population speaking the same language. . . . Unity of language and unimpeded development are the most important conditions of a genuinely free and extensive commercial turnover corresponding to modern capitalism . . . ; finally, they are a condition for the close connection between the market and each and every proprietor and petty proprietor, seller and buyer." [5] The greatest Marxian authority on nationalism, Joseph Stalin, put the same idea more bluntly, "The chief problem for the young bourgeoisie is the problem of the market. Its aim is to sell its goods and to emerge victorious from competition with the bourgeoisie of another nationality. . . . The market is the first school in which the bourgeoisie learns its nationalism. A nation is not merely a historical category but a historical category belonging to a definite epoch, the epoch of rising capitalism." [6]

The Marxians are not alone in this economic interpretation of history and the nation. The predominantly bourgeois thinkers of the eighteenth century and French Revolution formulated a somewhat similar analysis which was one source of the later Marxian interpretation. Here, of course, was no façade of dialectic materialism but rather forthright declaration, stemming from the philosophy of natural rights, that a nation was simply a joint-stock enterprise originated by men of property, the stockholders, and that it ought to be directed by them. Political philosophers like Locke and active politicians like the Abbé Sieyès and Alexander Hamilton thus created a concept of the nation-state existing to protect and foster the goals they desired, liberty and property. The Abbé Sieyès made perhaps the classic exposition in his famous pamphlet of 1789, "What Is the Third Estate?" When he answered "everything" he meant not the people but the property owners. This view was written directly into the French Constitution of 1789-1791 and indirectly into the American Constitution of 1787. The active (propertied) citizens were, according to this widely held view, the only real shareholders in the great concern which was the nation. In the minds of many the nation-state, hence, became something like a corporation established in hope of dividends by the economically interested.[7]

Both the "bourgeois" and the "proletarian" interpretations have won many adherents.[8] The first is not unknown and the second vigorously argued in the contemporary world. There is no gainsaying a substantial measure of historical truth in both these economic versions of the nation. Modern nations and the bourgeois classes often rose together. Many of the most ardent nationalists have been of the middle classes. Members of these middle classes did demand markets, national markets, and their clashes over trade, profits, and raw materials have stimulated and sharpened national loyalties and antagonisms. Those Western nations in which the middle classes have dominated have often been governed much like modern corporations are supposed to be—for the benefit of interested financial and commercial groups. But an exclusively economic interpretation, like all other exclusive approaches, is too simple, ignores too many facts, leaves out too many other possibilities.

The drive of the monarchs and dynasties of early modern times, the Henry VIII's and Louis XIV's, their predecessors and their successors, for power, land, and wealth was a major force in nation building. Nationalisms like those of Yugoslavia, Hungary, Rumania, and above all Russia, where Marx's dream was tried, came into being without a strong middle class, and in Russia the pre-Marxian dynasty found strong support for its national ambitions in the aristocracy, the landed nobility, and the orthodox clergy. Human frailties, geographic space, and difficulties of communication limited dynastic ambitions and hence the size of the political units so that boundaries were established at what came to be those of the nation rather than those of continental state or world empire. Language alternately smoothed the way for the formation of a national consciousness and acted as an obstacle to its spread. Propagandists for nationalism have been not only of bourgeois origin but of aristocratic and in recent times even working-class and peasant origin.

Economic determinism, whether bourgeois or proletarian, oversimplifies a complex historical process. The hypotheses of Adam Smith and Karl Marx are among the most useful conceived by men in their desire to understand how human societies evolve. But they make too little explain too much, contain something less than a full answer. There may be a divine key to Heaven; there is no economic key to history. Nations are the product of all the historical forces, political and social and economic—in short they are one product of modern human culture and that culture in its entirety.

As the economic factors have been sometimes over-emphasized so have the political. That power-seeking monarchs were instrumental in building the early nations, that wars largely political in nature deepened national consciousness are facts that require little proving. The search for power certainly led to the building of nations, for the nations were objectives of power as well as the means of obtaining more. Again, wars between states and the propaganda accompanying them have taught men to glorify the nation and hate national enemies. But the emphasis on power and war has been carried too far.

Among the foremost modern advocates of the power theory was the nineteenth-century German historian, Heinrich von Treitschke. To him the state (and he meant the nation-state, particularly Prussia) was "the people legally united," a unity "inherently necessary," the result of the "political capacity innate in man." As a collective personality this unity was "capable of willing" and therefore of exercising power. Through and only through the exercise of this state power (concretely in Germany the power of Prussia) was the way cleared for the nation and the national character established. "All historical study" had, therefore, to "return finally to consider the State, for there can be no will without a being capable of willing. . . ." [9] Exactly what all this means is as difficult to ascertain as it is to determine what Hegel, upon whom Treitschke leaned heavily, meant by the state as the "power of reason realizing itself as will." If it means what it seems to mean, that the state is prior to all else and creates everything including the nation, it is absurd. In point of fact the power of the Prussian state was perhaps the catalytic agent in the creation of Germany. But the state is nowhere a mystical or supernatural force above society except in the imaginative minds of those who so will it. Nor can it be proved to be higher or more basic than any other form of social organization, than family or church for example. The state is only what historical processes and the individuals which comprise it make it. It has no being of its own, can create nothing of its own. As an instrument of those in control, its organization has, in modern times, been used to build nations but these nations could not have been built had not economic and social institutions and forces, had not individuals been working in the same direction.

Another of Treitschke's theses was that war created the nation. "Again and again," he shouted, "it has been proved that it is war which turns a people into a nation." [10] While it is far from proved that war turned peoples into nations, war helped create and certainly has accentuated national consciousness. Guizot (1787-1874), the eminent early nine-teenth-century statesman and historian, was not far from a correct diagnosis of his own age of nationalism when he perceived that consciousness of national unity arose out of "enmity and war." [11] In war both loyalty to one's own group and hatred of the enemy group are intensified. But again the idea has been carried much too far.

After Darwin numerous students applied the concept of struggle for existence to human societies and saw the nation as arising out of this struggle. In, for example, the view of Homer Lea (1876-1912), the American military adven-turer and writer, nations like individuals were subject to the evolutionary law of competition, a "Social Darwinism" which depicted nations arising when they became "mili-tarily strong and falling when they were militarily weak." [12] The English journalist Walter Bagehot (1826-1877) fully developed the idea in his *Physics and Politics,* first pub-lished in 1869. Prehistory, he declared, bound men to-gether into groups through "coarse, harsh custom." Out of these first "hereditary co-operative" groups those conquered who had "the most binding and invigorating customs," the "best customs" while the others perished. Nations thus sprang into existence, lived through and evolved out of struggle.[13] Karl Pearson (1857-1936), the famed English

scientist, summed up the argument with unscientific finality: Nature, he was certain, had decreed that the struggle
for survival was in groups, and the national group was the
only one able to cope with conditions.[14] Henri Hauser, a
recent French historian of nationalism, showed what this
meant concretely in the history of his own country when
he wrote, "It is the struggle, the armed conflict between
human groups which has created the nations. To force the
invader out of the territory is the elementary form of patriotism, the instinctive reaction of the invaded. It is enough
to recall the role of Jeanne d'Arc in the formation of the
French national consciousness." [15]

Now the doctrine of a struggle for existence, like Marxian economic determinism, is a fertile hypothesis affording
insight into the mechanisms of human evolution. But it is
only one among many possible and perhaps necessary hypotheses, and it is not supported by the empirical proof
required were it to be *the* interpretation of human development. An opposite hypothesis, that men are gregarious,
and seek therefore to co-operate among themselves,[16] possesses as much and as little validity. If men's actions were
solely controlled by struggle, then they might not form
groups but fight fiercely and alone with only the law of the
jungle (whatever that is) as their guide. Or if men were
solely dominated by their quest for survival and in the
process formed groups for this purpose, then they certainly
would not form nations but other types of political organization, for nations have often warred and millions of men
have been killed in their name. Actually the phrases "struggle for existence" and "survival of the fittest" have often
been no more than slogans used to bulwark the arguments
of those who wished to prove men by nature selfish and
belligerent, and thus provide a rationalization for a particular kind of society, the predatory. No one knows what
"fittest" means or if competition in struggle is more significant than co-operation in peaceful ways. Probably both
hypotheses must be used. Today we *know* only that the

survivors have survived. No other inferences are as yet more than inferences.

Even if the Darwinian hypothesis of struggle were fully valid for individuals, it would not follow that it would also apply to groups, to nations. Often nations have been described as if they were individuals. While analogies of this kind may be enlightening and helpful to poets, cartoonists, and orators, they can never substitute for concrete fact and logic. Individuals are born, they proliferate, they die. A nation is not born but develops slowly through hundreds of years. It does not create other individuals like itself. Its parts are in no sense related to each other as are the parts of a biological individual. If it dies, it does so slowly. A nation is not an individual. The same conditions do not mold it, it is not constituted in the same way, it does not act as one person.

While struggle has been a factor in nation building it does not explain why nations vary, why some have become strong, or why they originated. Jeanne d'Arc, a symbol of the French nation, rose out of the French and English dynastic struggle over territory and prestige in the fourteenth century. But the French nation is not only the result of struggle of patriots but of language and literature, of custom and idealism, and of a thousand other forces. Struggle sharpens and deepens national consciousness. It does not explain why it begins, what causes the common resentment at invasion, what gives the common feeling that there is a common enemy.

Among the stronger forces making for the nation has been common language.[17] Almost every student of nationalism has believed language a basic element in its formation, and this is not to be denied. But it must be emphasized that language has been only one element and certainly not always a decisive one. Language differences do not clearly separate nations. Two are spoken in Belgium and Canada, four in Switzerland, and many in the Soviet Union and India. German is spoken on both sides of the

Rhine; Portuguese and English on the east and west sides of the Atlantic. English, French, and Spanish are each the dominant tongues in many nations. Nor do language lines correspond with those of so-called race or with those of culture. Within Germany, for example, "where there is uniformity in language" there is "marked diversity" in the physical characteristics of the people, and in the "non-German part of central Europe where there is marked diversity in language" an approach to uniformity in some physical characteristics.[18] And languages of the same basic stock, *i.e.,* the Aryan, may be spoken by peoples of widely different cultures as widely separated by geography as India, England, and the United States.[19]

Nationalists like to think of their language as the common heritage of their nation, as the natural tongue of their people. Here again fact must be distinguished from fantasy, history from illusion.[20] In new nations like the United States where the immigrants are many there is no common *historical* language for many of the nationals. Their ancestors spoke another language, German, Norwegian, Polish, Yiddish, or Italian. And what is true of new nations was also true of the older if one looks back far enough. Many of the ancestors of the people who now habitually use French as their native tongue once spoke Latin or one of the Celtic or Teutonic languages, and many an ancestor of those who now speak English once spoke Welsh or one of the Germanic tongues.

In fact, not fantasy, languages are always changing, growing, dying. They are never stable, never the same as they were or will be. Probably an ordinary Englishman of the twentieth century would have trouble understanding the King's English even of the sixteenth century. French, one of the most refined and static languages today, can be traced in basic fundamentals to medieval times and to Latin but it has never ceased expanding and contracting; modern spoken and written French is quite different from the French of the fourteenth century, when it became the official language of France.[21] All modern languages can be traced to their respective origins but none sprang into being all at once and all are medleys built upon older languages which in turn are derived from still older languages. All, like the French and English, have been enlarged and invigorated through constant influx of foreign words and new words to describe new things in the natural and social environment.[22]

For some peoples in each nation the language cannot be described as native in one further sense. In no small measure languages have been imposed upon peoples by conquerors and rulers. French was not naturally spoken by many who were the ancestors of modern Frenchmen nor was English or German by many of the ancestors of modern Englishmen and Germans. The various governments, monarchical and republican alike, often forced the official language upon peoples they controlled by violence or threats of violence, by making it materially advantageous to speak the language, by provision for education in the official language only. Thus French governments forced the inhabitants of Brittany and Flanders to speak French just as the British governments compelled the Welsh, Scots, and Irish to use English and the German governments made Poles and Czechs learn German. Hence the *langue d'oïl* of the Seine governmental region became French, the East Midland dialect used by the English government became "proper" English, and the *Hochdeutsch* of the Hohenstaufens became German.[23]

Language differences, then, are not native in any long-time historical sense. They are native only in the sense that a man is born into a group using a language, acquires this language, and learns to use it habitually in early childhood.[24] As he learns the speaking habits of his family and neighborhood, he learns to think this language his. He is enabled to communicate with others speaking the same language while at the same time he encounters difficulty understanding others who use different words. He tends, in consequence, to feel a tie, a loyalty to the group using his "mother tongue." In this limited way language is a factor in the development of national consciousness.

Since human history has been recorded, men have formed groups. While psychologists no longer believe in "instincts" such as the "social," empirical evidence indicates that men have always needed and desired a group of some kind for the expression of personality, and, in fact, it is through their groups that they acquire a human personality. The smallest of the social groups, the family, is necessary to continued existence. A man alone is apparently not a man but an atomistic creature without meaning.

From these premises the conclusion has been drawn that the nation is an outgrowth of men's social needs, that it is simply a larger family through which men find an outlet for their gregariousness and a group in which they form and express their personalities. As Adam Smith argued in his *Theory of Moral Sentiments* published in 1759, the nation is thus conceived to be a natural development of man's social affections, a "particular portion" of mankind within the sphere of his "abilities and his understanding." [25]

To the writers of a French *cahier* of 1789, for example, the *patrie* was "a single family, whose elder members use their superior intelligence and powers . . . to increase the happiness of the younger." [26] Ardent nationalists as well as more dispassionate scholars of later periods went further and saw the nation as a means, perhaps the chief means of stimulating aspiration and creating and transmitting culture. Friedrich Schleiermacher, the German Pietist, believed that only within his nationality could a man make himself completely understood, and work with all his energy to serve the good.[27] To Maurice Barrès, French ultrapatriot, the nation was "the only complete, and the most solid and broad of all social forms." If nations were wiped out, the highest and most precious spiritual and economic relationships of man would be endangered. Nationalism was not just a fact of sentiment but a rational and mathematical obligation.[28] An English authority on international politics, Alfred Zimmern, believed nationality the one force capable of stimulating and maintaining self-respect because it was "the one force whose appeal is instinctive and universal." [29] Other students were less dogmatic but still saw the nation and nationality as basic expressions of social life. T. H. Green (1836-1882), the Oxford idealist, believed that the love of mankind had to be particularized somehow. He considered "the man whose desire to serve his kind" was not "centered primarily in some home, radiating from it to a commune, a municipality and a nation" had no "effectual desire to serve his kind at all." [30] And a famous American anthropologist, Franz Boas (1858-1942), who was no friend of narrow racialism and belligerent nationalism, was of the opinion that nationality was the "community of emotional life, that rises from our everyday habits, from the forms of thoughts, feelings, and actions, which constitute the medium in which every individual can unfold freely his activities." [31]

From the eighteenth century onward many writers have thus held the nation a necessary medium for human thought and action. Man alone, they have stated, is nothing.[32] He must have some group through which he can grow, think, create, gain human characteristics. This, to them, could only be the nation. While men had progressed beyond the simple family group, they could not comprehend a universal society or state. These were too vast, remote, and insubstantial, affording them neither the social outlets they needed nor a basis for their loyalty. During the cosmopolitan eighteenth century Herder satirized the philanthropists and citizens of the world who associated with one another "all completely equal, cultured, polite, very happy" with no fatherland, no one for whom to live.[33] The English clergyman Sydney Smith during the Napoleonic wars likewise ridiculed them, asserting "it would be difficult to say, whether complete selfishness, or universal philanthropy is the most likely to mislead us from that sound, practical goodness, in which the beauty of Christianity, and the merit of a Christian, consist." He thought that men might "speculate on worlds" but had to act in families or nations or they would "only sacrifice deeds to words" and rule their lives by the "maxims of the most idle, and ostentatious sentiment." [34] Herder and Smith were echoed often during the nationalistic nineteenth and twentieth centuries.[35] And as late as 1947 a French critic of the United Nations Educational, Scientific and Cultural Organization (UNESCO) scoffed at the internationalists as men "without color, race, or sex." [36]

No one can doubt that the nation has been a vehicle for the social growth of the individual and has served men's need for an object of devotion. No one can doubt that some kind of a group is a sociological necessity.[37] But these truisms explain little about the nation. Why the nation as the requisite social entity rather than a class, a church, an empire? Does not, in fact, the individual basically find expression in and acquire his human personality from his family and local community? The nation is not the inevitable, the only, or even the necessary result of his gregariousness. Moreover, even in the contemporary world where nationalism is intense and continually expressed, ordinary people in peacetime are less conscious of their nationality than of their individuality and their family. When they create—write books or paint pictures or compose music— they do not do so because they are Americans, Englishmen, Frenchmen, but because they as individuals have to live, want to write, paint, and compose. A nation may be one result of man's need for a group, but it is only one, and one that has, historically, arisen for many reasons.

The nation and nationalism are obviously products of history, since history is everything man has thought, said, and done, and everything in man's present must in basic form have evolved out of man's past. But all this is to mutter only pompous platitudes, and platitudes no matter how pompous explain little. History may supply the answers but history is not a cause of nations; it is simply the time during and the circumstances under which they evolved. The questions must be *what* in history brought the nations into being, and why did they develop. And this is to ask: How did groups of individuals acquire the belief in different common histories, or more pointedly, come to think they constituted a group?

Historians and nationalists alike have fallen into at least two errors when they have seen history creating the nations:

(1) That all the individuals within a nation really have had a common past;

(2) That the "commonness" originated much earlier in history than it actually did.

Possibly, as John Stuart Mill wrote in his *Representative Government,* the strongest of all forces creating a nationality is "identity of political antecedents; possession of a national history, and consequent community of recollections; collective pride and humiliation, pleasure and regret, connected with the same incidents in the past." [38] But this explanation is circular; it does not clarify what in history brought the common consciousness of the common history into being or what created the common history. As a matter of hard fact many individuals in each contemporary nationality, particularly new ones like the American, can scarcely be said to have a common past unless imagination is reckoned reality. The ancestors of a great proportion of living Americans did not participate in the victories of the American Revolution or in the tragic American Civil War or in any of the American "antecedents" before 1870 or 1890. They were in Ireland, Germany, Italy, Poland, and Norway. What is true of the peoples of the United States is likewise true of the nationalities of, for instance, South Africa, Canada, Brazil, and the Argentine. As in the United States many of the inhabitants of these nations, being descendants of recent immigrants, could not share in a common past unless one were fabricated for them. In older

countries the situation is different only in that the ancestors have lived on the same soil for more generations and
perhaps arrived at some conscious common group feeling
earlier. Here, too, care must be exercised. Inhabitants of
France before 1789 thought of themselves first of all as
Bretons or Provençals, as members of one of the three
estates or at most as subjects of a common king.[39] They
were seldom, except for a few intellectuals, deeply conscious of a common national past, and indeed for many
there could hardly have been such a past. Before the Napoleonic wars few inhabitants of what is now Germany primarily thought of themselves as Germans but rather as
Prussians, Bavarians, Hanoverians, Saxons, and citizens of
a hundred other states, cities, and bishoprics. For most inhabitants of the region there was no significant common
heritage; it neither existed in fact nor in their consciousness. A common group history then, if it goes back much
beyond the nineteenth century, is for most contemporary
peoples almost fictional. It is real only in the sense that
they have come to believe in it. The belief is real; the actuality never existed. In the new nations the ancestors were
from many countries, had diverse experiences and loyalties.
In the old the same was true further back in history, and
before 1789 most were illiterate peasants who were conscious of little beyond their village, their class, and their
own present.[40]

Some historians, catering to "the vanity of mankind,"
have been able to divine common histories long before the
facts of history permit such divinations and long before
the peoples themselves have been aware they had anything
in common.[41] As a distinguished American historian, J.
Franklin Jameson remarked, one of the chief tasks of modern scientific historians has been "to clear away those legends of fabulous antiquity, with which each nation . . .
invested the story of its antiquity." [42] Early national historians, indeed, saw their nations beginning far back in
history. Spanish kings were traced back to Tubal, grandson

of Noah. English history was supposed to begin with the giant Albion and Brutus of Troy or with Brut, grandson of Aeneas.[43] Later historians may have been more sophisticated but they, whatever their national origins, have sometimes looked far beyond the evidence.[44] The historian Treitschke gazed into the crystal ball of the past to see two strong forces always at work: "the tendency of every state to amalgamate its population in speech and manners into a single mould," and "the impulse of every vigorous nationality to construct a state of its own." [45] Bernard Joseph, seeking the nature of nationality, was by some intuitive insight able to perceive it "always in process of formation and development." [46] A recent student, Julian Benda, searched in medieval history to find Frenchmen then "willing" their nation into existence.[47] Good historians could even set a specific date for the beginning of their nations. Augustin Thierry (1795-1856), whose letters on the history of France won him fame, put the beginning of France in 888, the year of the final dissolution of the Carolingian Empire.[48] J. R. Green (1837-1883), whose texts on English history were long standard works, could perceive the beginning of England with the landing of Hengest, the Jute, in 449.[49]

Historians are obliged to seek the earliest evidence concerning the group which is their subject. But in seeking origins they are guilty of anachronism when they see in the origins all the characteristics of the later group, when they assert that a nation or nationality is beginning when only some events or ideas occur from which the nation or nationality might later seem to stem.[50] England did not yet exist in the fifth century nor did the English nationality. As late as the fifteenth century Jeanne d'Arc, the greatest symbol of French patriotism, fought not so much for her nation as to restore her rightful king and stop the fighting in France so that the Christians could unite against the infidel.[51] That model of German valor and manliness, the brave Arminius described by Tacitus, did not know he was a German nor did most of the inhabitants of what came to be Germany until 1,800 years later during the Napoleonic wars. Both nation and nationality are the result of long growth and the accumulation of ideas, sentiments, events, traditions, and customs. To ascribe, however, a common history to a people before they are a group, to supply a nation a common history long before any evidence of a common consciousness appears, is only violent and often dangerous exercise of the imagination. As Paul Valéry observed, belief in this kind of history "turns races into daydreamers and drunkards; it gives them false memories, it renews old wounds and leaves them no peace; national glory or national persecution mania drives them into collective unconsciousness, renders them bitter, conceited, and generally unbearable." [52]

A common past, except for folk song and legend, is chiefly the possession of but the literate *individuals* in any nation. Even for many of these it does not really extend far back. For citizens whose ancestors were recent immigrants, the common past must be created. Institutions, ideas, governments, languages become common to a group because of chance, political force, and diplomacy, favorable economic circumstances, social needs, and because historians write national histories. Nations, nationalities, nationalisms exist, not because of any inevitable, inexorable historical laws or metaphysical historical phenomena but because of the total culture of modern times and that historical series of events and ideas which happened to produce them in this culture.

Section III

NATIONALISM IN HISTORY

HOW NATIONS AND NATIONALITY DEVELOPED FROM THE TWELFTH TO THE EIGHTEENTH CENTURIES

ɔ|c

To write a full history of nationalism would be to write a multivolumed history of the Western world since the twelfth century and the history of the rest of the world for at least the last hundred years. This chapter attempts only to survey the origin of basic historical forces and ideas which contributed, often later as they developed in another context, to the rise of nationalism in western Europe and the United States from roughly the twelfth to the eighteenth century.

Beyond the vast mass of material which had to be examined, three major difficulties arose. Often students of nationalism, as pointed out earlier, have tried to find simple explanations for the rise of national feeling and have employed "either-or" instead of the conjunction "and." The present writer would be happy to find an explanation, a single hypothesis which would definitively explain why and how nationalism arose. But the reasons for nationalism are many, complex, and intertwined. The difficulty is not to find the *one* explanation; rather it is to be certain that many are examined. The writer is under no illusion that this difficulty has here been entirely overcome. Secondly, since the factors which have led to nationalism cannot be resurrected, they cannot be isolated, and

59

their causal validity cannot be tested. Those described here
are those which in our present state of knowledge and
climate of opinion seem to have contributed most. The
historian can only present what he hopes are the best
guesses on the basis of the evidence the past has left us.
Thirdly, historians and patriots often have tended to see
forces which later might develop into nationalism as the
thing itself, or to see a direct line of development from
certain possible origins to the full flowering of the ideas
when such development may not have occurred. To avoid
this kind of erroneous thinking is not easy. But the evidence seems to tell us that modern nationalism developed
slowly and became evident in the full sense only with the
eighteenth century and the French Revolution. When,
therefore, this chapter goes back into the late medieval
period, this does not mean that nationalism is to be found
there but only that certain institutions and ideas then arose
or existed which *later* became part of modern concepts of
nation and nationalism.[1]

Sentiments akin to nationalism are possibly as old and
as prevalent as man and society.[2] Each people, from primitive tribe to modern nation, seems to regard itself as the
center of the world, as somehow distinct, as "real men,"
and each seems to have evidenced some kind of group
feeling. Some men, especially the more primitive ones,
have been intensely loyal to a tribe. Some have, as in fifth-
century B.C. Athens and Sparta, been united by a common
devotion to a city-state.[3] Some have looked up to and jointly
served an emperor like the Roman Augustus or the sixteenth-century Charles V. Some, in ancient Israel or medieval western Europe, have possessed a common faith in
a creed or in a religious leader. Some have held it an honor
or duty to be a member of a feudal class as in tenth-century
France. Because of loyalty or compulsion, some have followed an absolute king such as Louis XIV. Some have
lived and fought unitedly, as in Nazi Germany, because
of a belief in a master race. Some, the Marxian commu-

nists, for example, have believed themselves bound together as a class by inexorable material law. Men have been, then, united by belief in or loyalty to tribe, city-state, emperor, creed, feudal class, monarchy, race, and economic law.

These loyalties are chiefly to be distinguished from modern nationalism by the object of the loyalty. In some of the ancient Greek states the patriotic devotion of the citizens (not the slaves or other inhabitants) to their city, possibly cannot be distinguished in any other way. They are also different because today not just some but nearly *all* men are principally and most significantly united and divided by their devotion to only *one* object, their own nation.

The nation as institution and symbol, it must be emphasized, has meant different things; conceptions have varied with time, place, and the individual. Usually, however, the word refers to (1) a definite state which in early modern times was dynastic and in modern times has been democratic or dictatorial,[4] (2) a definite territory though it has varied in size and seldom has been considered large enough, and (3) a group of people who possess a distinctive common culture—language, literature, history, and a common hope to live together in the future.[5] The major problem here is to determine how, for our own time, the common state, territory, and culture became established and how men became devoted to them, that is, loyal to the nation.

Historically it is possible to trace the origins of modern nations at least to the break-up of Charlemagne's empire when western Europe was roughly split into Latin and Germanic sections.[6] But neither well-developed nations nor widespread national feeling can be said to exist for hundreds of years thereafter. As Professor Joseph Strayer has observed, "The scale of allegiance [during the Middle Ages] of most men would have gone something like this: I am first of all a Christian, second a Burgundian, and only third a Frenchman."[7] A few of the Western nations, par-

ticularly England and France, began to emerge into some
definite form beyond the local feudal state or domain before the end of the twelfth century, and national consciousness arose still later.[8] No definite dates, of course, can be
set; both the extension of government and territory and
the realization of a common culture necessary for the creation of the nation were slow, occurring over a long period
of time. Nation building began without planning or design, and usually proceeded that way; it was not a continuous but an intermittent and sporadic process; and it still
goes on.

While the forces which early built the nation cannot
be precisely isolated and evaluated, the royal dynasties
which were at first but strong feudal families were of major significance. If René Johannet, the French historian
of nationalism, exaggerated, he was partly right when he
wrote, "The cause of the statue is not the marble but the
artist. In the case of nationality, it is primarily the dynasty." [9] In France and England as well as later in Spain,
Germany, Italy, and Russia, the strongest and perhaps
luckiest noble families won the territory and, with their
supporters, created the monarchical governments which
became national.

At the beginning and through their history these families
primarily desired territory, wealth, prestige, and power.[10]
They did not think that they were creating nations and
certainly during their early years little national feeling
existed anywhere in their domains. In France especially,
and in England usually, the chief feudal lord, the king,
simply tried to enlarge his own domain and his own feudal
power. The first he accomplished through war and conquest, diplomacy and duplicity, marriage and purchase,
inheritance, legal and illegal confiscation of feudal vassals'
property, and perhaps through fortuitous circumstance.
The second he gained through the provision of royal laws,
the levying of royal taxes, the creation of an official class
(especially lawyers) dependent upon the monarchy, and the

general substitution, whenever possible, of royal authority
for what had been the rule of lesser and more local feudal
princes or for the claims of the universal Church.

The process is most clearly to be seen in France from
about the reign of Philip Augustus (King, 1180-1223) to
the final consolidation and glorification of monarchical
rule of Louis XIV (1643-1715).[11] Slowly pushing out from
Paris the Capetian kings and their successors,[12] the Valois
and Bourbons, acquired in piecemeal fashion nearly all
of modern continental France by the end of the seventeenth century. During the same period they were able to
establish effective royal control over it. One acquisition
led to another; each one made the central monarchy relatively stronger than its rivals and better able therefore to
acquire more territory, more power. Success facilitated further success. As the monarchy won territory, it acquired
greater and more diversified resources. The new territories
and resources supplemented the old. The original domain
of the Capetian kings was chiefly agricultural. The conquest of Normandy (1204) opened the lower Seine Valley
and the acquisition of the Midi (1226-1271) brought
wealthy southern towns and an outlet on the Mediterranean. When the dynasty obtained the province of Champagne, it obtained a center of trade and a major trade route
and further enriched itself beyond most of its rivals. As
the dynasties brought their widely scattered territories into
one continuous area, they could defend the boundaries of
their domains more easily and concentrate their energies
better than other feudal lords.[13] The more the royal holdings grew in comparison with those of rivals, the more
likely they would grow further. Larger territories usually
meant more power and more power enabled more conquests.

This aggrandizement of the French monarchy took five
hundred years. The process was halting and was not without rebuffs and retreats. Territory once gained was often
lost again in war or by inept bargaining, and it was often

given away to a younger son or favorite for his personal domain or to a daughter as a dowry. The French kings were not all competent, strong, aggressive. But from Philip Augustus they were often shrewd in building their terri- tories. So successful were they that one could imagine in their history, as have a good many French historians, either unbelievable luck or the work of mystical forces.[14] How else, except, of course, by their obvious biological potency, could the circumstance that the Capetians did not fail to have direct male heirs in the family for over three hundred years be explained?

The story of the growth of the domain of the Capetian, Valois, and Bourbon kings is well known and need not be retold here except briefly to illustrate the creation of the territorial basis of the French nation. Starting with divided and scattered small bits of land in the north center of what is now France, with little more than the Ile de France around Paris, they expanded slowly until their lands reached the Pyrenees, the Rhine, the Atlantic, and the North Sea. Decisive progress began toward the end of the twelfth century when Philip Augustus acquired vast lands in ways that were to become typical.[15] Through his mar- riage and by force of arms he obtained Artois and the counties of Amiens, Vermandois, Valois, and Montdidier. On the excuse that the English King John, his vassal, would not appear at the French court to answer accusa- tions against him, Philip confiscated John's fiefs on the continent [16]—Normandy, Anjou, Maine, Touraine, and Poitou. He took the county of Alençon on the death of its lord, Robert IV. Thus Philip controlled the valleys of major rivers—the Seine, the Oise, the Somme, and the Artois—covered Paris to the west, opened communication to the sea on the north and west, and ruled domains run- ning through the middle of France from the north through Auvergne in the south.

Subsequent kings, through early modern times, Philip III (1270-1285), Philip IV (1285-1314), Louis XI (1461-

1483), and Charles VIII (1483-1498), added peaceably or forcibly nearly all the rest of what is now France except scattered lands to the north and northeast.[17] The otherwise insignificant Philip III (the "Bold") took the remainder of Languedoc when the feudal rulers died without an heir.[18] His son's marriage to Jeanne of Champagne brought that rich eastern province as well as southern Navarre to France when the son became Philip IV (the "Fair"). By a legal decree Philip the Fair confiscated La Marche and Angoulême in the southwest. After victories in an early war against the Count of Flanders he annexed Lille, Douai, and Bethune in the extreme north. And through the marriage of his second son he acquired a claim to Franche-Comté, though this province was not permanently won until much later. When the Capetian line ran out in 1328, after more than three hundred years of continuous rule, only the Holy Roman Empire provinces of Dauphiné, Franche-Comté, Provence, Alsace and Lorraine, and the feudal provinces of Burgundy, Brittany, Guienne-Gascony, and Flanders, and scattered minor cities and fiefs were partially or wholly outside the domination of the monarchy. Dauphiné was purchased in 1349.

During the Hundred Years' War, 1337-1453, lands changed hands often and rapidly. Several times the French kings, now of the Valois family, seemed about to lose all or much of their domains. But at the end the French pushed the English almost off the continent, took their last important continental possession, Guienne, and the Valois dynasty remained in control with its lands, France, vastly expanded.

When Louis XI ascended the throne in 1461 feudalism might have reasserted itself and one great lord, the Duke of Burgundy, might have become more powerful than the King of France. But again fortune favored the French royal family. Louis XI, his daughter Anne de Beaujeu, who served as regent for his young son, and the son, Charles VIII, were astute and ambitious rulers. Louis crushed his feudal opponents like the Duke d'Alençon, the Duke de Nemours, and the Count d'Armagnac, most of whom were not too able. He obtained Provence when its last ruler died without an heir. And after the overly ambitious Duke of Burgundy was killed in a battle against the Duke of Lorraine, Louis was able to take possession of much of his domain through confiscation, clever diplomacy, and the betrothal of the dauphin, later Charles VIII, to a Burgundian princess. The next territorial objective of importance was Brittany. In the so-called "Foolish War" of 1486-1488, the Duke of Brittany, Francis II, was defeated and compelled to promise he would not give his daughter in marriage without the consent of the French king. When the Duke died soon after, Charles VIII saw the opportunity. Whoever married the daughter Anne would obtain Brittany. While the future emperor of the Holy Roman Empire, Maximilian, bargained for Anne's hand, Charles secretly negotiated marriage for himself. That Anne was forty and he was only twenty-one made no difference. Land meant more than a woman. The prize was Brittany and the enlargement of the royal territory and power.

For the next half-century the French monarchs vainly tried to expand further, particularly in Italy, while defending what they had already acquired. For another half-century weak rulers, internal dissensions, and disputes over the succession to the throne rendered further expansion impossible. Even the man who restored order to the kingdom, Henry IV (1589-1610), the first Bourbon, could do little more than validate and consolidate the claims of the monarchy. Not until the rule of Richelieu (1624-1642) and the reign of Louis XIV did territorial accumulation of consequence begin again. Intervening in the Thirty Years' War, Richelieu increased the royal territory by the Three Bishoprics and Alsace (except Strasbourg). Through four major wars against much of Europe and through not always clever diplomacy Louis XIV pushed France's frontiers still further north and east, gaining part of the province of Flanders, Franche-Comté, and a few cities—Strasbourg and Dunkirk being the most important. With the exception of Lorraine, acquired in 1766 on the death of its ruler, the father-in-law of Louis XV, and minor border rectifications, the European territory of the French nation was complete. The "national" frontiers of France, the Alps, the Pyrenees, the Rhine, the Atlantic, could now become "natural," though they had been attained by means other than nature—by force, guile, marriage, inheritance, and purchase. They were natural only in the sense that a particular group of creatures of nature, Frenchmen, had attained them.

The role of the dynasties in building the territorial foundations of other nations may not have been as obvious nor as decisive as it was in France. In England, however, and later in Russia, Germany, and Italy, royal families played vital although differing roles as they sought to enlarge their personal domains. In every case it was not so much the extension of national "royal" power as the enlargement of the king's personal domain which created the territorial basis for the nation. The kings were seldom nationalistic in any modern sense.[19]

So important was dynastic striving for territory in the early history of nation building that it would be easy to overstress it and ignore other forces of equal importance. As the dynasties extended their domains they usually also built personal governmental agencies, executive, legislative, judicial, and administrative institutions.[20] These *later* would become the national agencies and institutions. Sometimes, it is true, national political institutions were beginning to grow, partly in opposition to the royal power, as in the case of the English Parliament. But in France and England early, and in Russia, Germany, and Italy later, the monarchical state tended to shape the society and attempted with great success to centralize and to unify and thus to make the society over into a unit that was powerful and could be conveniently governed and led.[21] Here

again, as in the case of territory, the monarchs were seeking not national but personal power and glory. Often they
would have preferred to be building a personal empire
like that of the Hapsburgs and Charles V in the sixteenth
century. Perhaps it is to be regretted in the light of subsequent events that geographic space, poor communication,
and intense personal rivalries prevented one ruler for all
of Europe. As events happened, no one ruler could become
strong enough, and any one monarch who so threatened
immediately became the object of attack by the others.
The result was not one empire but a series of independent
monarchical and later national states.

The chief object of the monarchs was to enlarge their
domain and intensify their sway over it. It was to build a
state, a dynastic state for the purpose of furthering the
power and glory of the prince. It was primarily *étatism,*
not nationalism, which characterized the governments of
the Bourbons and Tudors and most other dynasties.[22] If
the national interests were considered, they were regarded
as synonymous with those of the monarch. While no kings
ever said, *"La nation, c'est moi,"* they often so thought
and acted. And when they did they were establishing the
governmental as well as the territorial foundation of the
modern nation. In order to gain and retain power they
had to create central governmental agencies. They had
to obtain money through centrally levied and collected
taxes, to establish a royal army and navy, and to erect a
superior court system. And to carry out their will and government they had to have a great number of loyal royal
officials. While the taxes, armed forces, courts, and officials
were not national at first, they would become increasingly
so. Without conscious design, then, the nation-state was
coming into being.

Again, these developments took place in different ways
at different times in different countries. In early Norman
England, but not in the France of the same period, all
vassals were directly responsible to the king, and, except

in border lands, did not possess the rights to administer high justice, coin money, or wage private war. Later in England the nobility and upper middle class shared the royal power more than in most countries, while in France the monarchy, with its allies from the middle classes, played a more significant role, the aristocracy usually opposing centralizing tendencies. So far as the nation-state was concerned, the result was much the same. As the royal central government became more extensive and powerful, the governmental bases of the nation were being laid down.

In England the kings from the Norman William the Conqueror (1066-1087) to the Stuart James I (1603-1625), though they at times were forced to share their power with a parliament representative of the upper classes, used their ancient feudal rights as well as their military might to strengthen the central government.[23] William the Conqueror, treating England as a feudal property, forced all fief holders to swear allegiance directly to him. He collected the facts for the old Danegeld tax in a survey so closely made "that there was not one single hide nor rood of land nor . . . was there an ox, cow or swine that was not set down in the writ." Henry II (1154-1189), though no trueborn Englishman, made possible the continued growth of English common law by enlarging the power and scope of the royal courts from the *royal curia* on down, thus reducing those of the local, feudal, and church courts.[24] He began the practices of regularly using juries and of sending down itinerant justices to enforce the royal laws, and their decisions were a significant source of the developing common or universal law of the realm. While his judges were as much interested in collecting royal revenue as in enforcing justice, the royal central government was strengthened in either case. In pressing need of revenue he succeeded in levying royal taxes upon all personal property and incomes. And in his Assize of Arms of 1181 he commanded what weapons all Englishmen should possess for the royal service, thus reducing the power of the nobility and enhancing his own. Henry II thus "left England with a judicial and administrative system and a habit of obedience to government." [25] Henry III (1216-1272) continued to send down royal commissioners, the "General Eyre," to examine the financial and judicial business of the shire officials. In order to get taxes for his war with Philip IV of France and expand his own royal power, Edward I (1272-1307) called what was later termed the "Model Parliament," and this Parliament was the prototype of the body which much later became the chief agency of the British national government and took the place of the monarch in unifying Britain. Under Edward also began the English Statute Law which, among other things, restated and more precisely defined the feudal real property laws and made them uniformly applicable to the whole kingdom.[26] Edward III (1327-1377) appointed justices of the peace to interpret royal law and justice in every county; these royally appointed officials by Elizabeth's time concerned themselves with nearly all local legal matters from petty offenses to the building of roads and the enforcement of the poor law.

By the close of the medieval period the English monarchy had strengthened the central government, established national institutions, begun English national law, and created a class of governmental lawyers and officials who were always interested in protecting and advancing the interests of the royal nation-state.[27] More important here, it had taught the English people to look to the central government rather than to lord or priest for protection and security. If the "King's Peace" was indifferently enforced, it was better than any the lesser feudal lords could offer. Hence, under royal aegis the nation-state in England was well on its way to acquiring unlimited sovereignty. Even when opposition to the monarchy's absolute power arose as in the reigns of John (1199-1216) and Henry II, when English constitutional government may be said to have its beginnings, the result was to stimulate interest on the part of the nobility and burgesses in the central government, a government that was primarily royal but that could become national.

The Tudors in the sixteenth century completed the edifice of royal national government, though the first Stuart king, James I, was to provide the most reasoned argument for royal absolutism by divine right. Henry VII's (1485-1509) "Star Chamber" made the royal power everywhere feared if not respected and it brought order if not always justice after the anarchic years of the Wars of Roses. Henry VIII (1509-1547) founded the Royal Navy which was to become the chief instrument of England's power throughout the world.[28] What is of even greater importance for the growth of the nation, he broke with the Roman Catholic Church and established an English or Anglican Church and religion. This break had been long in coming. Popes and kings had disputed their respective powers in England since the twelfth century reigns of Henry I and II. The statutes of *Provisors* (1351) and *Praemunire* (1353) in Edward III's reign had stemmed the influx of alien clergy and forbidden appeals to papal courts. During the latter part of the fourteenth century John Wyclif (?-1384) had advocated a national church. And the lands and wealth of the Church had long been much coveted by the crown and nobility. In the 1530's for both personal and political reasons, and with much support from all classes, Henry VIII made himself "Protector and Only Supreme Head of the Church and Clergy of England." Probably the national interests were not uppermost in Henry's mind; nevertheless his action established a national church. England was now independent of any foreign control. Another stone had been laid on the foundation of the English nation-state. When James I claimed for the throne absolute dominion over England he was but rationalizing what the Tudors had done.

Though the names and incidents are not alike, the

French monarchy established effective royal control of its domains in much the same fashion. From about the twelfth century the kings began to institute royal governmental institutions and controls. Payments in kind from their domains were commuted into annual money payments; royal direct and indirect taxes were established,[29] and collectors were sent to the provinces to gather these revenues. With their permanent income from taxes and from the revenue of their own domains they were able to hire soldiers and set up a royal standing army; thus they could dispense with unreliable and divisive feudal levies. They established royal courts, such as the *parlements,* above those of the feudal lords and the Church, and made possible appeal to these courts from anywhere in the kingdom. They hired lawyers who substantiated and extended the royal claims to power and territory.[30] They convoked a representative body, the Estates General, which while it would lack the power of the English Parliament, nevertheless would become a national body and one day, in 1789, would declare it represented the nation. Not without great difficulty the kings forced all vassals to be directly responsible to them and prohibited private war. At last, in the seventeenth-century civil wars of the Fronde, they and their ministers, Richelieu and Mazarin, broke the political power of the nobility almost completely, and through royal intendants made the royal hand felt in even local affairs. The royal conquest of power extended also to the Catholic Church. From the beginning of the fourteenth century monarchs contested the claims of the papacy in France. In the attack (1302-1303) on Boniface VIII, Philip the Fair and his lawyers (Nogaret, for example) argued on both feudal and national grounds as they asserted Boniface was trying to injure France. If the French kings did not break with the Catholic Church, they established control over the clergy in France and a Gallican rather than a Roman Church through measures like the Pragmatic Sanction of Bourges (1438) and the Concordat of 1516. In the

first half of the seventeenth century they crushed the embryo state within a state that the Protestant Huguenots
tried to establish. Though even by Louis XIV's time they
had not been able to end diversity and bring uniformity
in France, they had brought all France under their domination and through the royal power built the governmental
framework of the nation-state.

To a considerable extent, then, the governments of both
France and England had become national before the end
of the seventeenth century. In France the monarch reigned
supreme. In England the kings were forced to share their
power with Parliament. But in both countries the sovereign central authority could no longer be effectively challenged. This central authority extended to the borders of
what became the modern national boundaries. Vestiges of
feudalism remained especially in France, and the Church
there was not as subject to the state as in England. If in
England, Parliament decisively wrested control from the
king in the years from 1640 to 1689, the central, the national government continued and grew more powerful on
much the same foundations as it had grown. By the end
of the seventeenth century, as Grotius had argued earlier
in 1625, everywhere in the West the national state, though
still monarchical, was sovereign and supreme. As an authority on the seventeenth century, G. N. Clark, stated, "Energies which had previously been controlled from a variety
of centres—feudal, ecclesiastical, communal, or what not—
were becoming polarized about the state. . . ." And the
conception of national state sovereignty "had been completed by jurists and political theorists . . . had almost
established its domain in international and 'municipal'
law." [31]

In most other European countries the royal families
established central governments which would become national in the same way, though at a later time. In Branden-
burg-Prussia, which became the nucleus for Germany, for
example, Elector Frederick William I (1640-1688), King

Frederick William I (1713-1740), and King Frederick II (the "Great," 1740-1786) during the seventeenth and eighteenth centuries laid the foundations of universal military service, general liability in taxation, and a compulsory school system. These the nineteenth-century nationalist historian Treitschke would quite accurately call "the threefold group of general civic duties by which the people of Prussia have been trained in an active love for the fatherland." [32]

Louis XIV told his grandson, the Duke of Burgundy, that the nation resided entirely in the person of the king.[33] In one contemporary sense he was accurate. In his reign as well as during the reigns of many earlier and contemporary monarchs the interests of the nation, if considered, were believed to be the same as those of the monarch, and as the sovereign the monarch was synonymous with if not actually the state. He was wrong otherwise. Before a nation could come fully into being there had also to be a people who consciously possessed some common customs and ideas, some common history and hopes. The dynasties helped mold these customs, ideas, histories, and hopes. Loyal subjects, as those of France in the time of Louis XIV, worshiped the king, thought he ruled by divine right, and saw in him the instrument and symbol of the nation. But the late medieval and early modern monarchies were only one factor in nation building.

During the same centuries as the monarchs of France and Britain were establishing their nation-states, other forces were arising which would both evidence the trend toward the national organization of society and further stimulate national feeling. Certainly among the most significant of these was the gradually developing belief that the inhabitants of a country should pursue a common economic policy. This belief, to be sure, was already incipient in some of the monarchical economic measures such as those concerning royal taxes, and kings such as Philip the Fair and Louis XI in France and Edward III in England had attempted to control shipments of goods out of their kingdoms. But as an expressed policy it would develop somewhat later than the idea of monarchical supremacy. Only in the seventeenth century would it become generally accepted and fully practiced.

About 1436 an English Bishop of Chichester, Adam de Moleyns, outlined a plan for English commerce and a navy to protect it, foreshadowing the future policy that was to contribute to England's commercial greatness. He wished to "cherish merchandise, keep the Admiralties, that we be masters of the Narrow Sea." [34] The idea took hold. The English monarchy and its supporters followed it. About 150 years later Richard Hakluyt published a classic exposition of the view—with not the "Narrow Sea" but the whole world in his purview, the *Principall Navigations Voyages Traffiques and Discoveries of the English Nation.* His purpose was not only to recount but to foster interest in the commercial development of England. It was, he began the preface to his second edition, "for the benefit and honour of my Countrey" that he had "zealously bestowed so many yeres, so much traveil and cost, to bring Antiquities smothered and buried in darke silence, to light, and to preserve certain memorable exploits of late yeeres by our English nation atchieved, from the greed and devouring jawes of oblivion. . . ." [35]

With De Moleyns and Hakluyt appear the preconceptions of the seventeenth-century state economic policy which came to be called mercantilism. Though mercantilism was primarily conceived as a way of strengthening the state and monarchy, it was also a national economic policy. [36] The ideas behind the policy promoted the national interests and at the same time they afford us additional evidence of the growing national consciousness. In search of power the state now, as in the France of Louis XIV and Colbert, attempted to build and control economic life within the country and all trade with other countries. As it molded internal economic life through governmental assistance and regulation, it reduced or destroyed feudal, provincial, guild, and municipal restrictions upon agriculture, commerce, and industry, and thus tended to make national rather than local interest paramount. It assisted national trade by royal or parliamentary edict, by building national systems of communication, banking, and money, and by aiding agriculture and business through bounties. At the same time it tried to so regulate foreign trade, with measures like the English Navigation Acts of the seventeenth century, that the home country would have a favorable balance of trade and thus would become richer (according to the current theories of wealth) while foreign countries had to ship out their precious metals and thus became poorer. The state, therefore, in the economic as well as the political spheres, now combatted the "medieval combination of universalism and particularism." [37] As it did so, it tended to centralize and unify the internal economic activities of each country, and, at the same time, to divide and set off the interests of each nation from every other nation. Though the end was state power, the means had to be national. The state had to strengthen the nation economically to be strong itself, and it had to try to weaken other like nation-states so as to be comparatively stronger. The result was stronger national states and a greater stress upon national interest.

The political and economic trends toward the creation of the nation, of course, reflected or were part of the whole historical development in western Europe. Common group cultures were taking root and these, as people became aware of them and desired their growth, would further accentuate national feeling. In middle and southern Europe, in Germany and Italy in particular, the emergence of national cultures preceded actual political unity to a greater degree than was true in western Europe. But as with the chicken and the egg it is impossible to tell which came first. Politics, in fact, are as much a part of culture as language and religion. In general the common cultural characteristics took form during the same centuries as political unification proceeded and as the monarchical governments extended their hold upon domains and peoples. As each group developed its common culture, its language, its religion, for example, it usually grew more and more conscious of it, and more desirous of a sovereign central government.

The precise time of the emergence of national languages in western Europe cannot be determined.[38] Languages do not spring fully formed into existence; they grow and become distinct through hundreds of years. In spoken form the western European languages were developing by Charlemagne's time, though not for centuries were they to be thought of as national tongues or to be used by all the peoples within what would become the separate nations. The Oaths of Strasbourg of 842 mark one of the first significant evidences of the official use of the vernacular. In common opposition to Lothair, their emperor brother, Louis the German (King of the East Franks) and Charles the Bald (King of the West Franks) swore loyalty to each other. As they did, Louis used the *lingua romana* (Roman-French) so that his brother's retainers might understand him; and Charles spoke in the *lingua teudesca* (Deutsch-German) for the same reason. But these languages were certainly not yet modern French and German nor were they kingdom-wide in usage.

During the twelfth to fourteenth centuries the trend becomes much clearer.[39] Then in France and Britain, as well as in the territories which in the future would become Italy, Germany, and Spain, both the spoken and the written languages were assuming their more definite modern forms and were becoming so widely used that they may, somewhat inaccurately, be termed national. As the common people spoke, during the long medieval centuries they established common patterns of speech; these were fairly clear for extended areas in western Europe by about 1200. And as the intellectuals increasingly thought and wrote in the vernaculars from about the same time, they tended to determine and fix the more exact forms of the languages. Dante (1265-1321), though he did not so intend, made it likely that Tuscan would become Italian when he wrote the *Divine Comedy* in that dialect.[40] As poets and story-tellers like Cavalcanti, Petrarch, and Boccaccio wrote in Italian they fixed the language ever more firmly. The fifteenth-century Renaissance humanists might again stress classical Latin. The writings in Italian and the customary speech of the commonalty prevailed.

In France the *langue d'oïl* of the court, Paris, and sur-rounding regions began to obtain some pre-eminence in the eleventh century.[41] Writing in French began princi-pally in the twelfth and thirteenth centuries when long versified narratives like the *Brut* and the *Rou,* the satire *Roman de la Rose,* Villehardouin's *Conquest of Constanti-nople,*[42] and Joinville's *Life of Saint Louis* were written. Historians in France, it might be noted, began to use the vernacular earlier than historians elsewhere.[43] The first offi-cial documents in French appeared about the middle of the thirteenth century. In 1539 by the Ordinance of Villers-Cotterets the official administrative language became French instead of Latin.

The story in England parallels that of France, though the literature in the vernacular starts somewhat later. Out of the East Midlands, the dialect spoken in Oxford, Cam-bridge, and London became the English tongue while the use of French and Latin tended to diminish. In the second half of the fourteenth century Langland's *Piers Plowman,* Chaucer's *Canterbury Tales,* and many of Wyclif's religious pamphlets appeared in the vernacular, and Wyclif with others translated (completed in 1388 after Wyclif's death) the first English Bible.[44] By 1375 William Nassington could note,

> *But lerid and lewid* [learned and ignorant],
> *old and young*
> *All understanden English tongue.*[45]

About the same time English was beginning to be taught in the schools. John of Trevissa noted in 1385 that "in alle the gramere scoles of Engelond, children [now] leveth Frensche and construeth and lerneth in Englische." [46] And in 1362 because French was "much unknown in the said realm" of England, the city of London petitioned for and Parliament passed a statute requiring that all pleadings and judgments in all courts including Parliament itself be in English.[47] By 1450 English instead of Latin or French became dominant in legal documents and was used by all classes as their customary tongue, though the historical chronicles remained for the most part in Latin until Tudor times.

Thus the foundations of the Western national languages were well built just before the use of movable type in printing made possible the wide diffusion of books. Printing made it likely that the already developed languages would find wider and wider acceptance until they actually could be said to have become national.

By the sixteenth and seventeenth centuries the vernacular tongues had won a clear victory. The use of Latin, except in Church documents and services and to some extent in the universities, declined rapidly all over western Europe. In France writers like Ronsard (1524-1585) and Joachim du Bellay (1525-1560) not only wrote in French but praised and defended it while the translator and publisher Henri Estienne (1531-1598) satirized the use of Italian words by Frenchmen and extolled the excellence of French.[48] Across the channel Sir Thomas More, the Christian humanist, wrote his *Utopia* (1516) in Latin, but there also most writing was now being done in the native tongue. At the end of the century the "glories of the English language" were being created in the comedies, tragedies, and poems of Shakespeare and a half-century later in the sonorous prose and poetry of Milton.[49] In the seventeenth century French became, even more than English, a definite, fixed language when the classic writers Corneille

(1606-1684), La Fontaine (1621-1695), Molière (1622-1673), and Racine (1639-1699) wrote their plays and fables. In 1694 the French Academy, itself an evidence of growing national feeling, commenced its monumental first diction- ary of the French language. Voltaire was right when he wrote, *"C'est dans le siècle de Louis XIV que cette élo- quence* [the French] *a eu son plus grand éclat, et que la langue a été fixée."* [50]

To say that the general and basic forms of English and French were fixed and that the languages were generally used is not to assert that French and English were every- where spoken and understood in the respective countries even by the seventeenth century. In both lands widely dif- fering dialects and even different languages were used by sizable minorities. A Parisian might still need an inter- preter at Marseilles, and the poet Racine, traveling in the provinces, could not make himself well enough understood to obtain *"un vase de nuit."* Nevertheless national lan- guages had evolved and they provided one more basis for national unity and consciousness.

The potential significance of the emergence of national tongues for national consciousness and unity was seldom apparent to contemporaries. Few demanded that all who spoke the same language be within the same political group- ing or believed that a common language was a major social tie. But that the significance for the nation-state was com- ing to be realized is shown by a reported speech of Henry IV of France to deputies of newly acquired provinces: "As you speak the French language by nature, it is reasonable that you should be the subjects of a King of France. I quite agree that the Spanish language should belong to the Span- iard and the German to the German. But the whole region of the French language must be mine." [51] In spite of the absence of much evidence, it probably can be inferred that the already developed language differences served to sharpen the incipient national consciousness while dawning awareness of a common language stimulated some feeling of national unity.

It would be a mistake, nevertheless, to assert that the development of common vernacular languages within groups of people in western Europe before the eighteenth century indicated a high degree of national feeling just as it is wrong to see in the language differences the sole key to modern nationalism. National languages grew; they did not originate by divine command in a Tower of Babel. They slowly grew out of older languages, out of contact with other contemporary languages, and out of the everyday experiences of the common people. They developed because the monarchs and their governments tended to force a common tongue upon their peoples with their laws, taxes, and armies. They won speakers because the peoples found it convenient in their political, economic, and social lives to speak a common tongue. Once a language was well established and came to be used for writing, it grew of itself, became habit. Usage stimulated more usage.[52] But it was long before patriots realized that language could be used both to unify and to separate peoples.

While language would come to be regarded as perhaps the chief distinguishing mark of nationality, language cannot alone explain the emergence of nationalism. In point of fact the sentiment could later develop where a common language was not present, as in Belgium where two languages have lived side by side for hundreds of years.[53] And sometimes the sentiment has not evolved where the same language is used in two different countries, as in Britain and the United States. Probably language differences help explain why national consciousness arose, but more than common languages were necessary before nationalism, cultural as well as political, could become strong.

The growth of national feeling can be measured in part by the emergence of national religions and churches as has been indicated above. Here again the danger of overemphasis arises; the national religions may be as much result as cause. The splintering of the traditional (for western Europe) Christian faith and Catholic Church in the sixteenth century was as much an effect of national feeling as a stimulus to more. If, however, the Roman Catholic Church had not lost its power and appeal, modern nationalism would have been much weaker and less prevalent. Conceivably a world state based upon religious principles could have arisen. When the Church no longer held the predominant place in men's lives, they sought security and salvation elsewhere—in the monarch, in the nation.[54] Some men, especially those of the more emotional Protestant groups like the Pietists of Germany, transferred to the nation much of the enthusiasm and loyalty their ancestors gave to the Church.[55]

The medieval Roman Church held its doctrines to have universal application. At the same time it had wide territories to administer. For administrative purposes—for government and for the collection of dues and donations—it had to divide these into districts. These were called, for example, Gallia, Germania, Italia, and Anglia. The districts sometimes roughly corresponded to areas which later became those of national states. Within each district the administration tended to centralize and unify.[56] In this way even the Roman Church may have contributed to the rise of nations. The ethics and the laws of the Church, however, were equally applicable to all who acknowledged the Church. The faithful could equally achieve earthly blessing and heavenly salvation regardless of the district in which they happened to live, regardless of their "race" or nationality.[57]

The Protestant revolt against the Church was only in part based upon national grounds. Dynastic materialistic interests, intellectual enlightenment, and spiritual dissatisfaction were probably at least as significant. One profound modern scholar, Ernst Troeltsch, has failed to see any connection whatsoever between the establishment of national churches and the principle of nationality.[58] Nevertheless, national sentiment in some countries contributed to the establishment of national churches, and encouraged the nationalizing of religion. The national churches, once created, encouraged further national consciousness. While Protestantism in itself was not inherently nationalist, most Protestants wanting their own religion to become universal, the revolt denied the universal creed. It accentuated national habits of thought and speech, and, by so doing, it enabled the nation to take the place of the Church as the instrument of salvation and as the chief object of earthly loyalty.

Some of the reformers, like Luther (1483-1546), simply preached the supremacy of the prince or state over the Church.[59] This was a kind of *étatism,* not nationalism. While Luther spoke of German interests as opposed to Italian and preferred to speak and write German rather than scholarly Latin, he was scarcely a nationalist.[60] But until his kind of secular supremacy was achieved the nation-states could not fully command supreme allegiance. A few of the early reformers went further. John Wyclif, far in advance of his times, wanted a national church subordinate to the national state.[61] The Hussite leaders of Bohemia came close to identifying their religious cause with the national interest. Appealing for aid in 1420 they cried that the emperor "wishes to despoil us of our salvation, foist upon us his heretical creed as proclaimed in Constance and lead us to damnation. Should you, despite it all, wish to take his side, we should be forced to believe that you also favor the extinction of the Bohemian nation and to treat you, with God's help, on a par with the Lord's and our nation's public enemies." [62]

The identification of religion and nation occurred most completely and clearly in the seventeenth-century Puritan revolt against royal Catholic absolutism in England.[63] From their study of the Old Testament and their own deep sense of righteousness they drew the conviction that Englishmen, like the ancient Hebrews, were a chosen people.

To Cromwell, the English, and of course he meant the Puritan English, were "a people that have had a stamp upon them from God; God having, as it were, summed up all our former honour and glory in the things that are of glory to nations, in an epitomy within these ten or twelve years last past." [64]

When other early reformers protested, they were seldom so motivated by national loyalties.[65] When Henry VIII broke with Rome he was not thinking so much of English as his own interests. Yet national interest and religious feeling often became identified. This was especially true where the Protestants, such as the Presbyterians, insisted upon individual and local group responsibility for human action and its consequences. No longer for most Protestants was there a priesthood and a central divine representative on earth to intervene for them with God. They had to make their own life, their own future. While they approached God directly for their soul's salvation, increasingly they turned to the state, to the nation as a source from which all earthly favors could flow. A new way to a kind of mundane immortality was thus opened to them. As the German nationalist Fichte (1762-1814) declared much later in his *Addresses to the German Nation* (1807) an individual could now find permanence "promised . . . by the continuous and independent existence of his nation." [66] Men had had in western Europe the guaranty of the authority of the universal Church. When this was challenged and shaken, they could gain a sense of belonging and a feeling of security from a new authority, the nation-state.[67]

Of course the Protestant revolt was not alone accountable for the loss of a universal spiritual authority nor for the increasing importance of the nation-state. Perhaps it was but another phase of the trend toward secularization of society. Once successful, however, it tended to accentuate the similarities among the people within each of the dynastically formed nations and to sharpen the external differ-

ences among them. The various state churches had national
heads, national administrations. They usually supported
the monarchical governments which were becoming national governments, and strengthened the hold of these governments upon their peoples. And they were, at the same
time, one more cultural force fostering national cultural
uniformity and unity.

The national churches increasingly employed the vernacular in sermons, ritual, and hymn and thus spread the
use of the national tongues.[68] The most important book for
most Protestants, the Bible, was translated and published
and read in these languages rather than in Latin. The German of Luther's Bible became to a large extent the literary
as well as the spoken language of the people in north central Europe. The English of the King James version, the
"King's English," fixed still further the language of Wyclif
and Shakespeare for Englishmen. In Sweden and Denmark
the publication of Bibles in the vernacular helped establish what is now Swedish and Danish.[69]

To assess exactly the influence of these Protestant usages
upon national consciousness is impossible. National consciousness was emerging in all western Europe, in Catholic
as well as Protestant countries.[70] It was a French Catholic
king, Philip the Fair, who quarreled with Pope Boniface
VIII (1294-1303), denied the authority of the papacy in
crucial matters of salvation and taxation, dealt the papacy
an almost fatal blow when he established at Avignon a
French pope "surrounded by a French court," and began a
"captivity" of the popes which lasted seventy years. The
"Gallican liberties" of the fifteenth and later centuries
were national liberties of the French Catholic Church only
a little less indicative of a desire for independence of Rome
than the series of acts which separated the Church of England from the papacy. But whatever the effect of Protestantism, it was not negligible. If nothing more, religion,
then as now, supplemented and reinforced other beliefs
and prejudices. This was especially true during the wars

of the time. The wars of the sixteenth century were usually dynastic and religious in origin. But as they were fought, they became, like the wars of the seventeenth century, increasingly national, with religion contributing to the feeling of national differences on the one hand and national unity on the other. Protestant Englishmen could kill Catholic Spaniards more zestfully because they were both Catholic and Spanish. The Dutch fought for their independence because they were Dutch Calvinists opposing Spanish Catholics as well as because they wished to trade without Spanish controls and resented absentee taxation. And much of the Irish national opposition to England resulted from Irish Catholicism's opposition to English Protestantism.

Dynasties were establishing the territorial and governmental bases of the nation; national languages were taking form; national religions were coming into being. Universal church, religion and empire, and atomistic feudalism were alike losing their hold upon the individual and society. All this does not prove, except through tenuous deduction, that national consciousness and loyalty were either widespread or intense. In his play *Saint Joan,* George Bernard Shaw dramatized the Hundred Years' War by having a nobleman declare to a chaplain: "Men cannot serve two masters. If this cant of serving their country once takes hold of them, goodbye to the authority of their feudal lords, and goodbye to the authority of the Church. That is, goodbye to you and me." But if a fifteenth-century nobleman thought this, he was a prophet looking perhaps two hundred years ahead.

Of what the common people were thinking or believing we know little. They were for the most part illiterate, and there were no public opinion polls. Only when they committed violent acts as in the peasant revolts are we aware of their ideas at all. On the basis of what little evidence they left we may fairly guess that they were seldom aware of national issues, had little if any interest in them, and possessed little national feeling. The hard facts of their daily lives took all of their attention. When they thought or acted in groups it was only on a local scale, for family, for their village, or perhaps against their lord. If in thought or action they went beyond the confines of the narrow community, it was only because some high authority like the Church or monarch compelled.

On the other hand much isolated evidence can be collected to show that national consciousness was sometimes appearing among the nobles and the bourgeoisie, and among the poets and officials who sprang chiefly from them and may have represented their views. Occasionally individuals exhibited a high degree of national feeling and the number who did so was growing.

From the twelfth century onward the persistent historian can cite illustrative examples of national consciousness from literature and official documents. These examples, rare until the fifteenth century, become more and more numerous until they become commonplace by the end of the eighteenth century. As long as they are not torn from context and represented as typical of opinion, they may be used to demonstrate the dawning of national consciousness. For nearly every aspect of modern nationalism a possible origin before the eighteenth century may indeed be found. Western Europeans slowly, very slowly, acquired dislike of foreigners, respect for the national state, love of native country, a pride in their group's past, and an interest in its future. It would be wrong, however, to assert that all of modern nationalism appeared so early or that a continuous development of national feeling can be traced from the Middle Ages to the present.

When in the twelfth-century *Chanson de Roland*, the hero saw himself surrounded by the Saracens he cried, *"A Dieu ne plaise que la douce France tombe jamais dans le déshonneur."* As his companion, Oliver, fell, he cried again, *"O douce France, tu vas donc être veuve de les meilleurs soldats."* Arriving before the body of Roland, Charlemagne in tears moaned, *"Il est mort, celui qui était toujour*

à notre tête. Ah! douce France, te voilà orpheline." One
cannot be certain that the poet was not here expressing
feudal honor and dynastic loyalty rather than national
patriotism.[71] Possibly all three were present as they often
were even much later. But that here a kind of incipient
national sentiment was present cannot be doubted.

In the late medieval period it is often difficult to isolate the national from other sentiments. The various loyalties fade almost imperceptibly into one another. The same
individual might feel different loyalties, religious, feudal,
and national, at the same time; one might be uppermost
at one moment, another at another time. Few gave their
loyalty deeply and persistently to the nation. Jeanne d'Arc,
long the most sacred symbol of the French nation, was a
Christian and royalist rather than a nationalist as we have
pointed out before.[72] The 100 per cent patriot or integral
nationalist was centuries in the future. Still, national feelings were slowly emerging, and the various attitudes which
form modern nationalism were appearing, often separately
and mildly, it is true, but appearing.

Dislike of aliens, a feeling appearing among old and
primitive peoples, occurs early. In the middle of the thirteenth century Matthew Paris (1200?-1259) evinced hatred
for all foreigners, reporting that the Spaniards were "the
scum of mankind, ugly in face, contemptible in behavior,
and detestable in their morals," and telling the most hair-
raising and bloodthirsty tales of the destructive Tatars who
were then overrunning eastern Europe.[73] A participant in
the Fourth Crusade wrote the Pope, "It is very important
for this business that the Germans should not march with
the French; for we cannot find in history that they were
at accord in any momentous common enterprise." [74] During
the Hundred Years' War (1337-1453) especially and
throughout the numerous wars of the sixteenth and seventeenth centuries like statements of national antagonisms
are not difficult to find. The French and English were often
bitter in their denunciation of each other. A French hu-

manist and diplomat, Robert Gaguin (1433?-1501), was possibly as accurate as he was rhetorical when he wrote, "It would be easier to reconcile a wolf and a lamb than an Englishman and a Frenchman." And he could have been right when he said that he had heard of English children being given a bow and a figure of a Frenchman and told, "Go, my child, learn to kill a Frenchman." [75] The antagonisms so often expressed may not have been so much national as personal and it is certain that they often arose out of the temporary discomfort of battle rather than any deep-rooted permanent prejudice. The fact remains that distrust and dislike on national grounds were taking root. François Villon (1431-146?), poet of the Parisian streets and taverns, was quite modern, though his figures of speech were medieval, when in his "ballad against the Enemies of France," he asked that they suffer the most awful torture, encounter monsters belching fire, and have molten coin poured into their bellies.[76]

Love of the state and native country appears equally early. As the state became more secularized, so paradoxically it became more and more the subject of a worship akin to the religious. During the late medieval period, possibly as early as the thirteenth century, the political community, for a few men, began to take the place of the Church as a "mystical body" for which the individual might make the supreme sacrifice. Henry of Ghent at Paris in the thirteenth century compared the "death of a citizen for his brothers and his community to the supreme sacrifice of Christ for mankind." A French poet of the same age, Richier, "styled the crown of France the most precious of all relics and declared that those who were killed in protection of the crown should be saved in life after death." [77] This high esteem for the state, particularly as it was personified by the monarch, became more intense in succeeding centuries until by the seventeenth century kings like Louis XIV both demanded and received worship from all classes.

Dante's love of Italy is well known. Petrarch's (1304-1374) sonnets upon Italy reveal a deep attachment to native land:

> *Is not this my own nest*
> *Where I was nourished and was given life?*
> *Is not this the dear land in which we trust,*
> *Mother loving and kind*
> *Who shelters parents, brothers, sister, wife?*

and great sorrow for Italy's woes:

> *My Italy, though words do not avail*
> *To heal the mortal wounds*
> *That in your lovely body I see so dense*
> *I wish at least to let my sighing sounds*
> *With Arno and Tiber wail*
> *And Po, where now I sit in deep suspense.*[78]

At the beginning of the fourteenth century the chronicler Robert of Gloucester sang of England as a "right merry land, of all earth it is the best. . . ."[79] In 1380 to the French poet Eustache Deschamps, France was a *"pais tres doulz pour demourer."* [80] About the same time another French poet, Alan Chartier, who was also a royal official, revealed deep national patriotism as well as feudal fealty when he wrote, "After the bond of Catholic faith nature binds you above all else to the common welfare of the country of your birth and the defense of that ruler under which God has caused you to be born and to live. . . . And since this is the law that nature has established no work should be grievous for you, no hazardous adventure should be foreign to you if it supports this country and saves this ruler who sustains and nourishes you among the living and receives you in burial among the dead." [81] After the invasions and disorder of fifteenth-century Italy, Machiavelli (1469-1527) pleaded for a princely savior with a patriotic devotion to Italy that seems almost out of place in his hardheaded analysis of contemporary politics. "Italy left as without life, waits for him who shall yet heal her wounds and cleanse those sores that for long have festered . . . she prays to God to send some one who shall deliver her from these wrongs and barbarous insolencies." [82]

In the late sixteenth century Shakespeare occasionally revealed deep pride in England's strength as well as its natural beauties.[83] The bastard Faulconbridge concludes *King John* with the boast

> *This England never did, nor never shall*
> *Lie at the proud foot of a conqueror. . . .*

And his Faulconbridge was willing to challenge "the three corners of the world in arms." Nothing could harm England if it "to itself do rest but true." To the bard's dying John of Gaunt (*Richard II*) England was, "This royal throne of kings," "this other Eden—demi-paradise," "this happy breed of men," "this blessed plot." Shakespeare was not alone in his devotion to England. For the seventeenth-century Trimmer of George Savile (1633-1695) the "earth of England" had "divinity in it and he would rather dye, than see a spire of *English* Grass trampled down by a foreign trespasser. . . ." The Trimmer thought there were "a great many of his mind, for all plants are apt to tast of the Soyl in which they grow, and we that grow here, have a Root that produceth in us a stalk of English juice. . . ." [84]

Pride in nationality is more difficult to find until the eighteenth century. It does not early seem to have been as prevalent as dislike of foreigner or love of native land. That such pride was incipient may be deduced from some of the above quotations. On occasion it was overtly expressed. In Henry VII's time (1485-1509), for instance, one of the keen Venetian envoys declared that Englishmen believed no other men like themselves, that whenever they saw "a handsome foreigner" they thought he looked "like an Englishman," and that it was a greaty pity he was not.[85] About the same time and after Poggio Bracciolini's discovery of the manuscript of Tacitus' *Germania*, some German

humanists like Jacob Wimpheling (1450-1528), Konrad
Celtis (1459-1508), and Ulrich von Hutten (1488-1523) began to speak highly of German character, especially its
military virtues.[86] Hutten, who was not only a knight and
a humanist but something of a national patriot, wrote a
poem entitled "Why the Germans Are Not Degenerate in
Comparison with Former Times." [87] During the next century Milton (1608-1674) in his *Areopagitica* eloquently
exhorted the Lords and Commons of England with his
famous "consider what nation whereof it is ye are, and
whereof ye are the governors; a nation, not slow nor dull,
but of a quick, ingenious, and piercing spirit; acute to
invest, subtile and sinewy to discourse, not beneath the
reach of any point the highest that human capacity can
soar to." And the great philosopher-mathematician Leibniz
(1646-1716), far ahead of his time in this as in other ideas,
would soon be telling the Germans they were superior in
the practical arts and sciences and that God gave them
reason above all other peoples.[88]

There are still other ways that the beginnings of national
consciousness can be illustrated before the eighteenth century. One of the most significant of these is the writing of
national histories, histories which reveal an interest in the
common past and not uncommonly a didactic hope to improve the common future.[89] The chronicles, annals, and
histories written during the late medieval period in England and France are many. In one sense some of them could
be called national histories. When they do not treat of the
purely local affairs of, say, a monastery, they are often lauda-
tory accounts of the national monarchs. Often they begin
with the then believed myths concerning the origin of the
country and come down through the reign of the king with
which they are contemporary. Henry of Huntington (d.
1155?) wrote, for example, a *Historia Anglorum,* which
starts with Caesar's invasions and ends with the reign of
Stephen (1135-1154).[90] William of Malmesbury, William of
Newburgh, Ralph (Abbot of Coggeshall), Geoffrey of

Monmouth,[91] Bartholomaeus de Cotton, the St. Albans his-
toriographers Roger of Wendover and Matthew Paris, and
many others wrote or compiled chronicles and histories of
England and the English monarchs during the late twelfth
and the thirteenth centuries. In France from the time of
Louis VI (1108-1137), of whom his chief minister, the
Abbot Suger of St. Denis, wrote a biography, similar eulo-
gistic chronicles and histories were compiled. From about
this time and through much of the fourteenth century, the
monks of St. Denis acted as semiofficial biographers of the
French kings.

How widely these histories were read or how great was
their influence in creating a national spirit one cannot say.
Since they existed only in manuscript and few copies were
made, they were not widely known. For this reason and
because they devoted most attention to the dynasty and not
to the embryo nations, they probably do not evidence
widespread national feeling nor did they serve to create
much consciousness of national unity. Yet these histories
were often more than accounts of local feudal lords, and
later more national-minded historians would draw upon
them to create or re-create a common past for each nation.
As Voiture, the French court wit and man of letters, surmised in 1636, when those who came later read history they
would become enamored of their countries.[92]

Historians who might be called national with more accuracy than these early chroniclers appeared only with the
vigorous intellectual life of the Renaissance. Only a few
need be briefly mentioned here by way of illustration. Paradoxically an Italian humanist, Polydore Vergil (1470?-
1555?), wrote one of the first truly modern national histories
of England. Requested by Henry VII to write a history,
he spent twenty-eight years of industrious research upon
it. A greater sixteenth-century national history of England
was William Camden's (1551-1623) *Remaines concerning
Britaine*. Written out of "love of country" the book nar-

rated not only the lives of the kings but also described "the country and its inhabitants, languages, names, arms, coins, clothing, high roads, towns and cities, natural scenery, and natural resources." [93] Camden was concerned with not just the customary details about the feudal dynasty but with the affairs and interests of the whole nation. In the same spirit a group of English historians founded the Elizabethan Society of Antiquaries in 1572 to study and preserve old manuscripts. And five years later a William Harrison (1534-1593) published a work with the significant title, *An Historicall Description of the Iland of Britaine*.[94]

In France numerous national histories appeared during the latter half of the sixteenth century. Those of Du Haillan, Du Tillet, Hotman, François de Belleforest, and Lancelot Voisin de la Popelinière might be cited.[95] The title of the work by La Popelinière is indicative of the trend toward treatment of the secular affairs of the country: *Histoire de France enrichie des plus notables occurrences survenues en Province de l'Europe et pays voisins, soit en paix, soit en guerre, tant pour le fait séculier que ecclésiastique depuis l'an 1550 jusques à ces temps*. While Italy was not unified, nevertheless it acquired a national historian in the sixteenth century when Francesco Guicciardini (1483-1540) followed his *History of Florence* with a *History of Italy*. In long and boring sentences he treated the affairs of all Italy from the invasion of Charles VII in 1494 to the election of Pope Paul III in 1534. While Spain was unified territorially but not culturally, it, too, obtained a patriotic historian in Juan de Mariana (1536-1624), whose *Historiae de rebus Hispaniae* was first written in Latin to acquaint Europe with Spanish history and then translated so that his ignorant compatriots could know Spanish history as well.[96]

Perhaps the early growth of national consciousness is best summed up in the evolution of the word *patrie* or fatherland. For a good medieval Christian the Latin word *patria* meant as much the city of God as any place on earth. In Saint Augustine's words Heaven was the "common fatherland" for all Christians. During most of the Middle Ages in feudal France, for example, the word might denote the local province or town or village, but never the whole of France. While the old meanings of *patria* did not disappear, new meanings begin to appear in the twelfth and thirteenth centuries. Occasionally men now applied it to the national kingdom or crown, and to these as a "visible symbol of a national territorial community" for which they were increasingly willing to die.[97] By the fifteenth century the French words *patrie* and *patriote* were introduced. Soon French humanists like Etienne Dolet, Guillaume Bude, Joachim du Bellay, and Rabelais were using the first to denote almost what the modern man means by "fatherland." [98] In the late sixteenth century, two hundred years before the French Revolution, an obscure Jewish rabbi of Prague, Loewe ben Bezalel, foreshadowed modern conceptions of national self-determination when he asserted "that every people has its own nature and its own character or form [Gestalt], that every people has a might of its own and ought not to be subject to any other people, that every people has its natural habitation and a right to live there, and that it must be granted to every people to choose its own God according to its own ideas." [99]

But the foreshadowing of modern ideas by a few learned men did not mean that modern nationalism had arisen. Most people, as late as the eighteenth century, were seldom aware of "nation" and nationality, though these can be said to have come into being. The national welfare was not yet their paramount interest. Most men still had other loyalties, to church and religion, to kingdom and monarchy, to class, province, and village, which bound them much more strongly than those of nation. National governments did not yet try to regulate and control all life, and men did not yet primarily look to them for the solution of basic problems. Not until the latter part of the eighteenth century would nation and nationality become of supreme importance for most western Europeans. And until they did nationalism cannot be said to have been more than incipient.

Chapter VI

THE NATION BECOMES THE PEOPLE
(1715-1815)

ɔ|c

Modern nationalism is a product of as well as a decisive element in the shaping of the total culture. Men do not become nationalists because of biology. They are not born nationalists. They acquire national consciousness and become national patriots because the political, economic, and social conditions and thought of their time make them so. Probably men are social by innate disposition but gregariousness could lead and has led to many types of association and degrees of unity. The nation became the dominant social grouping in modern times because ideas and institutions—the culture—determined that men might live in a larger social grouping than family or tribe but did not permit them to comprehend an international or universal state.[1]

Eighteenth-century culture produced the first full flowering of the national sentiment. This is not to assert that popular nationalism then burst full grown into existence, that nationalism by the end of the eighteenth century was everywhere the same, that the sentiment was equally shared by all western Europeans, or finally that it had completely eclipsed, even where it was strongest, all other group loyalties. The nationalism that came into being in the eighteenth century grew out of the historical conditions of

97

earlier centuries as these have been described in the previous chapter. As conditions varied in European lands
during the eighteenth century, so did the degree of development and kinds of national feeling. Nationalism grew
strong in France and England by 1815; it was still in its
early stages in Germany, Italy, and Spain; and only indi-
cations of its eventual rise were evident in most of eastern
and southeastern Europe.[2] Further, the evidence indicates
that the Enlightenment of the eighteenth century influenced the national patriotism of the French, English, and
Americans more than it did that of the middle and eastern
Europeans while the Romantic movement of the late eighteenth and the early nineteenth centuries left a greater im-
press upon German nationalism.[3]

In spite of these differences nationalism was becoming
the dominant social sentiment in all western Europe and
America. By the end of the eighteenth century Western
civilization had produced, in western Europe, the basic
national institutions and loyalties which were characteristic of later developments in most of the world. Nationalism from this time on would win more and more adherents
and its intensity would continue to deepen until *la patrie*
or *das Vaterland* would become the final end of most men's
endeavors and almost the sole object, other than immediate family, for which they would willingly die.

Conceivably men could have turned in the eighteenth
century to other institutions and loyalties to find satisfaction, status, and security. There was, indeed, among the
intellectuals of the eighteenth century a cosmopolitanism
that meant loyalty to all humanity, rather than to a particular nation. Men like Goldsmith and Hume in England,
Voltaire, Diderot, and Helvétius in France, Goethe,
Schiller, and Kant in the Germanies, and Jefferson and
Franklin in the American colonies regarded themselves as
citizens of the world. In their writings they stressed universal natural law, the rights and duties of man, friendship
and peace among peoples, and tolerance for all men. With

Goethe they believed "Above the nations is humanity." [4]
Perhaps only hindsight enables us to see the eighteenth
century and earlier historical trends as trends toward nation
and nationalism. Possibly in a century or two historians
will be able to see in them the origins of a new universal
state which encompasses all nations and swallows up all
lesser loyalties. As yet this hindsight is not possible. Here
it is the intention only to describe the conditions, the institutions, the ideas which led to the further evolution of the
nation and that devotion to it which is called national
patriotism. In the eighteenth century more and more men
were becoming national patriots and for these devotion
to the nation was becoming the supreme loyalty.

The reasons for this development were many. History
had already brought into existence some national institutions and ideas and thus had determined in some degree
those to which men would now turn. The preceding centuries had created forms into which the culture of the
eighteenth century was poured. The early modern dynasties, as those of England and France, had united territories and peoples and extended somewhat uniform and
centralized governments over them. These dynasties had
evolved political and economic policies in their own interest which furthered unity and uniformity within their
possessions. To a limited extent within these possessions
common languages and cultures had developed. And the
intellectual leaders of the various peoples, particularly in
the West, were slowly acquiring a common consciousness
of their developing common problems, institutions, and
cultures.

During the eighteenth century more men were becoming
literate and hence more aware that they were oppressed by
nobility, clergy, or a foreign power, and that they might
reduce or eliminate this oppression through common (or
national) action. At the same time the findings and method
of seventeenth-century science from the time of Newton,
the whole eighteenth-century Enlightenment and the

slightly later Romantic movement provided reason to hope
for a better and more glorious future to be achieved likewise through common (national) action. Encouraged by the
new science of nature and man the intellectuals reinvig-
orated the old idea of progress. Everything became possible if men were able to act together to improve their
condition. The seventeenth-century English poet Dryden
anticipated later sentiments when he tied this future to
his nation:

> But what so long in vain, and yet unknown,
> By poor mankind's benighted wit is sought,
> Shall in this age to Britain first be shown,
> And hence be to admiring nations taught.[5]

Relief from oppression, progress toward a good society,
how could men realize these? By devotion to the national
welfare which after all was but devotion to their own welfare. For the late eighteenth century in western Europe it
would not be inaccurate to equate roughly the word "popular" with the word "patriot." The desires, personal as
well as social, of the vocal part of the populations of western Europe, particularly the bourgeoisie, were now increasingly focalized in the nation which consisted at least
of all the propertied individuals within the state. Through
the nation the ideal society of the middle classes and, much
later, most of the working classes could be established.

Once this conception was firmly implanted, the nation
tended to perpetuate itself. More and stronger national
institutions and ideas meant still more and still stronger
national institutions and ideas. Peoples who were not national minded were forced in their own defense to become
so, and those already so found it expedient and helpful to
become still more so. Those who were in power in the
nation-states wanted more power; this meant greater and
more powerful national governments and a further intensification of national patriotism. Peoples who did not
yet possess national institutions and national governments

found they had to get them or remain oppressed by peoples who did. As the national governments expanded, exercised more control, and determined the lives of an increasing number of people, increasing numbers looked to them for the solution of present difficulties and the way to a better future. Almost everything worked toward the intensification of nationalism. Men were now born into national societies; they were often educated in national schools; their justice was obtained chiefly through national courts; their taxes and civic duties were mostly national; their culture conditioned them to think in national terms; and their leaders usually taught (or propagandized) them to worship national idols and ideals.

The bourgeoisie was the chief though not the only medium for these national ideas. Neither this middle class nor its national mindedness, it is true, were phenomena exclusively of the eighteenth century. Nor was the nationalism limited exclusively to the middle classes. It is because of their power in the eighteenth century that we stress them here. The bourgeoisie's modern origins can be traced to the twelfth century and so can some of its national attitudes. From this time onward, especially in western Europe, the class grew in wealth and numbers. From this time, too, it tended to ally itself with the national monarchies.[6] Through this alliance the middle classes and monarchs obtained mutual benefits. They were each, for different reasons, often opposed to the privileged orders. The kings wished to extend their powers at the expense of the nobility and clergy. The middle classes desired privileges, those concerned with property and those having to do with social equality with the nobility. The kings wanted the supplies, wealth, and taxes which the bourgeoisie could provide.[7] The bourgeoisie hoped for security of property and freedom for trade which the king could provide. Thus both monarch and middle classes often found mutual benefit in the joint extension of their mutual interests which they also could conceive of as *the* national interests. If ambitious members of the middle class carried trade to far-flung places, if they discovered new lands, this meant increased profits and hence increased royal (national) wealth and taxes. And the royal (national) government provided naval protection for the trade, gave bounties for colonial products like naval stores, and safeguarded the home market for patriotic members of the bourgeoisie.

The alliance between monarchy and middle class was never complete or solid. It was not born out of mutual affection but came primarily from the interests of the monarch in power and taxes, and the interests of the bourgeoisie in security for property and the opportunity to gain both more wealth and higher social status. When absolute monarchy could not, as in England in the seventeenth century and France in the late eighteenth century, defend the old social order as well as protect property, and afford opportunities for gain as the bourgeoisie desired, the bourgeoisie plus some aristocrats limited the monarchical power by constitutional provision and when this was not enough, removed the king's head (Charles I, Louis XVI). When the kings were limited or dethroned, the propertied citizens became sovereign, and they, the Cromwellians and French Revolutionaries, calling themselves the nation, ruled in the name of the nation. Men, propertied men, could now be patriotic and at the same time serve their own interests, for were not the national interests their interests and their interests those good for the nation. What served the nation, served them. What helped them was good for the nation, for they were the nation.[8]

All this, of course, is oversimplification of a complex story. True in substance the interpretation needs modification in detail. The alliance between the bourgeoisie and monarchs was not an alliance in the strict sense but a marriage of convenience. It was not between two equals, for in the early period the monarchs were the stronger, and in the later the bourgeoisie. The monarchs did not rely completely upon the bourgeoisie but at times allied themselves with priest and noble. These latter were not always at odds with the middle classes; in England the squirearchy and commercial nobility at times jointly fought the royal power. Many of the leading liberals of the eighteenth century were, in fact, of the privileged classes; the Baron Montesquieu, the Marquis de Condorcet, and the Abbé Sieyès are only three of the many who might be cited.[9] And during the Revolutionary era when nationalism was rising swiftly, nobles sometimes became as patriotic as any member of the bourgeoisie. No one could say that the Marquis de Lafayette, the Baron vom und zum Stein, or the Duke of Wellington were unpatriotic.[10]

If the bourgeoisie sometimes received assistance from the privileged classes, it is also true that they and their new idea of nation could not have risen to dominance without the material and ideological decay of the Old Regime. The age of reason was not only an age of the continued rise of capitalism and the formulation of the concepts of what has been called the liberal or bourgeois society. It also witnessed the continued decay of feudalism and the further decline of medieval Christian values. Nearly everywhere in western Europe the feudal nobles were continuing to lose their peculiar functions as intermediaries between rulers and peoples, as protectors of their vassals and serfs, and as civil administrators and military leaders. In England, to be sure, the nobility would open its ranks, share its responsibilities with the rising commercial classes, and in a sense enter the bourgeoisie. But more often, in western Europe as in France, the feudal lords were giving up their social functions to king and bourgeoisie. When this happened they were losing their *raison d'être* as a class and tending to be swallowed by larger entities, first the monarchical state and then the nation.

What was true of feudalism and the nobility was also true, possibly to a lesser extent, of the church and the clergy. The universal order they represented was broken and the values for which they stood partially discredited

and often ignored. The chief function of the clergy, salvation for erring man, no longer held so vital a place in the
scheme of human life. Compared with success on this Earth
in gaining wealth, prestige, or knowledge, heavenly bliss or
hellish damnation were no longer so crucial. As Luther had
asserted two centuries earlier the priest was no longer absolutely essential. Now to be a good man, to win acclaim,
to obtain happiness one paid less attention to heavenly salvation than to saving, to social prestige and political power.

While the middle classes rose, the old institutions and
loyalties declined. But the first was not always the cause
of the second. The decline was not purely the result of
those basic changes in the economic substructure of society
which gave rise to the middle class, though they were certainly of great import. The decline was hastened by the
increased political power of the monarchs and the acid
solvent of enlightenment. The question might again be
asked, as with the chicken and the egg, which was first or
was causal. But there is no answer except to say that growth
and decay took place during the same time and that out
of them both came the intensification and spread of the
national idea. One further complication must be added. In
much of central and eastern Europe nationalism also arose,
not so much because of the bourgeoisie (it was weak) as in
reaction to foreign oppressors and even sometimes as an
aristocratic reaction to the liberal, middle-class ideas of
the French Revolution.

If, then, it be stated with the economic determinists who
follow Adam Smith or Karl Marx that the bourgeoisie was
the agent of the modern national state, this is not only too
sweeping a generalization but inaccurate history. Nevertheless, when the western European bourgeoisie came to
share or to obtain full political power in the eighteenth
century, they did so in the name of the nation, and a national patriot was he who favored a government providing
liberty and protecting property. The nation was no longer
a king, his territory, and his subjects. It was now composed

of citizens, propertied citizens usually, who inhabited a common territory, possessed a voice in their common government, and were conscious of their common (imagined or real) heritage and their common interests.

With the rise of the middle classes to power, the nation and its welfare became the common denominator and the common end of thought and action. Through it the liberals of the eighteenth century, most of them of the middle classes, thought they could progress to the kind of society they desired and believed good for all men. Without conscious selfishness, and perhaps also sometimes without calculation, the middle classes conceived of themselves as the national societies and established national governments which chiefly favored themselves. When they did, the highest and most prevalent political loyalty came to be that devotion to their *own* society and government which is called national patriotism.

What was coming was foreshadowed in some of the philosophic writings (Rousseau) of the eighteenth century, and remarkably expressed in most of the French pamphlets and cahiers of 1788-1789.[11] The events of the French Revolutionary and Napoleonic eras and the reaction of other peoples and governments to these events spread, accelerated, and sharpened the national spirit among most Western peoples.

Both the writings and events reveal striking changes in the climate of opinion:

1. A rising consciousness of national unity at the same time as other unities and distinctions such as those of privilege and province tended to disappear.

2. A mounting opinion that all propertied inhabitants, sometimes all inhabitants, were part of the nation, and should have a voice in the sovereign national government, that is should be citizens, stockholders with voting rights in the common enterprise, the nation.

3. A growing belief that this sovereign national government of citizens (not just the monarch) should perform

national functions and carry on nationwide political, economic, and social activities for the benefit of all citizens.

4. An increased awareness of and a desire for a national culture, that is a common language, literature, religion.

5. A rising sentiment that not only all (at least all the propertied) inhabitants were part of the nation, should share its responsibilities and be subject to it, but that all should be completely devoted to it. The nation became an object of worship and national patriots sought converts at home and domination abroad.

Not only does the evidence reveal new and widening consciousness of and belief in the nation but it also shows that these were being increasingly translated into actuality, into political, economic, and social institutions which in turn further stimulated and shaped national patriotism. In France, during the Revolution, where the process took place in most sharp-cut fashion, those old religious, feudal, and provincial institutions regarded as obstacles to national unity were attacked and almost destroyed while the national government was given the functions they formerly had performed. At the same time the old royal government was reshaped until the executive, the legislative, the judicial, and the administrative powers represented the nation's, not the dynasty's, interests. Propertied (for a time all) citizens were charged with responsibility for the national government. Economic freedom and civil liberties were decreed (if only partially established) upon a national scale. Religion, military defense, and education were nationalized. Finally the national spirit expressed itself in the wars and imperialism of the later Revolutionary and the Napoleonic eras.

Other Western peoples in varying ways basically repeated the French experience. Partly for reasons inherent in their own history, partly in imitation of France, partly in reaction to French imperialism, they likewise established national institutions and strove to defend and extend them, even though this meant international war and the conquest of other nations. By 1815 almost everywhere in Western civilization the nation in idea and institution had become the real or desired supreme unit of society.

As with most ideas in history the origins of popular nationalism are to be found earlier than the first researchers believed, though not as early as enthusiasts would imagine. National patriotism began to be popular in France before the Revolutionary period, usually considered the time for its first manifestation. In England's North American colonies incipient national loyalty became evident by 1740 and, though it was not deeply felt by most until the next century, the Revolution of '76 galvanized it for increasing numbers.[12] In the England of a century earlier the Cromwellian revolt with its myth of "a chosen people" had nationalistic overtones. A good Puritan was a good Englishman devoted to England and to English interests at home and abroad. And his government, the national government, was supposed to and did work for the national Puritan and commercial interests, through moralistic repression at home, through navigation acts to aid British merchants abroad, and through war against Holland which increased the power of England by eliminating a national competitor.

Of what the common man thought, we have, of course, little or no record. But certainly by the eighteenth century intellectual leaders in the West were more than occasionally conceiving of the nation as a people united by common interests, as more, therefore, than a king and the subjects he controlled.[13] Further, they were beginning to speak of patriotism in the sense of devotion to this nation (not simply the dynasty) as a highly desirable virtue for all men. The word "patriot" appeared increasingly often with the quite modern meaning of "he who in a free government, cherishes his fatherland, is devoted to his fatherland, or more accurately the public welfare." [14] Moreover, intellectual leaders were beginning to believe that the propertied were or ought to be citizens who by right possessed interests and

voice in the national affairs and for whom the national government ought to govern. And as they came to believe this,
their national consciousness and sentiment quickened and
deepened.

The growing popular concern with the *patrie* becomes
apparent about the middle of the century. The Abbé Coyer
in 1755, for example, published his *Dissertations pour être
lues, la première sur le vieux mot Patrie, la seconde sur la
nature du peuple.*[15] Surprised and angered that the word
patrie was no longer used, he argued that soldiers should
be taught to die for the public good, and that everyone—
judges, priests, women—owed their first duty to the fatherland. While Coyer's was an early voice, it was not an
isolated one. About twenty years before, the English philosopher and unsuccessful statesman Bolingbroke had
published his *On the Spirit of Patriotism.*[16] In 1745 Henry
Fielding wrote for a newspaper called *The True Patriot.*
In 1750 a *Histoire de la patrie*—of the Dutch provinces—
appeared in France. In 1758 an anonymous author in Switzerland brought out a book entitled *Vom dem National-
stolze,* and in 1765 Friedrich Karl von Moser coined the
word *Nationalgeist* when he published his treatise *Von
dem deutschen Nationalgeist.*[17] In 1762 Charles Pierre
Colardeau wrote a poem called "Le Patriotisme," seven
years later a lawyer named de Rossel published a *Histoire
du patriotisme français, ou Nouvelle histoire de France* in
six volumes, and in 1771 Philip Freneau wrote his "Poem
on the Rising Glory of America." During the years 1760-
1780 the French Academy held contests for eulogies of
famous citizens and patriots like Michel de l'Hospital,
Bayard, and Colbert.[18]

As yet most writers on patriotic subjects retained their
belief in monarchy. A lover of the old days probably expressed prevailing opinion when he declared, "It is said
that the word *patrie* is quite modern, and very new. . . .
Please Heaven that it may always remain so. Our *patrie* is
in our king united with his subjects." [19] And in 1787 the

Academy of Châlons-sur-Marne offered a prize for a paper on "the best means for reviving and encouraging patriotism in a monarchy."

But conditions and ideas were changing. Questions were being asked. The answers given revealed the connection between popular government and popular patriotism. As early as 1710 the clever Bishop Fénelon would write during a time when France was threatened from the outside, "The affairs of the King are violently becoming ours . . . the nation must save itself." [20] Fénelon was ahead of his time, but he was not far ahead. The famous chancellor d'Aguesseau, pronouncing a panegyric on Louis XIV before the Parlement of Paris in 1715, asked whether "love of country" was only to be found in a popular state, whether it was an exotic plant in monarchies, a plant which grew healthily and produced precious fruit only in a republic where each citizen regarded the well-being of the state as his own.[21] Montesquieu, the philosopher-lawyer, noted in his *The Spirit of the Laws* (1748) the close relation between love of country and the republican form of government.[22] In 1754 the Marquis d'Argenson, a liberal jurist, wrote in his journal, "National opinions prevail and could lead far. Never have the words nation and state been so often repeated as today. These two words were never used under Louis XIV; the idea did not even occur to people. Never have they been so informed as today of the rights of the nation and of liberty." [23]

If for most men the *patrie* still meant the king and his subjects and patriotism chiefly devotion to the monarch, sentiment was changing. Bolingbroke's two essays of the 1730's, *The Idea of a Patriot King* as well as his *On the Spirit of Patriotism*,[24] marked a transition from the absolute monarchical to a more popular if still limited conception of nation. "The service of our country," according to this thwarted statesman turned philosopher, "is no chimerical, but a real duty." Every citizen who was a *real patriot* would bend "all the force of his understanding, and direct

all his thoughts and actions to the good of his country"—
that is "to the good of the people," "the ultimate and true
end of government." Duty to country, Bolingbroke believed, was best exercised with limited monarchy and an
aristocracy. In his England a constitutional king completely
devoted to his "country's interests" together with those who
were gifted with a "larger proportion of the ethereal spirit,"
should preserve and guide "human kind." "The true image
of a free people," in the mind of Bolingbroke, was "that
of a patriarchical family, where the head and other members are united by one common interest, and animated by
a common spirit." [25] But the patriarch's, the king's interests
were not just his alone. While to Bolingbroke the king was
to "most justly esteem" the nation's wealth "to be his
wealth, the power his power, the security and the honour,
his security and honour," he made it quite clear that the
reverse was also true, that the king should govern only in
the interest of the nation.[26]

Bolingbroke's "spirit of patriotism" apparently was not
a spirit to be equally shared by all, nor were all the inhabitants of a country equally citizens. To him, nevertheless, a
nation was not just a monarch and his subjects, nor was the
purpose of government just the promotion of narrowly
dynastic interests. The national interests were beginning
to be identified with those of the people who inhabited
the country, and the citizens of this country shared both
its responsibilities and its privileges.

Grimm, the literary critic, would ask why the Abbé
Coyer was surprised that the word *patrie* was never used.
He gave his own reply: orphans could not rightly use the
word and hence it was "necessary to continue to assert that
we serve the king and the state and not the *patrie*." [27]
Grimm's question and reply themselves indicate the trend
of opinion. The family of words stemming from the Latin
patria were entering more and more into common usage
because more men were more and more considering themselves members of a larger entity they called the nation. The

famous *Encyclopédie* of Diderot defined a citizen as "a member of a free society of several families, who shares the rights of this society and enjoys its privileges." There was "no *patrie* under the yoke of despotism." The *patrie* was a "father and children" in the sense of a family, a society, a free state, "of which we are members and of which the laws assure our liberties and our happiness." [28] This had little reality behind it when it was written in the mid-eighteenth century. After the revolts of 1776 in the United States and 1789 in France it would not be inaccurate, for nations composed of citizens were emerging.

If in 1789 in France opinion still favored monarchy, the nation nevertheless had come to be identified with the people who resided within its borders—at least with the propertied and lettered portion of them. All the adult propertied males were considered citizens, stockholders in the common enterprise, the nation. The nation of people was thus taking the place of the monarch as the sovereign, the legal entity,[29] and the symbol of unity and power. The sovereign "general will" of Rousseau's *Contrat social* was thus becoming the national will about which he was later concerned in the *Considérations sur le gouvernement de Pologne.*

In 1694 the French Academy defined the nation as "all the inhabitants of the same state, of the same country, who live under the same laws and use the same language." [30] A hundred years later the nation was often thought to be composed of citizens, including perhaps a monarch, who spoke the same language, inhabited the same territory, and also had a common government which represented and spoke for them.

What was the nation? [31] It was all the citizens. As they were, to paraphrase the Abbé Sieyès, everything, so the nation was everything. A French lawyer and pamphleteer of 1789, Lacretelle *aîné,* put down the new and prevailing concept as he wrote upon the coming convocation of the Estates General. A nation, he said, was the citizens who inhabited a territory, held property or performed tasks essential to those who cultivated the land, who obeyed the laws, paid taxes, and served the country. As these citizens possessed everything and collectively constituted the society they were the sole judges of what the society should do.[32] Robespierre's definition of the *patrie* in 1793 carried out the full implications of this idea. "What," he asked, "is the fatherland if it is not the country where one is a citizen and a member of the sovereign. The word fatherland in aristocratic states . . . means something only for the patricians who have usurped the sovereignty. Only in a democracy is the state truly the *patrie* of all the individuals who compose it, and able to count as many interested defenders as it numbers citizens."[33] The nation therefore, comprised the active citizens, and they could use the instrument of the national state to express their, the national, will. In turn they were to be devoted to their nation and willing to defend it.

The French patriots of '89 did not immediately overthrow their monarchy as had the American revolutionists a few years before. They waited until 1792; even in '93 there were many who opposed the guillotining of Louis XVI. The dynastic idea died hard. What had happened, however, was that the nation was no longer confounded with the king. It had evolved into a collective but single body, a being above the king, above clergy, above noble, above province, above manor and village, above any of the old unifying loyalties. Its instrument, the nation-state, could do anything. It could and did efface older but lesser distinctions, loyalties, unities. It could first argue with the monarchy, clergy, and nobility, then fight them and temporarily destroy them. It could weld together all the provinces and mold their diversities [34] into a whole.

And more. As the citizens were the sole arbiters of the nation, so the nation was independent of other nations.[35] Just as the king had been sovereign within his domains and he and his domains were independent of outside control, so now the nation was sovereign and independent. Citizens not only comprised the nation; in their collective national activities they were not subject to any control beyond their own will. In 1793 Carnot, the French organizer of victory, put accurately in words what was becoming practice. "Actually the nations are among themselves in the political order what individuals are among themselves in the social order." [36]

Each citizen possessed rights and privileges within the nation and each nation had the right to determine its own destinies. With these fundamental propositions, men could acquire a fatherland. They were legitimate children, no longer orphans as Grimm had declared them, and they could be devoted to the nation in the way Grimm had implied they should be.[37] During the 1770's the economist-statesman Turgot told Louis XVI that the orders of France were so engrossed by their personal (class) interests that no common interest was apparent, that hence the monarch had to do everything himself.[38] After 1776 and 1789 in the United States and western Europe this was no longer as true as it had been. Citizens possessed a common interest, the national interest which was but their own. When they acted patriotically to perform the public duties they were but serving themselves. National patriotism could now be as deep as the citizen's interest in his own welfare. As Alexis de Tocqueville later remarked of the United States, patriotism grew by "exercise of rights, and in the end, it is confounded with the personal interest of the citizen. A man comprehends the influence which the prosperity of his country has upon his own welfare; he is aware that the laws authorize him to contribute his assistance to that prosperity, and he labors to promote it as a portion of his right. . . ." [39] Even in those countries where kings continued to reign, they now had to do so in the name of the nation. The monarchical interests, as Fénelon had long before remarked of Louis XIV's, became violently the people's.

At first this was not in practice but only in public opinion. Practice followed, first in England, the American colonies, and France, and then later and always in varying
fashion in the rest of the world. In England a king was
beheaded in 1649 because he thwarted the will of the
dominant Puritan group which considered itself the nation, and from 1689 propertied Englishmen represented
the nation. While the monarchy still symbolized the national unity, it was severely and increasingly limited by
the will of the propertied who acted as if they were the
nation. American colonists of property threw off the rule
of their legitimate monarch in 1776, and, though they
were first tempted to establish a monarchy, created a constitutional republic in 1787. From this time onward in the
United States the national will, if often shaken, always remained supreme. In France the king was at first, in 1789-
1791, limited by a national constitution made by the
propertied representatives of the nation, then guillotined
in 1793 by a National Convention. While one or another
type of monarchy was restored until 1870, nearly all the
rulers governed not because of God's or their own but the
national will. Even when they attempted to rule absolutely
they felt it practical to consult the nation in a plebiscite
or were forced to grant a national charter.

Not only were the kings limited or overthrown. The
ancient royal and clerical institutions and functions—the
armies, the churches, the educational systems—became nationalized.[40] In the France of the late eighteenth and nineteenth centuries what had been the king's, the noble's, or
the priest's actually became the nation's. In other lands,
in the Germanies and Russia, the monarchies continued
to play a greater role. But in these countries as well the
rulers could no longer ignore the national will, and in
much of Europe nationalization of institutions and ideas
proceeded during the nineteenth century at almost as swift
a pace as in the Western lands.

Popular nationalism was thus part of the general move-

ment toward republicanism and democracy, of the
movement against monarchical, aristocratic, and clerical
domination. The national idea and the nation-state became
the instruments through which men could obtain liberty
and pursue happiness. The chancellor d'Aguesseau had
asked in 1715 if love of fatherland was to be found only in
popular states. The answer of many later intellectuals and
political leaders was "Yes." They agreed with the seventeenth-century's La Bruyère that there was "no fatherland
under despotism" and they supported Saint-Évremond's
epigram that "love of father-land is truly love of self."
When the nation-state could afford protection, rights, and
privileges, then it became possible for more men to feel
themselves part of it, to love it and fight for it.[41] And as
the national state acquired more and more functions, national feeling deepened and widened. The nation became
the being, the entity through which the individual obtained what he wanted, a symbol standing for liberty and
property, and an institution that could triumph over the
arbitrary rule and aristocratic privilege that threatened
property and denied liberty. When the *patrie,* the individual's own nation, became something, then he owed it
something.[42] Private interest became public virtue. The
public, the national good became synonymous with individual welfare.[43]

All men were not immediately recognized as full citizens, as having equal shares in and responsibility for the
nation. And it seems certain that the peasants and new
industrial workers did not then become as patriotic as the
bourgeoisie. Only the propertied, it was then believed,
really had a stake in the nation. Voltaire in his essay on
the "Patrie" in his *Philosophic Dictionary* early expressed
what was to be the eighteenth-century's dominant view and
reality. Only those who owned a house and land, who had
a voice in the common affairs possessed a *patrie.* "When
those who possess like myself, fields and houses, assemble
for their common interests, I have a voice in this assembly.

I am a part of the whole, a part of the community, a part
of the sovereign. Here is my fatherland." [44]

Those who owned the nation's wealth, then, were the
nation and the nation was sovereign. When their representatives met, they represented the sovereign will. This
"will" was on its way to becoming omnipotent, perhaps
more pervasive and mightier than the seventeenth-century
divine-right monarch. Whatever the citizens willed, their
nation-state could do. They could hence look to the national government, their government, for establishment of
their rights, for improvement of their individual welfare,
for protection against their enemies, internal and external. This government's function, in short, was to care for
the national interests which were identical with the interests of the citizens. In most countries the national governments were in fact limited in their activities by historical
custom and in several by a constitution during the next
century and a half, though even these, as Edmund Burke
would point out, were national. But regardless of limitation
placed upon them the scope and reach of the national governments extended to all phases of life, and especially during internal crises and wartime these governments were
able in the name of national security to exercise almost
unlimited power.

The very magnitude of the problems faced by eighteenth-century societies compelled national solutions. Fewer
and fewer political, economic, and social problems could
be solved by individual or local group effort. Populations
increased and men were brought closer together by the
slowly but constantly improving means of communication.
Trade flowed beyond the provinces, ideas circulated beyond the courts and capitals. The action of Paris could no
longer be isolated from that of Bordeaux, of London from
Manchester, of Philadelphia from Charleston. Each individual life depended increasingly upon a growing number
of others. The nation-state became the institutional will of
the group and the idea of nation the symbol of their unity.

Especially was this true during the crises of revolution and war from 1776 onward. When the American colonies fought England from 1776 to 1783 they could not hope to win (though at times they tried) by individual action. When the French Revolutionaries from 1789 to 1795 faced counterrevolution at home and nearly all of the European monarchies abroad, they had to unite most Frenchmen by persuasion and propaganda if possible, by force and terror if necessary. To win a revolution or war required by the end of the eighteenth century the decisive action of a unified group acting in the name of the *patrie*, of a government acting for and through the nation.

Chapter VII

THE NATION-STATE NATIONALIZES
(1715-1815)

ꙮ|ꙮ

As these national governments took firm hold they directly and indirectly stimulated national patriotism. They were at once a result of national sentiment and a stimulus to more. Political theorists and practitioners alike understood this, and the latter acted as if they knew what the former had written.

In his *Considérations sur le gouvernement de Pologne* the otherwise romantic but here realistic Rousseau instructed the ruler of Poland, "It is the national institutions which form the genius, the character, the tastes and the morals of a people, which make them themselves and set them off from others, which inspire them with that ardent love of fatherland based upon ineradicable habits." [1] A few years later, in 1787, the authors of the *Federalist* papers, persuasively arguing for a strong national constitution, declared that American national government should address itself "immediately to the hopes and fears of individuals" and attract support from "those passions which have the strongest influence upon the human heart." [2] And the German Pietist minister and monarchist, Schleiermacher, was soon to assert that the purpose of the state was "to preserve the consciousness of the unity of the whole

118

people as a true and natural unity and to express this idea in all forms of life." [3]

The national states acted in almost every field of human activity. They attempted to reduce or eliminate all loyalties and divisions within the country which might stand in the way of national unity. They acted directly upon the hopes and fears of citizens by maintaining order, protecting property, establishing national churches and school systems, by encouraging the use of national languages, by creating national armies, by assuring national privileges like civil liberties, by offering national economic opportunities through tariffs, and by making national public improvements such as roads. What had been responsibilities of king, priest, and noble now became the national state's. And as the nation-state assumed more and more of these responsibilities, thereby acting directly upon the "hopes and fears of individuals," these individuals looked more and more for the fulfillment of their desires, for the solution of their problems to the national state.

In trouble and in hope citizens learned to rely upon their national governments rather than upon the older instruments of authority. In France, for example, the old governmental institutions and organizations like the pays d'élection, the bailliages, the châtellenies, disappeared before the uniform national administrative system decreed by a national will voiced by the Revolutionary assemblies. The nation-state thus became the chief means as well as the chief end of action. In the name of the nation feudal classes were abolished or their special privileges reduced. In the name of the nation, governments extended their control over the churches and church property, thus even in Catholic countries continuing the process begun in Protestant countries during the Reformation. As the Third Estate of Nemours wrote in its cahier in 1789, so these governments considered it "necessary that there be no state within a state, no corps which may cause trouble or

raise money by an authority independent of that of the
patrie. . . ." [4]

In France, as in England over two centuries earlier, the
church became a national church.[5] During the Revolution
the governing groups confiscated church property, declaring it part of the national patrimony and as such to be
used for the benefit of the nation. In a Civil Constitution
of the Clergy, the National Assembly made the clergymen
national servants, forced them to swear "to be faithful to
the nation," and almost severed the connection of the Catholic priests with their "universal" head, the Pope in Rome.
And with Robespierre the National Convention attempted
in 1794 to establish a worship of the national state where
festivals of reason inculcated patriotism for the Republic
of Virtue. Religious loyalties were tenacious, as Napoleon
later comprehended; they held firm longer than most of
the older ones. National loyalties, however, were becoming stronger. Even with the new ardent Protestants of Germany, the Pietists, national feeling was nearly as strong as
religious dogma. The belief steadily mounted that even
"Religions are national and modified according to the disposition of the people." [6]

With more success the governments nationalized their
armed forces. The king's mercenary and feudal armies became the nation's; some of these took the name, as in
France and later the United States, of national guards.[7]
In the words of Barère, the Jacobin orator, the soldiers
became citizens and the citizens soldiers. And all the citizens became soldiers. The famous *levée en masse* of 1793
called upon all the inhabitants to come to the aid of their
patrie. "Let everyone," cried Barère as he argued for the
decree, "assume his post in the national and military effort that is preparing. The young will fight, the married
will forge arms . . . provide subsistence, the women will
make soldiers' clothing . . . become nurses in hospitals
for the wounded, the children will make lint out of old
linen, and the old men will . . . be carried to the public

squares to inflame the courage of the young warriors and preach the hatred of kings and the unity of the Republic." [8] The chief and highest duty of man became bearing arms for the nation-state, fighting for the defense of what was "dearest and most sacred, the nation." [9] Once the subjects had taken little interest in war unless their own city had been attacked, because after all it was the king's and not their war. [10] Now, increasingly, all war was theirs because they were citizens, they formed the armies, and the armies defended and extended *their* interests. Hence the state could and did call upon them.

What France began here, other nation-states could ignore only at their peril as the wars of the Revolution and Napoleon proved. When, and only when, the English, German, and Spanish armies became in large part armies of patriots defending their fatherlands, could the French be defeated and sacred English, German, and Spanish soil and interests be defended. [11] From the 1790's onward armies became increasingly armies of citizen-patriots, the more patriotic, apparently, the more effective.

But how could patriots for these armies or to serve the nation in any way be created? Men were not born with inherent love of country, with the "national character" implanted in them, or speaking their "native tongue." Unlike geniuses, patriots had to be made. Nature was credited with much by the eighteenth century, but it could not be trusted to develop men unassisted. Those already patriotic and the governments which came to represent them by the end of that century understood this. By the eighteenth century significant cultural similarities, in language for instance, had already grown within the various groups. More were "discovered" and when they did not exist they were to be created through national education. But cultural similarity was not enough; men had to be made loyal. For this, education was also helpful and necessary. Through public-school education, national holidays and festivals, the publication of patriotic histories and collections of folk-

lore, national ideals could be inculcated, the national character molded, and above all national loyalties created. As
Rousseau had advocated, the late eighteenth century made
a tremendous effort to make men national patriots. So
great a governmental effort was required that biology and
nature could not have been more than neutral. Men did
not, contrary to Herder's belief, apparently carry their
God-given group character within them as did the plants
and animals.[12]

All during the century intellectual leaders, particularly
in France, encouraged the teaching and use of the national
languages. The reasons they gave were varied. People could
learn their "native" language and understand it more readily than Latin. They needed it in their daily lives, in their
businesses, and in their relationships with one another.
Latin was "dead," could not express meaning as accurately,
and hence was impractical except for scholars. Perhaps
these arguments were in part only rationalizations of the
bourgeoisie, who saw the various patois as obstacles to
trade and found learning Latin a waste of time and money.
But whatever the motive the belief mounted that each
nation should have its own language which all the nationals should use. Toward the end of the century the
arguments became more obviously the patriotic. The national language should be uniformly employed throughout the national territory to enable men of the same nation to recognize and understand each other, the spiritual
wealth of the nation was stored in its language and could
only be tapped by those understanding it, and the true
spirit and character of a nation could only be expressed
in the national tongue.[13]

In France from the time in the early 1700's of the great
Jansenist leader of the University of Paris, Rollin (1661-
1741), through the Revolution, the demand grew for the
teaching of French and the use of French in all instruction in the schools. In 1763 Elie Bertrand in his *Dictionnaire universel des fossiles propres et des fossiles occiden-*

tales expressed a common view: "All our masters teach us Latin and Greek which are never known perfectly and soon entirely forgotten; none teach us to be useful to the fatherland by employing our time, our money, our talents to practical things." [14] After the closing of the Jesuit schools about the same time, French was increasingly taught and used, even in those citadels of conservatism, the colleges and universities.

Almost everywhere in the Western world, though usually a bit later than in France, the same tendencies prevailed. While French dominated in court and diplomatic and Latin in academic circles, Herder, Fichte, and Schleiermacher in the Germanies pleaded for the use of German,[15] just as Noah Webster desired an American language in the United States and Alfieri demanded Italian for Italians. In southern and eastern Europe as well, movements for the exclusive employment of national tongues began. In Greece Adamantios Korais was creating modern Greek with his numerous publications of the Greek classics. Josef Jungmann in Bohemia wrote a Czech grammar, a history of Czech literature, and a Czech-German dictionary, proclaiming language the supreme criterion of nationality. A Bishop Mïcu (Samuil Klein) published a Rumanian grammar. In Hungary John Ribyini asserted the superiority of Magyar, while in Russia Lomonosov in his Russian grammar (1755) declared Russian the most expressive of all languages.[16]

With the French Revolution the national languages became a matter of governmental concern.[17] Again it was France which led. During the Revolutionary years Mirabeau, Grégoire, Talleyrand, and Barère, for example, tried in various ways to spread the use of French among the inhabitants of France and thus stimulate patriotic ardor. The National Convention provided that the laws be read to the people in French, and that a teacher of French be appointed in all districts such as the Breton where French was not customarily spoken.[18]

All Frenchmen were to speak French. This, it was believed, would reflect their unity and perpetuate their liberty. A correspondent of the governmental Bishop Grégoire in 1790 wrote, "Unity of language is not only useful
for public assemblies; the safety, the public actions, the
execution of the laws, the unity of the regime all demand
this reform. . . . The great number of dialects could have
been useful in the ninth century and during the long
reign of feudalism . . . but today we all have the same
law as master, and are no longer 'Rouergas' or 'Bourguig-
nons' . . . we are all Frenchmen [and] should have only
one language, as we have only one heart." [19] The Jacobin
Barère, reporting for the Committee of Public Safety in
January, 1794, declared that the dialects and foreign languages spoken in France "perpetuated the reign of fanaticism and superstition, secured the domination of priests
and aristocrats . . . and favored the enemies of France."
Calling it "treason to the Patrie to leave citizens in ignorance of the national language," he demanded that "the
language of a free people" be "one and the same." [20]

Possibly the greatest stimulus to the use of French during the period was not the result of the direct efforts of
individual patriots and the national governments but of
the change in the nature of government and the enlargement of its functions. As more people participated in government, more had to understand what was being done on
a national scale. As radical and new laws were rapidly
promulgated, it became advantageous to understand them
—for self-protection if for no other reason. As men entered
the national services, military and civil, they found it necessary and expedient to understand and use the language
of the law, the language of command.[21] In 1812 a prefect
of the department Seine-Inférieure summarized these reasons for the increased use of French. "(1) The habit and
necessity of reading these numerous laws, the decrees of
every kind posted on the walls of all the communes, these
public announcements which come daily to excite and feed

the curiosity of all citizens. (2) The establishment of municipal duties which oblige so many peasants to write in an intelligible style in order to correspond with superior authorities, especially those of the popular societies, of which all the members must often speak from the rostrum to colleagues as ignorant as they but who are usually disposed to ridicule them if they speak in popular dialect. (3) The military conscription and levy which, taking from home a good part of the youth, places them in position to purify their language through the habit of attempting to speak better or differently. Thus it results that when they return to their homes, they bring with them a way of speaking, which though it deteriorates a little, nevertheless has some effect upon those with whom they associate." [22] Indirectly, too, the employment of national languages was fostered by the new roads and bridges built, often for military reasons, during the eighteenth century. Facilitating communication among regions these made a common language more desirable and stimulated its use as they increased awareness of national unity. Probably, as Brunot, the historian of the French language observed, the engineers of bridges and roads "served" the cause of national languages better and more than many academicians. [23]

As it was with languages, so it was with all education. More and more the objective came to be the making of national patriots, good citizens. Here again republicanism and national patriotism were closely tied. In his analysis of government in a republic Montesquieu foresaw clearly the problem that would face later statesmen. If despotism and monarchy were eliminated, they could no longer rely upon the old principles of fear and honor to bind men to the state but would have to use education to instill love of laws and country and thus preserve the government. "Everything," Montesquieu thought, "depended on establishing this love in a republic, and to inspire it ought to be the principal business of education . . ." [24] But even in a monarchy some were beginning to think education for patriotism vital. Believing that the first fundamental of public morality was childhood instruction, Turgot in 1775 urged Louis XVI to establish a Council of National Instruction to assure "uniformity of patriotic views." [25]

The great popularizer of patriotic education was, of course, Jean Jacques Rousseau. In his *Considerations on the Government of Poland* and the *Letter to d'Alembert* on the theater, he proposed a Spartan (Lycurgus) molding of citizens through training in the home, the school, and through public celebrations. He pleaded for an education which would place constantly before men, from mother's milk to death, the idea of the nation and thus awaken in them ardent love of their country.[26] To form a patriot (Polish in this particular case) Rousseau would have the child learn to read by reading about his own country, at ten years know all the products, at twelve all the provinces, roads, and towns, at fifteen all the history, and at sixteen all the laws. There would not be a great action or illustrious man of whom the child did not have "full memory and heart and of whom he could not instantly give an account." His teachers would not be foreigners or priests but patriots, "married if possible, and distinguished by their morals, honesty, good sense, enlightenment. . . ." [27] To arouse patriotism and consciousness of unity, the citizens, in adulthood as well as childhood, would be edified by simple public spectacles, pageants, and folk games.[28] The effect of these would be "to reinforce the national character, augment natural inclinations and to give a new energy to all the emotions." [29]

Whether many of the French Revolutionary leaders actually read Rousseau may be questioned. Some, like Barère,[30] did, and many had similar views on patriotic education which they attempted to put into practice. The Constitution of 1791 provided for a system of free public instruction and for commemorative days to develop "the spirit of fraternity among citizens and attach them to the Constitution, the country and the laws." [31] The Convention of

1793-1794 decreed the establishment of public primary schools to teach French and train for citizenship. The orator Barère, who so often led in patriotic zeal, expressed a popular view when he declared that the purpose of schooling was to create "love of country," that each man should prepare himself for service to it. Children, he asserted, belonged to the "general family before the particular families, and when the great family, the nation, calls, all private spirit must disappear." [32]

To issue decrees was easier than to establish schools which inculcated patriotism. Until Napoleon acted, not much was done about state primary schools, though many plans were broached and some initiated. The movement had begun, however, and during Napoleon's regime French children and teachers were swearing allegiance to him and to France. Possibly the Revolutionary patriots were more effective with their patriotic commemorative days, from the great festivals of Federation in 1790 to the celebrations for Robespierre's Supreme Being and Republic of Virtue in June, 1794. There can be little doubt that many Frenchmen experienced an intense feeling of unity in the Federations in Brittany, Alsace, Dauphiné, and particularly Paris in the first half of 1790. On July 14, 1790, perhaps 15,000,000 Frenchmen attended celebrations all over France and many of them swore loyalty to the nation, the law, and the king. [33]

What began in political or patriotic education with the Revolution spread widely in Europe and America. For the most part, the greatest strides were made in the nineteenth century when every great and small nation moved to make education universal, free, and compulsory in order to create "good citizens," a term which in practice meant citizens more devoted to the nation and more willing to sacrifice themselves for it. Often the first stimulus to these educational reforms arose out of opposition to some real or potential oppressor, as in the German reaction to the Napoleonic conquests after 1806. But everywhere teachers

and scholars, as at Berlin in the 1810's, were appointed and
paid by the various governments to teach civic duty and
devotion to the national welfare.[34] Everywhere, as in the
young United States with its Jeremy Belknap, Nicholas
Pike, and Noah Webster, the attempt was made to create
a national character through the teaching of the national
language or even national spelling and national arith-
metic.[35]

Formal schooling and public festivals were but two
phases of the new national education. To inculcate patriotism anything from folklore to clothing could be utilized. Percy in England, Burns in Scotland, and Herder,[36]
and, a little later, the Grimms in the Germanies collected
and published national lore and songs, inspiring in this
way a love of a common past. French and Spanish acad-
emies as well as individuals began to publish dictionaries
and grammars of their respective national languages, and
this practice spread to eastern and southern Europe, to
what would later become Czechoslovakia and Yugoslavia,
for example. In eighteenth-century Germany Klopstock
called for a German poet (himself?) to "bestow honor upon
his German fatherland," [37] and Karl Friedrich von Moser
helped create a *Nationalgeist* with his *Patriotisches Archiv*.
Patriotic histories, such as had appeared in England and
France earlier, began to be written even in backward Russia (Karamzin's) and yet unborn Bulgaria (Paisi's). During the Revolution the French adopted a patriotic dress—
the long trousers, the cockade, the tricolor—and in Austria
in 1813 a Caroline Pichler pleaded for "German costumes"
for German women that they might "break away from foreign dictates." [38] If, with these stimulants and pressures, all
men did not become patriotic, it could only be because
some were perverse, incapable of emotional ties or loyalty.

To a superficial observer it might appear that liberal
eighteenth-century views on economics and civil liberties
ran contrary to the nationalistic trends in other fields, such
as religion and education. It is true that leading philos-

ophers and reformers believed with Adam Smith and the French physiocrats in *laissez faire* and opposed the governmental restraints of *étatism*. It is equally true that liberties of speech and religion essentially meant individual freedom from control by outside institutionalized authority. *Laissez faire* and civil liberties seem hardly consonant with strong nationalism. As these were considered and established in the eighteenth century and later, however, this presumption is not precisely accurate.

If men wished to speak or worship freely, only the national governments were able to guarantee these privileges. If merchants desired to trade without restriction or hindrance, it was only the national state that could establish *laissez faire* and hence promote trade in the wide area enclosed by the national political boundaries.[39] If the freedom to own property or gain profits was threatened anywhere within the country, it would be threatened everywhere within the country; therefore the right to property had to be guaranteed by the only institution capable of exercising nationwide control, the nation-state. Only from a national government that could cut across or ignore local boundaries and that was more powerful than a feudal order or a trade guild was the solution to the problems of economic or any freedom then to be found.

In this significant sense, then, national sentiment was strengthened at the expense of other older religious and feudal loyalties as the drive for liberty intensified and became realized. *Laissez faire* meant in the historical pattern of the time not only freedom from governmental control to seek profit but also freedom from all kinds of hindrances —from tax inequalities based on ancient privileges, from feudal dues, from local and provincial tolls and tariffs, and from craft guild regulations on quality. Individual freedom meant not only freedom from the arbitrary rule of monarchs like Louis XIV and James I but also from religious conformity and from the social inequalities arising out of aristocratic privilege. In these circumstances only a national government, a government with authority above all authorities, could effectively act. While the national governments were not supposed, according to the bills of rights incorporated in the new constitutions, to interfere with the individual's liberties, they were the chosen instruments or policemen through which these liberties were won and preserved.

Few, however, thought of the state as just a policeman, a negative restraint on economic privilege. The liberals of the Revolutionary era believed that the nation-state should be a positive force for the defense and promotion of the national interests. The state, for instance, was supposed to prevent any internal disorder which might harm trade, to establish those uniform conditions (weights and measures) and laws (of contract) which might assist trade, and to protect and subsidize the nation's foreign commerce as well as its domestic manufacture. It is notable that the most influential book of the eighteenth century, that published in 1776 by the archadvocate of *laissez faire*, Adam Smith, was called *The Wealth of Nations*. The economic welfare of nations (England in particular), not individual businessmen, was indeed ever in the forefront of Smith's argument. Did he ask for freedom of trade? This was because freedom increased the wealth of the nation. Did he desire complete freedom for the individual entrepreneur? No. He was quite willing even to limit individual profits in terms of national interest. The severely (in theory) regulatory Navigation Acts he called "perhaps the wisest of all the commercial regulations of England" because he believed "defence is of much more importance than opulence." [40]

If Smith was willing to restrict freedom of trade in the national interest, others were willing to use the nation-state economy in both old and new ways. The old policies of "provision" established by the monarchs were continued except that now the king's interests became the national. In the young United States Alexander Hamilton, the Sec-

retary of Treasury, pleaded with the national House of
Representatives to encourage manufacturing. "Not only,"
he argued, "the wealth but the independence and security
of a country appear to be materially connected with the
prosperity of a manufacture. Every nation, with a view to
these great objects, ought to endeavor to possess within itself all the essentials of national supply." The defense and
security of the nation, especially should war come, thus
often took precedence over complete freedom of industry
and trade.[41]

With the possible exception of Britain, which later, in
the nineteenth century, saw its national interest in free
trade as long as it (Britain) dominated in manufacture and
on the seas, all nations followed policies like those of Hamilton.[42] They not only established national uniformity in
weights and measures and in business law, they provided
for national currencies and banks. To encourage home
manufacture they continued and increased tariffs at the
national boundaries. At times they went further. National
governments in crisis, as the French in 1793 and 1794, set
prices and wages, confiscated land belonging to priest and
noble, and in general taxed and regulated as the leaders
thought the national interest dictated. While the huge welfare state was still a hundred years in the future, some
leaders like Barère in the French Convention in 1794 also
believed that the nation should care for the poor, the aged,
and the sick.[43] And in fact the national governments would
assume increasingly, if reluctantly, these old duties of king,
priest, noble, and guild.

For increasing numbers of Europeans the national government became the father and protector. The old world
of status and fixed values crumbled rapidly in the eighteenth century. As this happened men sought refuge in the
nation against internal threat and external enemy alike.
Now in revolution and war, some men still turned to old
authorities, to lord and priest. Oftener most sought protection in their national government and in the idea of

nation. As they did, they increasingly became national patriots. Again and again this cycle seems to have repeated itself. Society had become fluid and dynamic. Long-fixed loyalties were in dissolution; fear sharpened the desire for a new authority which would afford protection and offer hope; the nation provided these. As the nation acquired significance and its government acted, especially in times of emergency when need was great, national consciousness and feeling were strengthened.[44]

While this dynamic process was taking place, the philosophic cosmopolitanism of the eighteenth century tended to decline, and national prejudices and hatreds to become accentuated.[45] More often now men exalted their own nation, and placed its welfare first, though this might mean injury to other like groups. The Dantonist Robert declared with the applause of the Convention in 1793: "I desire that the Legislator of France forget the universe for a moment and occupy itself with its own country. I wish that kind of national egoism without which we betray our duties . . . I love all men, I love particularly all free men, but I love the free men of France more than all the others of the universe." [46] Speaking in 1798 a German rationalist (*illuminé*) named Weishaupt caught clearly the meaning of what was happening as he perhaps coined the word "nationalisme" in French. When men united in nations, he declared, "they ceased to recognize themselves under a common name—. *Nationalism* or *National Love* took the place of general love. With the divisions of the globe and with its countries, goodwill contracted within limits which it could no longer surmount. Then it became a virtue to expand at the expense of those who were not under our dominion. Then to obtain this end it became permissible to distrust, deceive and offend strangers." [47]

Weishaupt described widespread opinion in western Europe during the war years, 1792-1815. It developed in France from 1792 when patriotism became synonymous with the support of the Revolution against internal and external enemies, where patriotic loyalty in defeat and invasion turned into patriotic pride in victory and expansion. Because of the fear and hatred of France, particularly of Napoleonic France, it happened in England, in the Germanies after 1806,[48] and, though the evidence is less abundant, in the Italies and Spain. And because of the example of France and the oppression of foreign conquerors, this nationalism was arising in Poland and Greece, and in some degree almost everywhere in Europe and the Americas. How, more particularly, this came about in these years of crisis warrants further attention.

Chapter VIII

THE SPREAD OF NATIONALISM
(1792-1815)

ɔ|ɔ

Revolution and war stimulated national feeling everywhere in Europe during the years 1792-1815. In hope of
liberty, in fear of oppression peoples developed common
attitudes which led to the first widespread and intense expression of what may be called modern nationalism. In the
France of 1792-1793 the common danger to the Revolution
and to France represented by *émigré* and foreign prince
inspired both unity and defiance. As the historian of
French Revolutionary diplomacy, Albert Sorel, observed,
the great mass of Frenchmen "saw something very practical
and real in the Revolution, the abolition of the feudal
regime . . . they saw in the armed emigration an attempt
to reestablish by force this hateful regime. The Revolution
was being accomplished to assure Frenchmen free possession of the soil of France. The foreign invasion was taking
place to destroy the Revolution, dismember France and
subjugate Frenchmen. They quite naturally identified love
of France with love of the Revolution. . . ." [1] The revolutionary demands for liberty, strategic requirements for
defense, governmental financial needs, and the personal
ambitions of politicians further inspired vast conquests,
first to the so-called natural frontiers and then far beyond.
If other men would not revolt as had the French, then

they, as the Second Propaganda Decree of December 15, 1792, proclaimed, would be forced to be free, that is free in the French manner. Believing themselves the "benefactors of the human race" the French were eager to carry their "superior" national institutions to all of Europe and perhaps the world. "Associate yourselves with eternal justice," cried the Girondist leader, Vergniaud, calling in January, 1792, for war against Austria, "save liberty from the tyrants. You will be at one and the same time the benefactors of your country and of humanity." [2] That most of Europe and the world either was not ready for or was unwilling to accept liberty *à la française* made little difference. French national and Napoleonic ambitions grew more swiftly than even their rapid military conquests, expanding steadily as success succeeded success. The French people, first stung into greater unity by defeat, were now united by pride in military superiority and victory.

French victories, at first passively if not happily received by the vanquished, were finally met by sullen resentment and then patriotic fury. War, conquest, oppression by one nation meant the rise of national consciousness and loyalty among the conquered and oppressed peoples. While the patriotic desire to acquire, defend, and spread liberty animated the French, at least at first, the desire for freedom *from* French *"liberté"* animated much of the rest of Europe. One common result was increased nationalism. The reaction of the oppressed nationalities became indeed, as Byron later sang, "the very poetry of politics." Peoples became aware, often for the first time, of their respective common traditions, common language, and common interests. And where the "commonness" did not exist, it was created by patriotic historians, educators, and politicians. When national traditions became associated with the wars against the invaders in the minds of the various groups, then nationalism rooted deeply in the popular mind. What the French "organizer of victory," Carnot, feared in 1793, that war might become nationalized, came to pass. As he surmised, the name of France became not only feared but hated. And out of the fear and hate, as out of hope by the French earlier, came the intensified desire of many European peoples for national unity, for national institutions —for an independent national government, for patriotic citizen armies, and for national education.

Hope, fear, hate in a time of insecurity and disintegrating values, these were fundamental in the growing nationalism. The nation became an answer to men's anxieties, a solution for their frustrations, and a refuge in a time of trouble. For many it became the hopeful road to a heavenly city of the future upon this earth.

In Britain the "French scare" of 1792-1793 brought war against France. The war and the "scare" led to resolutions for "Preserving Liberty and Property against Republicans and Levellers," to royal proclamations against seditious writings, to trials for treason of agitators like Muir, Hardy, and Tooke who, favoring the French Revolution, desired constitutional reform in Britain, and to the hardening of "Toryism" in all aspects of British life.[3] Thus the French threat united the British in defense of and pride in the British way of life. That same Arthur Young who from his extensive travels knew France so intimately formed in 1792 a "Loyal Association" whose purpose was to unify all those who desired to prove "their content with the Constitution of this Kingdom as Established at Present and to secure the Blessings we derive from its Influence." [4]

Hostility to France's Revolution gave birth to those classic statements of British patriotism, Edmund Burke's famous *Reflections on the Revolution in France* and the *Letters on a Regicide Peace*. In these he developed his earlier idea that the state, and he meant the British national state in particular, was a historically evolved organism. The liberties of Englishmen he saw as an *"entailed inheritance* derived to us from our forefathers, and to be transmitted to our posterity, as an estate specially belonging to the people of this kingdom, without any reference whatever to any other more general or prior right." ⁵ A national society he described as a contract, "a partnership in all art; a partnership in every virtue, and in all perfection. As the ends of such a partnership cannot be obtained in many generations, it becomes a partnership not only between those who are living, but between those who are living and those who are to be borne." ⁶ The political institutions, he argued, ought therefore to be the object of "religious reverence." In time of trouble earlier statesmen might have turned to God. Burke, Whig and liberal, turned to a metaphysical contract arising out of the English past.

Burke but put more rhetorically and spectacularly the reaction of many British patriots to the French threat. Wordsworth, Coleridge, Sydney Smith, George Canning, Lord Grenville, and the younger Pitt all spoke against France and its destructive uprooting of the past as they defended British institutions. If the British leaders were seldom as vocal as the French about their patriotism, they were as proud of their nation and as desirous of its independence. The British, already territorially unified and not without patriotism when the Revolution hit them, became more nationalist under its impact.

The experience of the disunited Germanies varied quite naturally from that of Britain, though in so far as nationalism was concerned the reactions to the French threat were similar. Although German political disunity would continue, the French conquests and oppression in many of the Germanies, including Prussia and Austria, stimulated a national patriotism that finally achieved its goal of an independent German nation in 1871. The brutal Napoleonic execution of the patriotic Nuremberg bookseller Palm, the crushing defeat of Prussia at Jena in 1806, and the repeated humiliation of proud Austria from 1797 to 1809 aroused many Germans to hope for national unity.⁷ While we know little about this feeling among peasants and workers, a great many of the intelligentsia and political

leaders became ardent patriots. Not only did philosophers
like Fichte, Schleiermacher, Friedrich Schlegel, and Arndt
preach devotion to fatherland but also soldiers like Mar-
witz and Gneisenau, statesmen like Stein and even the
Archduke John of the polyglot Austrian empire.[8]

The Prussian soldier Gneisenau after his experience
with British troops in North America perceived early the
meaning of the Revolution and its conquests for the Germanies, and what national efforts even from a conservative
view were required to repel the French. "The Revolution,"
this Prussian officer wrote in 1807, "has set in action the
national energy of the entire French people, thereby put-
ting the different classes on an equal social and fiscal basis,
thereby transforming the vital strength of the people and
their resources into interest-bearing capital, thereby abol-
ishing the former relationship of the states to one another
and the balance of power. If the other states wish to reestablish this balance, they must open and use these resources. They must take over the results of the Revolution
and so gain the double advantage of being able to place
their entire national energies in opposition to the enemy.
. . ."[9]

This kind of analysis repeated as it was at Jena, Berlin,
and Vienna led to reforms within the German states, especially those of Stein in Prussia. Its greatest effect was to
awaken civic interest, and this interest, quickened always
by hatred of the French oppressor, created a desire among
many Germans for a union of all Germans into a common
nation and state. In 1809 Friedrich Schlegel, employed
by the Austrian government to write patriotic propaganda,
appealed to his fellow Germans, "How much longer will
you be crushed beneath the heels of a proud conqueror?
. . . Awaken! Awaken, Germans, from the stupor of shame
and ignominy! Awaken and act for the sake of German
honor!"[10] And Germans were awakening. Like Schlegel's
the passionate outbursts of Arndt are not unrepresentative.
In him the romantic emotionalism of Rousseau and Herder,

whom he had read, became transformed into a violent patriotism. "We'll redden the iron with blood, with hangman's blood, with Frenchman's blood. Oh, sweet day of revenge. That sounds good to all Germans; that is the great cause."

How could this revenge be realized? Only through patriotism to that German nation of which Klopstock, Herder, and Friedrich Karl von Moser had earlier dreamed. Philosophers, poets, historians, and soldiers discovered with the pietist theologian Schleiermacher that the "individual cannot stand, cannot save himself, if that in which each and all of us are rooted—German freedom and feeling—be lost, and it is these that are threatened." [11] They came therefore to demand with Arndt not only "hatred against the crafty foreigners" but also the growth of a "general love among Germans." And some of them would agree with him that it was "the highest religion to love the Fatherland more clearly than lords and princes, fathers and mothers, wives and children." [12]

This religion came to be shared by more and more Germans.[13] Stung into action by French example and French oppression, they, too, began to identify their interests with a nation and to wish for union within a national state to which they could be loyal. To them there would have been much right in the statement of the journalist Rudolph Becker arrested by Napoleon for subversive German patriotic activity: "This attachment to the nation, which could be called *nationalism,* agrees perfectly with patriotism devoted to the state of which one is a citizen." [14]

Except for a momentary coalition against Napoleon after 1812, German unity did not then materialize. The aroused national spirit, however, burst into flame from the Rhine to the Vistula during the next century and a quarter, a flame so vast and hot that it would almost consume the Germans as well as their enemies. For similar reasons the same flame burned also in the Italies with men like Vittorio Alfieri, who hated the French with fury and exhorted his countrymen "to liberate Italy from the barbarians." [15] In a like way, though sometimes with different oppressors, Polish, Hungarian, Greek, Dutch, and Belgian nationalism also began. In these cases the nationalist rebellions were against the Russians, the Turks, the Austrians, and the French, against, for example, attempts like the Austrian under Joseph II to impose foreign rule, customs, and language.[16]

In their efforts to throw off oppressors the aroused peoples always had the French as well as the earlier American example. If the French could win freedom through the nation, so could they. At times the influence of the French was direct. In their abortive Constitution of 1791, Polish patriots stated their purpose to be the "general good" and the freedom and defense of the motherland, and they held "dearer than life and personal happiness the political existence, external independence, and internal freedom of the nation." [17] Ten years later the Greek Adamantios Korais, sounding a Greek *Trumpet of War* against the Turks, envisaged another *levée en masse:* "Able bodied men will fight with their arms. Old men will bestow blessings and exhortations. Priests will pray for the success of the army. . . . All men will lend their assistance to the cause for the sake of religion, fatherland, and their homes, their wives, their children, and for the sake of the present and future generations." [18] Thus when the French were not hated, other groups emulated them in their striving for a nation.

Out of oppression and hope for a better future, out of the belief that men could and should govern themselves in national groups, the sentiment of nationalism assumed its modern form in western countries and spread into central and southern Europe. Through the nation and its state men sought and believed they found the answers to their dilemmas and dreams, to their quest for liberty and security both within their group and in the relations of their group to other like groups. Perhaps, too, as Professor Eugene Anderson has provocatively suggested, the growing nationalism in part arose directly out of individual frustrations.[19] The evidence is clear that many of the most ardent national patriots of the time were men like Rousseau, Robespierre, Fichte, and Arndt who found in nationalism a way to overcome their individual failures and a means of achieving significance and fame.[20] Nationalism from 1789 to 1815 gave patriots a way of identifying themselves with the community and thus of finding security, status, and fatherly authority in a time of extreme uncertainty.[21] In another age they might have turned to other authorities, to priest, king, and noble, or in our own time to the psychiatrist. But in the Revolutionary era nationalism was an answer. Possibly it is true that every human society must be bound together by some authority which may be either imposed by force or accepted more or less freely. If this be true, then nationalism had begun to supply this authority, and the nation-state and national feeling were becoming the means and ends of action, the chief way by which men sought answers to their individual and social problems. Nationalism was well on its way to becoming the dominant religion.

As a religion it defied the laws of physical phenomena. Propagating itself, it grew stronger, more pervasive and ever more widespread. Paradoxically it became stronger as it fed upon itself, and burned ever hotter and brighter. Patriotism created patriotism, patriots forced others to be patriotic. Reason might counsel cosmopolitanism and caution hesitancy; emotion proved stronger and deified the nation.

For a growing number of men the nation became an object, perhaps the chief object, of religious worship. As the eighteenth-century Enlightenment weakened the universal Christian church and the foundations of supernatural religion, men increasingly sought not Heaven but new havens on this earth. The nation proved to be the chief of these. Through it an earthly paradise might be obtained if men only possessed faith enough and performed the necessary patriotic works. A poetic son of the Enlightenment, the Revolutionary Marie-Joseph Chénier, revealed clearly the transition from the old to the new faith in a speech to the National Convention in November, 1793: "Wrest the sons of the Republic from the yoke of theocracy which still weighs upon them. . . . You will know how to found on the ruins of dethroned superstition, the single universal religion . . . which has neither sects nor mysteries [he was wrong] . . . of which our law-makers are the preachers, the magistrates the pontiffs, and in which the human family burns its incense only at the altar of the *Patrie,* common mother and divinity." [22]

Those who steadfastly clung to the old supernatural faith were usually less patriotic but even some of them would bring their faith to the support of the nation. Friedrich Karl von Moser told the Germans as early as 1765 that they must believe in their fatherland as they did the Christian church.[23] Thomas Lindet, the French liberal priest, in 1790 saw the interests of his country as identical with those of his religion.[24] And the Protestant Schleiermacher in his long series of sermons from 1806 to 1813 declared that "Christianity demands attachment to the nation" and that he who did not feel the unity of the nation always remained "an alien in his house of God." [25]

The loyalty and devotion once given to old dynasties now also turned to the *patrie.* Subjects lost their religious attachment to monarchs as they became citizens and believed that they, not the king, were supreme. And as the king lost his divinity, the nation acquired it. "How will you know a republican?" cried Barère. And he answered, when he speaks of *"la Patrie* with religious sentiment," and of "the majesty of the people with religious devotion." [26]

With the most ardent patriots the fatherland became the repository of all their hopes and fears, the source of all life, joy, and even, in Fichte's words, of "earthly immortality." "Oh France," spoke Carnot prayerfully to the Diplomatic Committee in 1793, "Oh my fatherland, oh great people, truly great people! On your soil I had the happiness to be born. Only in death could I cease belonging to you. You encompass all the objects of my affection: the achievements to which my hands have contributed, the upright old man who sired me, the family without a blemish, the friends who know the depth of my heart. . . ." [27]

In the circumstances of the time this development of religious attachment to the nation was logical. There was a substantial basis for it. In societies where Heaven and Hell were losing their appeal and power, where monarchs and aristocrats could no longer protect and assure, the nation and its government could and did provide for the common welfare and hence the welfare of each individual. Through its *national* legislature, courts, schools, and army, the nation-state was responsible for security, stood for justice, created opportunity, brought glory. In fact it had become the chief agency which could attempt to satisfy these age-old desires of men in society.

As patriots worshiped, fought, and suffered for their nation, they loved and exalted it still more. The staid, Girondin patriot Roland well exemplified this reaction when in 1792 he wrote of the *patrie* as a "being to which men make sacrifices, to which men are more attached each day because of the cares it brings, that is created by great efforts, that is raised up in the midst of anxiety, and that men love as much for what it costs as for what they hope from it." [28] In America Washington admonished his fellow countrymen in his Farewell Address of 1796 to support their country because they had "in a common cause fought and triumphed together," the "independence and liberty" they possessed being the result of "joint councils and joint efforts, of common dangers, sufferings and successes."

As men suffered and bled for their nation, it became more than just a group of people occupying a common territory. It became in their minds, as Burke and Schleier-

macher reveal, an organism above and beyond mere contemporary men, a kind of "organic, planetary work of
art" which men should worship as the source of everything
they cherished.[29]

While the new faith did not assure supernatural bliss,
it possessed many of the distinguishing marks of most religions. It developed a morality with rewards and punish-
ments, virtues and sins, a ritual and outward signs, and a
missionary zeal. Indeed, as Ferdinand Brunot remarked, a
great number of religious terms passed into the domain of
politics during the French Revolution, and many of these
had to do with the fatherland and patriotism.[30] Men began
to speak of altars, sanctuaries, and martyrs of the *patrie*.

In the minds of many Frenchmen the great reforms and
passionate hopes of 1789 became synonymous with the
patrie. In other lands the nation became the symbol for
relief from oppression both from without and within. So
much is this true that to separate the hopes concerning
liberty from love of nation becomes almost impossible.
But, since in the minds of contemporaries the distinction
was not made, no attempt is made here. The nation may
have been only the instrument of obtaining the heavenly
city on this earth but the means was not separated from
the end and in any case the nation was fast becoming an
end in itself.

The precise content of the religion of nation varied with
time and place. In England it might mean devotion to the
English past, to the "entailed inheritance" of English law
and liberties. In France during the Revolution it involved
worship of the principles of liberty, property, and equality
before the law. In the Germanies during the wars of libera-
tion it came primarily to signify deliverance from French
domination. In the newly independent United States it
usually meant opposition to the old ruler, England, and,
depending upon whether the believer was Federalist or
Republican, advocacy of strong central government or of
individual liberties. But convictions common and basic

to all were that the nation should be sovereign and independent, that it was a people with distinct characteristics
and a common territory, that its present and its destiny
were somehow different from and better than those of like
groups, and that it was a being above the individuals who
composed it, a father or mother giving life, protecting and
promising a better future.

From these basic beliefs flowed the moral code which
dictated in "Rousseauean" fashion that whoever helped
his own group even at the expense of others was good and
worthy of the highest reward, and, on the contrary, that
whoever harmed or threatened the sovereignty and unity
of his group, whatever the interests of the rest of mankind,
deserved punishment—death if the offense were severe. The
commandments might vary, obedience to them was obliga-
tory and brought reward. If the individual was an integral
part of the nation, when he helped or harmed his nation
he was helping or harming himself. Patriotism was thus at
one and the same time individual necessity and moral
duty. By its standards all men could be judged.

Whatever the code and however intangible, every good
man, that is every patriot, was expected to believe and to
prove his belief by his conduct, by works. If he was faith-
less and acted contrary to the national interests (whatever
the rulers conceived these to be), he made himself subject
to prosecution by his government and persecution by his
fellows. If he did conform, if he were willing to sacrifice
even his life, then he was virtuous, of the elect, and would
attain the ultimate joy found in service to the fatherland.
Perhaps he might attain the rank of national hero and
become sainted by his compatriots.

To enforce patriotism the British might use their courts
as they did during the reform agitation of the 1790's, and
the French the Terror as they did in 1793-1794. When they
did they were both repeating what many of their "enlight-
ened" philosophers had loathed in the Roman Catholic
Church. They were re-establishing the Inquisition, excom-

municating and sometimes sentencing to death men whose chief crime was heresy, this time to the fatherland. To be traitorous had long been a crime; to be a national traitor now became the most heinous of crimes. Frenchmen regarded Dumouriez and Americans saw Benedict Arnold not only as despicably disloyal but also as hellishly impious, and would have executed them had they not found protection in "perfidious Albion." Once a major crime had been *lèse-majesté,* now this became *lèse-nation.*[31] Henceforward the nation-state apparently had the moral and legal right to enforce a code of conduct which signified not only love of nation but conformity and uniformity in loyalty to it.[32] The French Convention on December 16, 1792, decreed death for anyone attempting to harm the unity of the French Republic,[33] and other national governments were sooner or later to act likewise.

Public sentiment voiced by the faithful probably played a more effective role in enforcing national loyalties than did the governments. Social pressures to become patriotic and to conform to the national will mounted steadily. A French newspaper in 1791 noted a patriotism akin to the religion of earlier times in its exaltation and ardor. And it pointed out similarities, even to the mysticism and fanaticism with which those of contrary opinions were persecuted in the name of the new "divinities"—liberty and fatherland.[34]

Neither government nor public opinion could have made men patriotic unless they themselves were ready. Increasingly in western Europe leaders taught and admonished them to serve their *patrie* with all the fanatical exaltation that the early Christians had exhibited in their cause. Bolingbroke in his essay *On the Spirit of Patriotism* spoke of service to the country as the greatest and most glorious of moral duties, and the Abbé Coyer in his *Dissertation on the Old Word Fatherland* declared it sweet to die for its protection.[35] The Bolingbrokes and Coyers became ever more numerous and more dogmatic. Moral duty came to demand sacrifice to the nation. More and more men were willing to offer themselves and their property in return for the protection and hope the nation gave them.

A 1793 letter of a young Jacobin soldier to his mother shows the intensity of feeling that was arising. "When *la patrie* calls us for her defense, we should rush to her as I would rush to a good meal. Our life, our goods, and our talents do not belong to us. It is to the nation, to *la patrie,* that everything belongs. I know indeed that you and some other inhabitants of our village do not share these sentiments. You and they are insensible to the cries of this outraged fatherland. But as for me, who have been reared in the liberty of conscience and thought, who have always been a republican in my soul, though obliged to live under a monarch, the principles of love for *la patrie,* for liberty, for the republic are not only engraved on my heart, but they are absorbed in it and they will remain in it so long as that Supreme Being who governs the universe may be pleased to maintain within me the breath of life." [36]

Patriotic outbursts like this were common during the Revolutionary and later wars. War much more than peace incited men to complete absorption in the *patrie.*[37] Few western Europeans or Americans became permanently so fanatical. Indeed some remained devoted to the older ideals and institutions of church, monarchy, and feudalism, and a few, like Goethe, retained their eighteenth-century cosmopolitanism. What is true is that the dominant belief came to be that all men were born for, should live for, and should be willing to make the supreme sacrifice for the *patrie.*[38] As Barère, the Jacobin, put it, now many believed that "all moral and physical faculties, all political and industrial talents belong to *la patrie.*" [39] Hence all men could be called to serve their country, and as they served they often worshiped it the more. The French Legislative Assembly in June, 1792, decreed an altar in all communes with the inscription, "The citizen is born, lives and dies for *la patrie.*" [40]

At the same time nationalism began to assume the outward forms of religion. To be a patriot was to be a member of the faithful, and the faithful were to be known not only by works but by signs. One striking illustration of this is the amazing growth in France of words based upon *le patriote* and *la patrie*. Brunot, the great authority on the French language, lists for the early Revolutionary period, *archi-patriotique, ultra-patriote, patriote exclusif, lèse-patrie, patriotiser, s'empatrioter, demi-patriotes, anti-patriotisme, impatriotisme, impatriotique,* and *patrioticide*.[41] The French Revolutionaries showed greater enthusiasm than most other nationals. But the outward signs, the songs and symbols of the faith, manifested themselves all over western Europe. "Rule Britannia" appeared in 1740 with its verse,

> *The nations not so blest as thee*
> *Must in their turn to tyrants fall*
> *Whilst thou shalt flourish great and free*
> *The dread and envy of them all.*

And "God Save the King" was sung at Drury Lane in 1745. Impressed with the effect of the song upon Englishmen Joseph Haydn wrote the music for what later became "Deutschland, Deutschland, über Alles." [42] The story of the "Marseillaise" and Roget de Lisle in 1792 is familiar to everyone, as is that of Francis Scott Key and the "Star-Spangled Banner" in 1814. These patriotic anthems were effective. They inspired man in the fashion the fiery Girondin Barbaroux recounted when he described a fraternal banquet held in his home in June, 1792. "My house was surrounded and filled with citizens. A group of musicians came. They sang Provençal songs written in my honor and the hymn of the *Marseillaise*. . . . I always remember with emotion that at the last verse where the words *Amour sacré de la patrie* are sung, all the citizens in the house and street bent and kneeled." [43]

Similar outward manifestations and stimuli to patriotic

feeling are evidenced by the adoption of national flags such as the Union Jack of Britain and the Tricolor of France. Patriots also showed their faith by the civic oaths such as Rousseau had proposed for the Corsicans [44] and those the French so often spoke during the Revolution, by the altars of the *patrie* and the civic baptisms originating during the festivals of federation in France in 1790, and by the creation of symbolic figures such as that of John Bull.[45] Everywhere men came to regard their particular laws, their declarations of rights, their newly won constitutions as sacred books, and they sometimes regarded their representatives as priests. The scene cannot be duplicated elsewhere, but the opening of the French Legislative Assembly in 1791 epitomized the new cult: "Twelve old men went in procession to seek the Book of the Constitution. They came back, having at their head the archivist Camus, who, holding up the Book with his two hands and resting it on his breast, carried with slow and measured tread the new Blessed Sacrament of the French." [46]

The nation had not yet become an absolute to guide and control all men in their quest for certainty. It had become a kind of common mother as well as father to whom men could go in time of trouble and find blessedness. As this happened, it is small wonder that the rituals of an older religion were transformed into the ceremonies of nationalism, and that these in turn influenced men to deepen their worship. No statistical calculations or scientifically controlled studies can be made to determine how effective the rituals were. The efforts made by contemporary patriots to win converts in this manner indicated that they believed in their efficacy.

The similarity to religion did not end here. Like the early Christians good patriots were zealous in spreading their doctrines and ways of life. Monarchical expansion had, of course, already taken place, and the great national imperialistic ventures were to occur in the next century. The eighteenth century witnessed the transition—from the basically dynastic to the nationalist motivation for aggrandizement. Behind the new national will for expansion the motives were, of course, mixed. Bourgeois entrepreneurs coveted trade and profits, politicians sought popularity, military men wanted glory, and some men hoped to propagate liberty while others looked for adventure. The national idea could include all of these, however, and all could be focused around the national interests. In the name of the nation and ostensibly for it businessmen, statesmen, generals, liberals, and adventurers could all pursue their own ends at the same time as they carried their national blessings to the less fortunate. That this might mean a denial of other people's right to a *patrie* made no difference.

Adam Smith, and many another Englishman from Hakluyt onward, advocated the expansion of the British Empire. Regarding it as inevitable that Britain "will perpetually colonize," Smith asked Britain to "expand her colonial empire seizing the islands from the Falklands to the Philippines" in order to gain control of the Pacific.[47] While it could have been in a "fit of absence of mind," what British patriots like Smith desired was done. During the eighteenth century and down to 1815 the British nation, not its divine-right Tudors and Stuarts, acquired lands on the several seas throughout the world, and in North America, Asia, and Africa it took treasured possessions of its chief rivals, France and Holland. During their Revolution the French, after first renouncing all wars of conquest, found the glory and security of France in continued conquest, first of the neighboring territories and then of nearly all Europe. And in the United States Jefferson would acquire Louisiana, quite in opposition to previously expressed principles, and then send Lewis and Clark to the Pacific to assure the western territories for the United States.

The almost classic example of nationalist desire for expansion came with the Second Propaganda Decree of the French in 1792. As is well known, the National Convention in its first Decree of November stated it would "grant fraternity and aid to all peoples who wish to recover their liberty." But a month later this Convention declared that it would "treat as an enemy of the people anyone who, refusing liberty and equality, or renouncing them, might wish to preserve, recall or treat with the prince and the privileged castes. . . ." [48] Thus the French forced "liberty" upon neighboring territories, annexing as they were able, Nice, the Austrian Netherlands, and Rhineland territories. The conquered peoples had to pay French taxes, follow French policies, and they were told they were "equally summoned to govern, to serve, and to defend" the *patrie*. So certain were the French of their national rectitude that they believed the Declaration of Rights was to become the model for all Europe, for the "entire world." [49] And so believing, the French nation was to crusade with more success than had its greatest monarchs of the past.

With less attention to liberty the later Napoleonic legions would conquer or dominate much of Europe in the interests of imperial France. Then the French would not be so anxious for the emergence of free or any other nation-states inflamed with national patriotism. And they, from their national point of view, would be right, for other peoples, their national patriotism aroused by French example and French oppression, rose to crusade against the French dream of a French dominated continent.

By 1815 peoples in the West had formed or were forming nations. Conscious of cultural similarities the peoples of these nations possessed or wished to obtain their own sovereign governments, their own nation-states. The people, the government, the state, long separated, were becoming one in the minds of many, particularly and at least in the view of the middle classes. The national governments unified their respective peoples still further, exacting from them devotion and service to the death. To all good patriots their national cultures, territory, and governments became sacred. The nationalism of the nineteenth and twentieth centuries built upon these foundations.

THE AGE OF NATIONALISM, 1815-1955

Chapter IX

THE FORMATION OF THE ECONOMIC
AND SOCIAL BASIS

ɔ|ɕ

By 1815 the nation had come of age. Not only politically but economically and culturally it was the dominant unit in western Europe and the New World. Nationalism, incipient at least, had been evidenced almost everywhere. Yet it would be a mistake to see then the kind of nation and nation-state existing today, or to read back into the historical evidence the intense devotion given to them by most men of our own day.

In France as the revolutionary passion died, so did the intense patriotism of 1789-1793. France in 1815 was a nation, one of the great unified nations. Most of its citizens undoubtedly were still loyal to it if not always to the restored Bourbon monarchy. But after twenty-three years of almost constant war, most Frenchmen were tired. Within France divisive rather than unifying forces were temporarily dominant. While the old institutions, the church and the monarch, again dominated, the revolutionary ideals were not forgotten by many who wished not to restore the Bourbons but the "rights of man." In consequence many Frenchmen, disliking each other more than they did foreigners, lacked that sentiment of unity basic in nationalism. In 1814 the great Carnot, who had served well both Republic and Empire, pleaded again, as he had so often during the Revolution, for love of country in which each man sacrificed his "own interests to the general interest," and forgot himself "for the safety and glory of the country" because he believed his "private fortunes linked to the public fortune." [1] But Carnot's voice was isolated and he himself declared that Frenchmen then so lacked a national spirit as almost to prevent thought about it.

If most Frenchmen loved France, their Mariannes differed. Conservatives and reactionaries thought of France much as had their ancestors in 1715, as a territory and a people headed by a monarch who ruled through and with the assistance of the privileged classes. The Vicomte de Castelbajac, speaking in 1815, meant by the word *patrie* "not the soil to which I am attached by shameful laws of usurpation and despotism, but the land of my fathers, with its legitimate government, a government which accords me protection by reason of my obedience to the laws and which I am obliged to serve with fidelity and honor. Thus for me, gentlemen, the *patrie* is France with the King; and King and France are inseparable in my eyes for constituting the Fatherland." [2] The various brands of liberals of 1815, momentarily stilled, looked back with fondness to the constitutionally limited monarchy of 1789, to the Jacobin republic of 1793, or sometimes to an idealized Napoleonic empire which brought not only glory but equality too. In these latter conceptions the middle classes were the nation, or at least best represented it, and the nation in turn was to act chiefly in their interest. The lower economic classes, especially the growing number of city workers, never evinced as much nationalism as the middle classes. Neither among them nor among the peasantry was there much evidence of it in 1815.

France in 1815 was a nation-state whose citizens considered themselves Frenchmen but they were neither agreed nor vigorously nationalist. As it was in France so it was in much of the Western world. England, if not Great Britain, was a unified nation, and the several peoples of the islands had often revealed great devotion to Britain during the Revolutionary wars against France. But while Englishmen agreed in 1815 that England "should ever be," they disagreed upon what kind of an England it should be, as conservative Tories sought to maintain their England and fought liberals and radicals with troops at Peterloo and with acts of Parliament (the Six Acts of 1819). Moreover, some individuals within one dissident group, the Catholic, still remained loyal to their church, and among minority groups in Britain, like the Irish, Scots, and Welsh, a good many often felt little or no devotion to dominant England. Most Irishmen, in fact, hated England and English ways and were beginning to develop their own nationalism.

In the United States national feeling had not as yet intensely and widely developed, though occasional patriots like George Washington had been willing to lay down their lives and fortunes for the independence of their states and their country, and statesmen like Thomas Jefferson were zealously expanding the nation's boundaries. Not even during their Revolution had nationalism become intense for most Americans. So far as many of them were patriotic they were to "county, province or section" or perhaps to state or party.[3] The States were not yet tightly knit, each, like the New England states in their opposition to the War of 1812, usually regarding its own interests before embarking upon any common action. Among the people many were immigrants with little or no attachment to the nation; it attracted them chiefly because it offered cheap land. The frontier's beckoning opportunity constantly drew thousands of old and new inhabitants away from the compact settlements of the East where they might have found satisfactions in the development of national rather than provincial institutions. In the expanding West Americans were chiefly interested in clearing forests, in making a living or acquiring a fortune. In doing these they had little occasion to look to the new city of Washington and its government. Except for the occasional and infrequent help the national government gave against the Indians, the British in Canada, or French or Spaniards in New Orleans, they were scarcely aware of it.

Elsewhere 1815 and the years immediately following presented varying but similar patterns. German intellectuals were not as ardent for unity once Napoleon's insolent domination had been overthrown, nor apparently quite so devoted to the dream of a German culture. Austria, Prussia, Bavaria, Saxony, and the various smaller states again usually obtained what loyalties the people spared outside their personal, local, and class interests. University students would band together in a *Burschenschaft* for honor and fatherland. But the dominant spirit and material fact in the Germanies, in the Italies, and in most of Europe was Metternich. He, of course, was no nationalist but a believer in the old Empire, in monarchy, and in the nobility and clergy so far as these aided in the maintenance of order and the *status quo*.[4]

All this is to say that the old order was not dead and that nation and nationalism were not yet completely triumphant. It is to say only that monarchy, church, feudal class, province, and locality still remained as objects of devotion, that king, priest, and noble still rivaled the nation of citizens as symbols of authority and loyalty, and that family and personal interest as much as national patriotism motivated men to action. It is also to point to the fact that the nation as institution and idea did not yet strongly attract most rural peoples nor the growing urban working classes, that the nation had not yet become *their* means to gain *their* wants, nor the father-object to which they would turn in time of crisis. Some men would still place king above country and find in his service the recognition and satisfaction they desired. Some, like Chateaubriand in his *Génie du Christianisme* published in 1802, would still turn to the age-old solace of the universal church and assert that the Pope and the Church Fathers were the supreme authorities. A few like the Englishman Bentham would yet dream of a cosmopolitanism where in universal brother-hood individual men stood free to think out their own solutions to life's problems. As yet the nation did not "in-tegrate" all men's thoughts and actions, nor had it become the totalitarian master, lawgiver, and father in whom they found being and meaning.

Nevertheless, the foundations of modern popular na-tionalism had been laid. Upon these the patriots of the nineteenth and twentieth centuries built the institutional and ideological structures of modern nationalism.[5] The nation and state would increasingly absorb men as individ-uals, and men in classes. The bourgeoisie, most of the rem-nants of the nobility including some royal families, many of the priests and ministers, finally even a large proportion of the laboring classes would look to the nation for their satisfactions and their security, their privileges, and their refuge in time of trouble. While each group would seek different things from their nation and seek to divert it to their own interests, the nation would become the consum-ing end of most men's endeavors and the loyalty they paid to it would generally and greatly eclipse all others. The old authorities clung desperately to the power they par-tially regained in 1815 and the old loyalties never entirely disappeared. But almost as soon as the Old Regime was re-established, it and the devotion it commanded began to disintegrate under the incoming tides of liberalism and nationalism.[6] In the end nationalism usually proved the stronger. The French and American declarations of the late eighteenth century were for the "rights of man." The declaration of the abortive 1848 Frankfurt Constitution spoke of the "rights of Germans." [7] Historians may well one day call the period from 1815, or at least 1848, to the pres-ent the "age of nationalism."

In the West, in France, Britain, and the United States, the nation-states demanded, acquired, and were given more and more power, and the national spirit became ever more pervasive and deeply felt. Elsewhere, in the Germanies,

Italies, and Balkans, patriots clamored for national unification and usually attained their goal. In these newly
unified nations the nationalism customarily became more
intense, vehement, and aggressive than among the earlier
united peoples. By the twentieth century the national idea
had integrated almost all of human life and values within
it while the national state had swallowed up all lesser
jurisdictions. In fact political and legal authority, society,
and culture, past and present, became identified and
summed up in the nation. In this section an attempt will
be made to trace these developments in quite general out-
line and to analyze in more detailed fashion the *many*
reasons they came about.

From 1815 the process of creating nation-states evidenced
in the earlier history of England and France repeated
itself with variations all over Europe, and, though this is
not our concern here, throughout Latin America and
among the older peoples of Asia and Africa. Inspired by
romanticism and liberalism as well as by nationalism,
peoples everywhere hoped through their respective nations
to win happiness and dignity, peace and prosperity, and
power and glory. They increasingly saw the nation, once
it was unified, independent, and sovereign, as the way out
of oppression, the way to a kind of Mazzinian paradise of
good men, a Cobdenian utopia of peace and prosperity, or
perhaps to a Hobbesian Leviathan of authority and security. These dreams constituted the great strength of
nationalism. Especially when coupled with liberalism, nationalism appealed directly to the hopes and fears of men,
to middle-class men first of all but later to almost all men.
Nowhere did nationalism grow steadily, nowhere was it
without enemies and obstacles, nowhere were the nationalist tendencies exactly alike. Everywhere the idea and the
institution became predominant in the minds and lives of
men.

During the nineteenth and twentieth centuries one
people after another found they had a common historical

culture and common aspirations, revolted and warred to establish a united territory and a sovereign state, and then usually attempted to expand their boundaries to include all the people and land that could by one standard or another be called theirs. From 1821 to 1830 the Greeks, stimulated by the earlier patriotic endeavors of intellectuals like Rhigas and Korais, began a long series of nationalist revolts when they rebelled against their Turkish rulers. By the latter date they were able, with much assistance from Britain, France, and Russia, to establish an independent nation with an autocratic and later a constitutional monarchy, and to begin a struggle to enlarge their territory.

From 1830 onward national feeling intensified and transformed itself into action again and again. The many uprisings in that year, both liberal and national in aim, were generally unsuccessful. But that of the Belgians against the Dutch and the stubborn King William I resulted in the establishment of the liberal Kingdom of Belgium. And everywhere, in spite of initial failures, national feeling sharpened. Three widely different phenomena illustrate this. Patriotic societies, of which Mazzini's "Young Italy" was only the most prominent, began incessantly to agitate against "foreign oppression" and for the unity and independence of their nations. The German states, Austria excepted, were closely tied together economically by the *Zollverein* or Customs Union of 1833. And scholars, conscious of the need for national roots, started to publish huge collections of historical documents concerning the origins of their nations like the *Monumenta Germaniae Historica*.

Nationalist ideas and actions burst the bounds of Metternich's Europe with the revolutions of 1848-1849. After the Revolution of February, 1848, in France, revolts broke out all over central and southern Europe, in Austria, Hungary, Bohemia, Poland, in what later became Rumania and Yugoslavia, in Prussia and in several of the lesser German states, and up and down the long Italian peninsula from Venice to the Kingdom of the Two Sicilies. While these revolutions, like those of 1830, generally failed to win immediately their objectives of independent, liberal national states, they destroyed once and for always the old regime that Metternich strove so cannily to restore and maintain. Though the liberals of 1848 more often than not were unsuccessful, the nationalists were soon to triumph. If at the Frankfurt Assembly of 1848-1849 the German idealists talked themselves into inaction, within two decades men of action, Cavour and Bismarck, united their respective nations and within seventy-five years nearly all the "subject nationalities" won at least temporary independence and nationhood. For a time during mid-century, "federalism" rather than nationalism seemed possible. But this was not to be. Though neither Cavour nor Bismarck was a strong nationalist, though both of them were most interested in strengthening their own small states, Sardinia (Piedmont) and Prussia,[8] they were forced, in order to accomplish their ends, to lead national crusades which ended attempts to set up federations of central European and Italian states.

With that firm believer in the "principle of nationality," Napoleon III, as his chief ally, Cavour instigated a war against Austria in 1859. On the verge of defeat he utilized the ardently patriotic Garibaldi's daring deeds in southern Italy, and united Sardinia, Lombardy, Parma, Modena, Tuscany, the Papal States (except Rome), and the Kingdom of the Two Sicilies. In 1861 Victor Emmanuel II became king of an Italy united except for Rome and Venetia (both to be acquired within the decade), and scattered border regions (*irredenta*) in the north and east.

In much the same fashion Bismarck succeeded in Germany. At the helm of a militarized Prussia he provoked wars with Denmark, with Austria, and with France. In each his undeviating purpose was to create a German state with Prussia and his own Junker class dominant. Through clever diplomacy and the efficient Prussian army he isolated and then militarily defeated Austria to win Holstein, Hannover, Hesse-Cassel, and Frankfurt for Prussia and to erect a North German Confederation composed of all the lesser German states north of the Main River. Through equally skillful diplomacy and the Prussian army he then isolated and defeated France in 1870-1871 to unite all the Germanies except Austria into the German Empire proclaimed at Versailles in 1871.[9]

Just as the earlier English and French monarchs had united their territories and built their nation-states through war and diplomacy, so now Italian and German statesmen had created the political and territorial unity of their nations. In widely different ways the process of nation-state making continued everywhere during the same and ensuing years, in the Balkans, in central and northern Europe, and in the United States. Arising out of revolution, war, and diplomacy one new state after another was created on the basis of nationality. Individuals of the caliber of Cavour and Bismarck seldom acted such decisive roles, and monarchs seldom played leading parts as they had earlier. Democracy and, after 1918, republicanism now became more prominent but the trend was the same though the conditions and the arguments might be different. Generally, a common culture, a real or imagined common race or past were said to give a right to nationhood, and unification of territory as well as independence was declared to be the democratic end of natural or historical law. Often, it was also true, the new states were as much the result of the great nations' efforts to gain power as of the inhabitants' struggle for national self-determination. Sometimes new small states came more or less full grown into existence as the great powers (like Russia in the creation of Bulgaria) sought to obtain satellites. In the case of the United States only a violent Civil War settled the long disputed question of whether the federal (national) government or the state governments were supreme. But what-

ever the variations, the end was the same, the establishment
of nation-states which united peoples and territory into
a sovereign unit. In the Balkans, Serbia, Rumania, and
Bulgaria became united and independent in the 1870's and
1880's after long exertions against the Turks.[10] While the
Czech and Polish peoples struggled temporarily in vain,
the Magyars in Hungary won semi-independence in their
compromise of 1867 with the Austrian Germans. In 1907
Norway peacefully gained its independence from Sweden.
Finally, as a result of World War I and the various treaties
of 1919-1920, Hungary, Poland, and Czechoslovakia as well
as the small Baltic states of Lithuania, Latvia, Estonia, and
Finland became independent nation-states.

In no case did these new nation-states believe that they
included all the people or territory that rightfully belonged to them if the principle of national self-determination were followed. In almost every case they continued to
feel themselves wronged because they did not possess some
territory that had been theirs in a real or imagined past,
or because their new boundaries did not include some
group which spoke the same language or which was alleged to belong to the same race. But by 1919 both the
fact and the theory of national self-determination had triumphed. The theory meant that each group of people that
called itself a nation had a right to a united territory and
a sovereign nation-state. In fact each people in Europe and
the New World, with but few and minor exceptions, now
possessed such a territory and state, and this was universally
judged to be right and proper. When, in June, 1914, the
young Serbian named Princip shot the Austrian Archduke
Ferdinand to start World War I, few thought it strange
that he was motivated by the nationalist desire to end
Austrian "oppression" and to include Bosnia-Herzegovina
in Serbia. During the war the major spokesmen again and
again declared for the national organization of peoples and
territories, and for Europe, if not for their colonies over-
seas, they proclaimed it a major ideal and purpose of the

war. The scholarly Lord Bryce represented the best of Western thought when he described the English ideal for the future as "a world in which every people should have within its borders a free national government, resting on and conforming to the general will of its citizens." [11] And the greatest idealist among the victorious statesmen, Woodrow Wilson, declared his nation was "fighting for the oppressed nationalities who submerged or standing alone could never have secured their freedom."

Hence it appeared quite right and logical to most men that the Treaty of Versailles (and associated treaties) enthroned the nation-state. Even the world organization envisaged by the victory at Paris was no more than a league of sovereign nations, each with its own territory and people, each limited in its actions not by any international power but only by its own capabilities and will.[12] Europe was now split into more independent fragments than it had ever been in modern times, being divided among twenty-seven nations speaking forty to fifty different languages.[13] Further, what Europe had done the rest of the world was doing. If a people like the Jews or Hindus did not have an independent state, they were, with their Herzls and Gandhis, persistently demanding and soon to obtain them. Even in the old British Empire, the Statute of Westminster in 1931 recognized the Dominions as "autonomous communities . . . equal in status, in no way subordinate one to another in any respect of their domestic or external affairs. . . ."

Once unified each of the new national states like the older ones moved to extend and consolidate its power. Whatever the type of government, these governments enacted national laws, established national court systems and military forces, created national treasuries, and collected national taxes. They made their power felt in the lives of every man. They registered his birth and his death, and certified his marriage. They protected him against disorder, defined crimes, and sentenced him to prison if he com-

mitted one. They could and did, in sum, take over all the
functions traditionally performed by former governments
and by the church. The older governmental units, local,
provincial, imperial, tended to lose their powers. What had
happened in France and Britain earlier now happened
everywhere. The feudal lord, the country squire, the village priest lost their functions and their privileges to the
growing national bureaucracies. At the same time, as will
be pointed out in greater detail later, the new national
governments being more efficient, were able to "nationalize" their peoples and to control them more effectively than
had the old national monarchs.

The national states and national feeling that arose everywhere did not, of course, spring into existence out of a
cultural vacuum. They were in part, as pointed out earlier,
built upon common cultures that had historically evolved.
In many cases a common language or the basis for one
existed before unification began in the nineteenth century.
In every case scholars and poets, especially during the
romantic era, dug into history, collected documents and
folklore to discover or create a common past of custom,
law, literature, and art, as well as political life. Particularly
was this true in Germany where Herder and Savigny "discovered" the historical basis of German literature and law,
but everywhere, in the United States, in Bohemia, in the
Balkans, in Denmark, peoples were learning they possessed,
though they might not previously have known it, a common culture peculiar to them.

As the realization of a common culture induced a group
to believe itself a nation, so it also made this group aware
of differences which set it off from other like groups. If the
individuals of one nation had a common culture, this signified to them that they were different from other individuals in other groups. When, in addition, there was
superimposed upon this common culture, a common political government and this government sought security
through power, then the differences between the groups

were magnified. As these differences sharpened and peoples became ever more aware of them, nationalism intensified or, to be more exact, the greater feeling of national exclusiveness and nationalistic dislike of others constituted a phase of the constantly intensifying nationalism.

Nationalism was now tied also to the *Realpolitik* that had emerged from the rivalries of earlier times. While neither Cavour nor Bismarck was an ardent nationalist, they both wished to build strong states. Employing shrewdly those means of diplomacy later deemed realistic, power and duplicity, they were successful. For the same reasons and purposes their kind of international maneuvering likewise became associated with the liberal and democratic states. In France Napoleon III, Ferry, and Delcassé, in England Palmerston and Disraeli, and in the United States McKinley and Theodore Roosevelt, for example, all attempted to strengthen and to enlarge their nations without excessive regard for moral niceties. The leaders of most nations, like Machiavelli, saw the aims of politics summed up in the national interest as they conceived it. This interest could only be attained, they thought, through the acquisition of land, manpower, and resources, and the relative weakening of other powers. Since every nation sought these ends, conflict was inevitable, and conflict meant that nation and nationalism became the means and ends, the reason for struggle and condition of survival. What absolute monarchs like Louis XIV had done to buttress and glorify themselves, the nations were now doing. When in the new democracies every man became part of the sovereign, he wanted that sovereignty secure and its glory enhanced just as had the monarchs of an earlier day.

By the twentieth century, in summary, four general forces made the nation the supreme community and nationalism the supreme sentiment. These were (1) the desire to unify and success in unifying territory and people, (2) the extension of the power of the nation-state, (3) the growth of and increasing awareness of national cultures, and (4) the power conflicts between the nations which further stimulated national feeling. Nationalism now involved unity, uniformity, conformity, exclusiveness, and aggressiveness. It meant that all activities had to be integrated into the national mold, that the national state had to be omnipotent and the citizens absolutely devoted. If these ends were not attained, the argument went, where else could men find well-being, how else, indeed, could they survive?

These, however, are big generalizations which much need amplification. Why did these forces arise and how did they operate in the nineteenth and twentieth centuries? For Marxists or nationalist doctrinaires the answers might be easy: the bourgeoisie simply used the nation and nationalism to forward its interest in profit making, or men naturally became nationalists because God, fate, or natural law so ordained. But these are not answers. They are only a priori guesses made in line with preconceived views. They are neatly created myths, not realities. The facts do not combine so easily and the interpretations to be drawn from them are not so simple. The answers are, in fact, manifold, pluralistic, and not all available.

There can be but little doubt that the most nationalist of classes was the middle class or that the nineteenth-century economic structure favored the rise of the national form of human organization. Whether the economic factors were more or less decisive than the social, psychological, or political, however, the historian has no way of precisely determining. All that can be said is this: while they did not *alone* determine the course of history, they were of such immense significance that they need further discussion.

All through the nineteenth and twentieth centuries economic and technological advances tended further to unify groups which already possessed a common territory and state. They also encouraged unity inside groups that were only potentially nations. As railroad, canal, telegraph, and telephone systems were built, they tied the economies of scattered regions together just as the military road systems of Louis XIV had the regions of France. In the United States the tremendous burst of railroad construction after 1840 brought diversified economic regions together, especially the East and Midwest and the Northwest.[14] It is not perhaps to assert too much to say that the railroad enabled the North to triumph over the South in 1865 and to establish a strong national government in Washington. And after 1869 the transcontinental railroads solidified the United States. In France and Britain when the railroads crawled out of Paris and London, they brought together widely differing interests and peoples, tying them more firmly together for sources of necessities and outlets for local production. Most clearly was this the case in the Italies, where during and after the 1840's the railroads, in Giusti's phrase, "stitched the Italian boot," thereby making possible an economic unit upon which the nationalist politicians and idealists could erect a unified political and cultural superstructure.

Now railroads and telegraph and telephone lines did not always stop at old or projected national boundaries. But for political and financial reasons they usually were built within them. Thus they buttressed the already rising national sentiment. Within each nation the various territorial groups west, east, north, and south tended to become economic counterparts of each other. At the same time they permitted individuals within nations to become better acquainted with each other through swift and cheap travel and communication, and they encouraged common speech, styles of clothing, and social customs in general. Later, extensive highway systems coupled with gasoline engines reinforced these same tendencies. Still later, advertising, the movies, radio, and television further accentuated national uniformities by inducing people to speak, dress, and act according to national patterns.

As technological advance promoted nationalism, so usually did class interest. While these class interests might have been divisive as the Marxists asserted and as at times they actually were, in the long run each class usually believed its interests could be best served through the nation. If, in the United States, Henry Clay in the 1820's projected an "American System," in which the various sections and economic interests supplemented one another, so statesmen in other countries dreamed of and worked for self-sufficient nations within which each region and class could find satisfaction and promote the national interest. Throughout the whole period the middle classes were able to use the nation-state for the achievement of their economic goals. Winning these they became ever more nationalist. Even if they desired to be unhampered by governmental regulation, they sought national governmental protection and assistance in the acquisition and ownership of property.

Nowhere is this more evident than in the tariff policies pursued by all the great countries after the 1860's. As economists and politicians like Friedrich List, Mathew Carey, and Joseph Chamberlain proposed, the national governments, even eventually free-trade Britain's, protected their domestic producers by limiting and taxing foreign imports. In the United States during and after the Civil War the federal government raised duties on foreign manufactures in order to encourage "infant industry" and protect it as well as most other American industry against foreign competition. One by one the nations followed the same policy: Italy in 1878, Germany in 1879, France in 1881, and finally and hesitatingly Britain after World War I. Among the welter of supporting arguments for these protective tariffs, one is certain: tariffs enabled manufacturers to obtain higher profits. But these profits were guaranteed by the nation, and were declared to serve the national interests, quite logically so if the premise were accepted, as it was, that the interests of business and of the nation were identical.

By the twentieth century not only middle-class desires

were being thus served. Other classes likewise became interested in acquiring protection and benefits from the nation in the same fashion. From the 1870's agricultural groups in each nation, hoping to pre-empt the national markets for themselves, also demanded and usually received protection against foreign competition. During the same period in the richer manufacturing nations, labor groups began to demand and sometimes obtained measures to insure wages and employment against "cheap" competition from abroad. Often all groups joined, as in Britain, to support national imperial ventures in the belief that colonies were essential to maintenance of the homeland's standard of living.[15] Each class within a nation, then, found reason to desire a free internal national market for its goods and services, and a national barrier against the goods and services of other nations. Just as for Germans the *Zollverein* of 1833 "brought the sentiment of German nationality out of the regions of hope and fancy into those of positive and material interests," [16] so for all groups in each nation, concrete economic benefits tended to create national loyalties. For within each nation the immediate economic welfare of all classes now appeared greatly to depend upon markets open to national but closed to foreign producers. If later, after World War I, tariffs were not considered sufficient to protect "national interests," then national quota systems and national exchange controls were introduced.

What was true of the tariff was also true of other economic policies.[17] If "sound money" and banking systems were desired for the benefit of business, then the national and only the national governments could establish and maintain them. The British, French, and American governments, so long as the middle classes could dominate, provided for the "gold standard," and for privately owned but nationally controlled banking systems. Both of these, it was fondly hoped, would stabilize money and investments so that a dollar (or pound or franc) would always be "worth a dollar" and dollars invested would always bring a high profit. Interest of class and interest in the nation thus coincided. When the heavily indebted farmers and wage-conscious laborers became more vocal, especially during the postwar and depression years of the 1920's and 1930's, "sound money" policies could no longer command solid legislative majorities. But then support for "cheaper money" also became patriotic as these classes, looking to the national governments for ways to pay off debts or to increase wages, found ways to appeal to the national interests in order to promote their own. The growth of national governmental debts likewise stimulated an increased interest in the nation, as Alexander Hamilton, the American financial genius of the 1790's, had prophesied. Particularly for national military reasons the national debts mounted in all major countries. For long it was the middle classes that chiefly invested in the national securities but during the great wars of the twentieth century the interest of members of all groups in the security of their nation mounted when ownership of government bonds spread among all except the very poorest. Though the exact relationship between class or individual dependence upon the nation and loyalty to it is not calculable, yet it followed that as men appealed to and received benefits from the nation, they tended to identify themselves with it and with the state that symbolized it.

Marx, Lenin, and Stalin saw the nation-state and nationalism as only the means by which the bourgeoisie had gained markets. When Marx began his grand analysis of society in the England of the 1840's this view possessed much validity. It retained validity, though in decreasing degree, through the ensuing one hundred years. When in 1917 the brilliant American economist, Thorstein Veblen, observed, "The American national establishment . . . is a government of businessmen for business ends," he came closer to the truth than many of the contemporary flag-waving politicians.[18] Through the years after the resurgence of conservatism in the first quarter of the nineteenth century, the national governments of Britain, France, and the United States chiefly represented the interests of the middle class and legislated for them. This was true in Britain especially under the Liberal party and with leaders like Macaulay and Gladstone, but also with Conservative party leaders like Neville Chamberlain and Winston Churchill. This was true in France during the monarchical rule of Louis Philippe (1830-1848) and Napoleon III (1852-1870) as well as during the Third Republic with the leaders from Thiers to Gambetta to Poincaré. This was true in the United States whether the Republicans or, less clearly, the Democrats were in power and of the political leaders almost without exception.

But, as we have already seen, workers and farmers also became nationalist. Not even the class-conscious socialists escaped. The nation-state, it appeared, could be used as a vehicle of winning benefits or even class victory by the proletariat. An expert on Marxian Communism, Franz Borkenau, was entirely correct when he pointed out that the worker could not be disinterested, "even in the purely material sense, in the fate of the nation-state which gave him protection." "The protection of the working classes through social legislation" was "partly dependent upon the position of any given industry as against its competitors abroad. Other elements of the standard of living, and in particular the wage-rate," were "directly dependent upon the international market, not only of labour, but of commodities." [19] As early as the 1880's the astute Bismarck deliberately tried to win over German workers with his social insurance laws. Obviously he did not fail completely. In the crisis of 1914 the German workers like those elsewhere remained loyal not to the ideals of the Second International but to their nation.[20]

Workers became loyal not only because paternalistic governments gave them crumbs but also because they expected and received substantial benefits. That they might have re-

ceived greater assistance from an international organization
controlled by themselves is hardly relevant. The workers
were no more farsighted than the bourgeoisie. The national
form of government and society provided, at least in the
minds of most trade unionists, concrete benefits here and
now, not in some remote future. From the last quarter
of the nineteenth century the nation provided public and
universal education through which the worker might better himself and his children. After Bismarck's Germany,
other nations enacted social welfare laws through which
the worker and his family might be protected in childhood,
old age, sickness, and accident. In times of depression and
unemployment the nation provided relief and at least
kept him from starvation. In 1848 it was the socialist Louis
Blanc who advocated "national workshops," and in the
great depression of the 1930's the national government of
the United States, the greatest capitalist nation, acted to
provide jobs and minimum subsistence. The Communist
Stalin might declare he believed in national self-determination after the social revolution.[21] In practice most radical
workers wanted it the other way and Stalin's Russia became
in the 1930's and 1940's as nationalist as any country.[22] It
was not only capitalism, therefore, that became nationalist,
communism did as well. By 1940 the phrase "national communism" could be more accurately applied to the USSR
than "international communism." "Modern industrial
labor" certainly did not, as Marx and Engels had predicted,
strip the worker "of every trace of national character." [23]

Instead of dividing workers and bourgeoisie, national
economic interests tended to unite them within the national boundaries against the bourgeoisie and workers outside the boundaries.[24] In 1914 and almost to as great an
extent in 1939 workmen and capitalists, regardless of political party, patriotically united in defense of their nations.
If French capitalists and workers of the 1930's sometimes
hated each other more than they loved France, the same
was not true in other nations. In fact many governments

from Bismarck's time consciously fostered and effectively used national patriotism to overcome the potential struggle between classes.[25] When Charles Maurras, the violent French nationalist, specifically advocated that a "strong and well-organized national doctrine" be employed to promote "social understanding," he was suggesting no more than politicians were already doing.[26] Conservatives everywhere found an appeal to national patriotism an almost unfailing method of preventing the rise of radical groups, just as in Stalinist Russia national patriotism could be used to unite the proletariat against capitalist "encirclement." Though many would think labor duped, both labor and capital in the capitalist countries and labor and the state in the communist found in the "necessities of the fatherland" a motive for collaboration and agreement.

Nationalism not only made possible collaboration between economic classes but provided an outlet for group and individual frustration as rising urbanism and industrialism shattered old authorities. The old village and family life had afforded a comparatively quiet and settled life, communities where each man possessed status based upon dependable age-old ties and customs. If he had to make decisions, the answers were few and could authoritatively be expected from his masters, the lord or the priest. As this old rural and agricultural society disintegrated, so did its loyalties and traditions. When men moved into the faster tempo and uncertainties of urban, industrial life, they were deprived of their old status while they did not achieve security. They lacked respected authorities and comforting myths at precisely the time they were sorely troubled. Particularly was this true in the first half of the twentieth century when because of great wars, economic depression and conflicting ideologies, sensitive men lived in almost a constant state of anxiety.[27] They often became, in consequence, homeless human atoms, seeking some nucleus, something to which they could belong. At the same time the new science and the new liberal and democratic

doctrines gave promise of a more secure, freer, happier life.
How could this be achieved? For many men nation and nationalism offered the way. They offered new deities, new
hopes, a way to attain a good life in a time of flux, in a
time when, possibly more than in any other historical
period, men felt oppressed and maladjusted. Men had
greater possibilities of freedom than they had ever had.
But freedom they did not want or thought they could not
get without the nation.

If a group such as the Greeks,[28] Italians, Czechs, Serbs,
Irish, or Jews were oppressed, they blamed foreign control
and they could envision the attainment of a utopia through
the establishment of a unified, sovereign nation. When
Greeks of the early 1800's formed their *Hetairia Philike*
to drive the Turks out of Hellas each one swore: "I will
nourish in my heart irreconcilable hatred against the tyrants of my country . . . and I will exert every method
for their injury and destruction. . . . I swear by the future
liberty of my countrymen, that I shall consecrate myself to
[my country]; that henceforth thou [it] shalt be the scope
of my thoughts, thy [its] name the guide of my actions, thy
[its] happiness the recompense of my labours." [29] A famous
Garibaldian song of the 1850's drives home the same ideas,
suffered oppression and visioned freedom: "We are spurned
and scorned by the centuries because we are not a real
people but divided. Let us form a united band, on a common hope." [30]

What was true of groups applied also to individuals.[31]
Though any generalization must be cautiously put, the increasing insecurity of the individual in the urban, industrial world probably led many to become strongly patriotic.
Particularly this seemed to be true of some individuals who
might feel insecure because of physical or other handi-
caps or because of abnormal tendencies to neuroticism.[32]
Treitschke, the German nationalist historian, would have
chosen a military career had he not been deaf, and Charles
Maurras, most fervent of French patriots, was deaf from

the age of fourteen. A good many of the most famous patriots were passionate and extremely sensitive men torn by years of exile, like Mazzini. Or like Gambetta and Kossuth they were oftentimes of a descent different from the nationality they so ardently defended, and perhaps therefore felt it necessary to prove themselves by becoming even more nationalist than their fellows.[33] In many lands, of course, highly emotional individuals, seeking solution for their troubles in violently patriotic attacks upon "aliens" in their midst, have become violent nationalists. Fanatics like the anti-Semite German chaplain Adolf Stöcker and the French writer Édouard Drumont as well as the later German Nazis found in the Jews a scapegoat for all their personal troubles and those of their compatriots. And demogogical American politicians in mid-twentieth-century United States sought popularity as well as an explanation for all the national evils in investigations of "un-American" radicals and their "foreign" ideologies.

There is, of course, no certain or necessary relationship between frustration and patriotism.[34] In our own time the vogue of Freudian psychoanalysis makes frustration seem the motivation for all action. Frustration thus becomes a catchall explanation just as divine reason explained everything to the theologians of the thirteenth century and natural law everything to the intellectuals of the eighteenth century. In fact there is no way of exactly correlating insecurity with nationalism. Insecure and frustrated men have taken many other escapes from freedom in our time, dogmatic religion, communism, suicide. Further, no scientific studies based on properly controlled experiments have been made. The whole explanation may therefore be based upon a fallacious *post hoc, ergo propter hoc* argument.

In spite of the impossibility of exact measurement there can be little doubt that nationalism offered a medium of hope to nineteenth- and twentieth-century men.[35] Arising out of individual needs, this hope was of many varieties, all of which might be caught up within nationalism and work together to strengthen it. By working for, having faith in, the nation a man could open the way to a happier, freer, more secure life not only for himself but his fellows.[36] Nationalism in this way offered what religion once gave to a good many men. Some who might once have become priests in hope of salvation now became superpatriots in pursuit of a national utopia.[37] For most the nation became the way to the future and that future they thought good. Through it individuals could personally achieve creative lives, a sense of belonging to a community, a dream of power, or even a feeling of immortality. Through it the ordinary man could find brothers who might work with him toward the good life. Through it democratic politicians could win respect, prestige, fame, power. Through it military and fascist leaders could obtain socially sanctioned outlets for aggressive drives, a feeling that they were of a superior group, and a way to elevate themselves above so-called inferior and obstructive groups. If men's major motivations are love, hate, and anger, all three could find satisfaction in nationalism, and out of this satisfaction hope for a future where, enemies eliminated, good patriots could live securely and happily.

All through the nineteenth century the liberal nationalists like Mazzini found high personal meaning in thought and deeds for their nations. Mazzini with his inspired humanitarian nationalism was, of course, unusual and outstanding. He, more than most men, devoted his whole life, most of it in unhappy exile, to work for his beloved country. Other men by comparison seem less inspired, less involved. And yet the whole history of the last hundred and fifty years is filled with individuals who identified personal hopes with striving for what they considered the national aims. Many a nineteenth-century statesman, the Englishman Palmerston, the American Henry Clay, the Frenchman Gambetta, realized personal ambitions in forwarding his nation's commerce, in building a national system of economy, or in defending his nation against an aggressive enemy. Though their personal objectives varied, twentieth-century democratic political leaders, like Lloyd George, Theodore Roosevelt, and Raymond Poincaré, likewise achieved their lifework through their nations. In democratic nations the political leaders had in fact to appear more patriotic than most of their constituents to be elected, for their constituents also pinned their personal hopes upon national successes. In twentieth-century fascist countries the Hitlers and Mussolinis, their henchmen and their general staffs, most obviously achieved their personal objectives through shouting and fighting for the supremacy of their nations. The cynic might ask: Were not these men, liberals and fascists alike, motivated almost solely by self-interest? The answer might be "Yes," but their personal ambitions were subsumed in the national and at the same time they made the national aims their own. Through their own policies they dreamed of making their nations happy, secure, powerful, supreme. The ends of self-interest and the national interest, individual career and the national welfare became for them the same.

Individuals could look forward to some better order, some finer society when their national aims would be attained. In the great nations this often meant not only the attainment of these aims within the nation but the spread of their particular national ideas and institutions throughout the world. Englishmen dreamed fondly of bringing Anglo-Saxon institutions to the world, Frenchmen of the civilizing mission of France, Russians of Slavic unity or international communism, Germans of the supremacy of their *Kultur,* and Americans of their manifest destiny.[38] Patriots in each of these great lands were sincerely convinced of the absolute necessity for mankind that their nation triumph, and of the consequent obligation of their nation to carry, by force if no other way, its blessings to other less fortunate people. In this they saw a mission for their nation, a mission they could pursue with messianic zeal. Being zealots they thought, as Michelet of France,[39] that only their nation could save the world and without their nation mankind would be doomed. Being patriots they equated love of nation with the welfare of all mankind.

Patriots of lesser or of yet ununified nations were seldom as boastful but just as hopeful. The liberal Mazzini sang paeans to the future when through the unification of Italy, through the revolution of "Nationality," the work of humanity would be organized.[40] To a young nineteenth-century noble, Count Szechenyi of Hungary, Magyar unity and independence would bring forth "finer blossoms."[41] To the Danish Bishop Grundtvig, love of country and nationalistic fervor were the roads to high morality and Christianity.[42] Apparently the nation could be the road to almost any destiny for any group.

To unite a people and a territory into a sovereign nation, to strengthen the already united nation and glorify it, these offered a way for the individual to serve, to win prestige—goals to live for, to die for. These indeed offered immortality. As that master of taste Matthew Arnold declared, individuals found in patriotism "the sense of self-esteem generated by knowing the figure which his nation makes in history; by considering the achievements of his nation in war, government, arts, literature, or industry."[43] Possibly patriotism in this respect was chiefly what Clutton-Brock, the English humanitarian, called "pooled self-esteem." Perhaps as the vitriolic American economist Thorstein Veblen defined it, patriotism was only a "sense of partisan solidarity in respect of prestige."[44] But in the Western culture of the nineteenth and twentieth centuries it afforded for many men a community of feeling in which they could find hope for greater security and happiness.

In America the young Daniel Webster affirmed that patriotism produced "an elevation of soul" which lifted men "above the rank of ordinary men. Above fear, above danger [the true patriot] feels that the last end which can happen to any man never comes too soon if he falls in defense of the laws and liberties of his country." [45] If men died, then, in the name of the country, they might feel, in the words of Maurice Barrès, "a magnificent sweetness." [46] They might, if the Belgian Cardinal Mercier of World War I were to be believed, by virtue of such an act of perfect love, "wipe out a whole life of sin." [47] Indeed with Kipling's Englishman they might ask: Who dies, if the country lives?

Nation and nationalism may in these respects have given modern men the same benefits that totem and totemism gave primitive men. If nationalism were not primitive magic, it was "an organized and cooperative system . . . designed to secure for the members of the community . . . a plentiful supply of the commodities of which they stand in need and . . . immunity from all the perils and dangers to which man is exposed in his struggle with nature." [48] Though *no* direct historical relationship between totemism and nationalism can be traced, nevertheless the last was the complex system through which modern men thought they could obtain what they wanted, a sense of belonging, a feeling of prestige, a way of avoiding dangers and warding off enemies. It gave them, in summary, protection, social significance, and hope for the future.

Chapter X

CULTURAL AND
INSTITUTIONAL PRESSURES

ɔ|ɕ

Accentuating and deepening the national social consciousness were the old and new social institutions and cultural
pressures which during the period from 1815 increasingly
became oriented toward national ends.[1] Family, school, the
teaching and writing of history and literature, the press,
and even sports and entertainment all exercised pressures
in the direction of nationalism.[b]

In late years some anthropologists and psychologists have
attributed national character to childhood training.[2] While
there is much dispute, supported by few facts, concerning
what has been termed the anal-oral explanation of personality, it cannot be denied that the child is conditioned by
his family in all respects, including that of loyalty toward
his nation.[3] The "child forms most of his ideas about the
world of humanity from his impressions of his parents. . . ." [4] When the parents become national-minded,
then, the child imitates and follows. When, moreover, the
child is loved in the home, he may be less intolerant of
others and less inclined to nationalistic dislikes. The un-
wanted child, on the other hand, may dislike other peoples.
The exact nature of the parent-child relationship in these
respects, however, we do not know, There is no evidence
that the child is born with inherent love of nation; indeed
until the age of eight or nine he scarcely understands what

the "homeland" is. The Swiss psychologist, J. Piaget, in his meticulous study of two hundred children was "struck by the fact, that . . . children in the initial stages of their development, did not appear to display any marked inclination towards nationalism." He found that a "slow and laborious process was necessary before children attained an awareness of their own homeland and that of others." [5] From his family, nevertheless, the child at an early age learns respect for the law, awe for the policemen, and love of national heroes. Very likely in his early family life he is conditioned to respond to the words and symbols representing the homeland, his reflexes being conditioned to automatic reaction in favorable patterns when he hears or sees them. A great many parents came to feel as Clemenceau, the French war leader, did about France: if there was a country which had a right to the love of its children and to obtain their first smile it was theirs. [6] In the nineteenth and twentieth centuries, then, as most parents became more aware of and loyal to their nations, the children, born into the parents' cultural outlook, absorbed patriotic attitudes which would remain with them through their own adult lives. [7] If as members of the human race they were already gregarious in tendencies, the home environments in which they grew shaped these tendencies toward their national group.

What family life began in this respect, the schools continued and shaped further in the direction of nationalism. [8] Possibly the most distinctive quality of man, compared to other species, is his "teachability." Governments and patriots everywhere employed the schools to teach national patriotism. If the school systems varied in detail from country to country, in every nation the trend was toward making education universal, secular, compulsory, and patriotic. [9] By the twentieth century such education existed everywhere in western Europe and the United States and almost all individuals in these areas were affected by it.

From at least the time of the French Revolution rulers

have realized the value of formal education in the inculcation of loyalty. All during the century and a half since then
universities and colleges have often been centers of nationalist education. In time of war especially, the profes-
sors, like those, for example, at Berlin during the Napoleonic
wars, at Paris in 1870, and at American universities in World
War I, have pleaded and propagandized for the national
cause. As early as 1827 the American states of Massachusetts
and Vermont required the teaching of American history
in the lower schools. From a study of over eight hundred
American textbooks of the period 1776-1865 one recent
American authority concluded that the elementary schools
"operated as a primary instrument for the inculcation of
nationalism in the United States," a nationalism that "not
only taught the child hatred and contempt for other nations but exalted a conservative brand of nationalism for
domestic use." [9] After the 1870's, with the rise of universal
public education, efforts intensified to make all the schools
centers of patriotic inspiration. In France in 1879 Jules
Ferry, that able exponent of secular education as well as
imperialism, made clear one of its national purposes. "The
State," he said, "is certainly not at all an instructor in
physiology or in chemistry. If it suits it in the public interest to pay the chemists and physiologist . . . it is not
in order to create scientific truths; this is not its concern in
fostering education; its concern is to maintain a certain
state morale, certain state doctrines which are important
for its conservation." [10]

Everywhere instructors and texts were increasingly expected by governments and officials who controlled appropriations, in democratic America, in monarchical and Nazi
Germany, in Communist Russia, to inculcate love of homeland by depicting the glorious history of the nation, by
weeping over its wrongs, by showing how other nations
were treacherous, cowardly, and dishonorable—especially
in war.[11] In practice they customarily did what they were
expected to do. In the United States, for instance, as Henry

Steele Commager pointed out, the readers, spellers, and histories in the American schools inculcated patriotism on almost every page through the repetition of "a common body of stories, hero tales, legends and maxims." [12] And Bessie Pierce's remarks about American texts of the 1920's generally fit those of all the Western countries: "Textbooks are permeated with a national or patriotic spirit . . . on the other hand the attitudes engendered toward other peoples through a reading of these books must, in many cases, redound to their ignominy in contrast to the glory of America." [13]

Text and teacher alike, with few notable exceptions, taught the student that his own country was high-minded, great, and glorious. If his nation went to war it was for defense, while the foe was the aggressor. If his nation won its wars, that was because his countrymen were braver and God was on their side. If his nation was defeated that was due only to the enemy's overwhelmingly superior forces and treachery. If his country lost territory, as the French lost Alsace-Lorraine in 1870, that was a crime; whatever it gained was for the good of humanity and but its rightful due. The enemy was "harsh," "cruel," "backward." His own people, "kind," "civilized," "progressive."

Again and again the student learned, "My country, right or wrong, but always my country." Again and again he was instructed that he should be "prepared to endure hunger, thirst and cold for the sake of the Fatherland," and "be ready to die rather than abandon" his post.[14] In the United States from the 1890's more and more school children were forced by law or social pressure to "pledge allegiance" to their flag.[15] In the schools everywhere they were taught to be good citizens which meant in practice that they were to love their own country, always put it first in their affections, have no other idol before them.

This type of education culminated during the two great wars of the twentieth century and became absurd in the practices of Italian Fascists and German Nazis. Adolf Hitler commanded and the German schools of the 1930's taught: "History must be regarded by the folkist state as an instrument for the advancement of national pride. An inventor must not only seem great as an inventor, but must seem even greater as a national comrade. Our admiration of every great deed must be bathed in pride that its fortunate performer is a member of our own people. From all the innumerable great names of German history, the greatest must be picked out and introduced to the youth so persistently that they become pillars of an unshakeable national sentiment." [16] Nazi education carried nationalistic education to the limit. Certainly in democratic countries, down to the 1950's at least, there was no such complete warping of knowledge to nationalist ends. But most schools in all the Western nations indoctrinated their students in national patriotism, desired to "kindle the fires of patriotism and feed them constantly," and this was one type of indoctrination that nearly always went unchallenged.

And the teaching was apparently effective. When in 1897 in France, examiners asked candidates for the modern baccalaureate, "What purpose does the teaching of history serve?", 80 per cent answered, "To promote patriotism." [17] When in the late 1920's Professor Bessie Pierce questioned 1,125 students in the public secondary schools of Pennsylvania and Iowa, she found that the great majority regarded defense of country as the highest form of patriotism and only four admitted that the United States "has carried on some enterprises which we can't be proud of." [18]

Along with attempts to "educate" patriots went persistent efforts to provide the materials for and to write national histories. These efforts were twofold in purpose. Patriotic historians desired to discover how their nations began and developed, and through this knowledge to create and foster love of and loyalty to the nation. The immense amount of historical research and writing in the nineteenth centry was thus, in part, a sign of nationalism and a reason for more. In the 1820's and 1830's English,

French, and German historians began monumental collections of their national historical sources. G. H. Pertz began to edit the great *Monumenta Germaniae Historica* in 1824, François Guizot commenced the publication of *Documents inédits sur l'histoire de France* in 1833, and the British Parliament in 1834 authorized the publication of documents concerning the early history of Great Britain and Ireland which began under the title "Rolls Series" in 1838. These early collections were followed by innumerable others during the century that followed until there were few "undocumented" periods in the history of any nation.

Using these documents as well as the multitudes that were yet uncollected and unpublished, individual historians devoted most of their attention to national, not local or world, histories. Though many of them were objectively "scientific," they nevertheless usually selected national topics on which to write. Often they were swayed by nationalist prejudices to speak highly of their own nation and deprecatingly of others, especially those with whom their own nation had recently fought or expected soon to fight. Michelet's advice to his fellow countrymen was not untypical of the point of view of some historians in many lands: "Frenchmen of every station, of every class and party, remember well one thing. You have on this earth, only one sure friend, France."

In France, among a great many patriotic historians, Henri Martin, Augustin Thierry, and François Guizot revealed the triumphs and tragedies of their nation as did the later Ernest Lavisse and Alphonse Aulard.[19] In the United States George Bancroft, John Fiske, James Schouler, John Bach McMaster, and many others lovingly depicted the rise of the American people. One famous school of American historians, among whom Herbert Baxter Adams, James K. Hosmer, and Moses Coit Tyler were notable, proudly discovered the roots of American (and English) institutions in the tribal organization of the Teutonic forests, thus at-

tributing to these institutions an ancient genealogy that
was somehow superior. In the United States from the mid-
nineteenth century historical societies were organized in
every state to fill the growing want for a national past, a past
that the States, compared to the older countries, lacked.[20]
English and German historians during the same period
were giving their nations histories of which they could be
proud. Among them were J. R. Green, Edward Freeman,
Bishop Stubbs, and Sir Henry Maine in England, and in
Germany Friedrich Dahlmann, Johann Droysen, Henrich
von Sybel, and Heinrich von Treitschke.[21] Many times historians, like the Germans just mentioned, helped create
and arouse national consciousness and led the way to national unity. Czechs learned of their common past and right
to nationhood from Palacky and the Bulgarians from
Paisi.

What these great historians began in the nineteenth century, twentieth-century historians generally continued.
Only a few of the better-known ones, like Charles Beard in
America and Friedrich Meinecke in Germany, dared to be
genuinely critical of the fundamental policies of their nations. Lesser historians usually popularized national views
of history until children in their schools and adults in their
homes and libraries could easily arrive at the belief that only
their own nation was great, only their own nation was brave,
only their own nation was inventive, in short only their own
nation had much history worth knowing.

Out of these national conceptions rose the famous national heroes upon whose lives the young were taught to
model their own: Jeanne d'Arc, Henry IV, Napoleon,
George Washington, Patrick Henry, John Paul Jones,
Robin Hood, Francis Drake, the Duke of Marlborough,
Admiral Nelson, Arminius, Frederick the Great, and Gneisenau.[22] Out of them arose magnificent traditions, national
symbols and faiths, to be fervently exalted by all good
patriots. Out of them likewise came hatred for the domestic traitors, the Benedict Arnolds, and the foreign oppres-

sors, the "Huns" and barbarians, who had tried vainly to harm the nation. As each group studied its own real or imagined common history, it learned of heroic achievements and awful agonies, came thus to possess common "sacred and memorable" traditions which it could revere.[23]

Such traditions were deepened and widened by stress upon national languages. Scholars of already united nations published philological works, grammars, and dictionaries in profusion to "purify" and develop the national tongues. Three quite different examples will illustrate. Noah Webster hoped to establish an American language through his dictionaries and spellers used so extensively in the American schools of the nineteenth century. The learned Sir James Murray edited *A New English Dictionary* (1908) to give all the possible historical meaning of the words of the English language. Ferdinand Brunot's monumental *Histoire de la langue française,* upon which he worked for half a century, was not only erudite but also a highly republican and patriotic work. Within groups not yet nations linguistic studies were among the first signs of rising national consciousness. They were also consciously made to stimulate it. The works of Korais in Greek to arouse Greek national feeling have already been mentioned. One Vuk Karajich (Karadzic) published a Serbian grammar in 1814. Soon after 1800 Czech scholars began to publish philological studies of their language. If a people did not possess a common language, scholarly patriots provided one.

Scholars, poets, and novelists all over Europe and the New World labored hard to develop their languages and literatures, to encourage national loyalties, to promote unity. In Germany, for example, as Bismarck's English biographer, C. Grant Robertson, observed, "Poetry, philology, comparative mythology and folklore, the comparative study of institutions, palaeography and the archives, the philosophy of law—history in its widest streams, explored and mapped by the severest science—were exhibited to enforce a single moral—the greatness of the German contri-

bution to the civilization of the past, a greatness in proportion to its fidelity to its racial and national character, and
the certainty that a similar fidelity in the future would
produce no less momentous results for Germany and humanity." [24] Sometimes the authors of these works set out
directly to make patriots by giving their nations a "pure"
language, by exploring the origins and showing the conti-
nuity of the national laws, by romantically recovering the
folklore which rooted the national character, or by inspiring their countrymen through poem and song.[25] In many
cases the writers did not primarily or even consciously aim
at this end. They nevertheless attained it when they wrote
not in the universal Western language, Latin, but in their
national tongue and about subjects almost solely national.
They attained it, too, when their "villains" were strange-
looking foreigners while their heroes, tall, strong, and cou-
rageous, were, of course, of their own nationality. Whatever
their motivation a Tennyson would sing about "Love
Thou Thy Land," a Swinburne of "The Commonwealth
and the Armada"; the Grimm brothers would edit German
fairy tales and *Deutsche Sagen,* and a Savigny would publish his learned studies on German laws; [26] a John Green-
leaf Whittier would write his poem, "Our Country," Oliver
Wendell Holmes his "Union and Liberty"; a Déroulède his
"Chants patriotiques," and a Maurice Barrès his trilogy,
Le Roman de l'énergie nationale. All of these instilled
patriotism on a high adult level.[27] For the children of every
country cheap and simple novels such as those of Tom
Swift and the Boy Allies series in the United States accomplished the same end.

So much did literature become national that the nationality of an author came to mean more than the content of
his writing. By the twentieth century the student seldom
studied drama, poetry, or novel as such but the English,
the French, or American drama, poetry, or novel. The
extreme was again to be reached in the totalitarian states
of the second quarter of the twentieth century when few

literary works or studies of any kind could be published unless they patriotically supported the policies of the national government. By 1955, even in a democratic country like the United States, popularly elected governmental officials were examining all forms of artistic production to root out any ideas that were "un-American." Again, no studies were available to indicate how effective the linguistic, literary, as well as political, efforts were in fostering nationalism. But if literate men read chiefly their own national literatures, if they read almost entirely in their national languages, if the sources of their information were almost exclusively national, they could scarcely avoid becoming national patriots.

Almost every cultural activity in the nineteenth and twentieth centuries pointed toward increased nationalism. A few writers might stress economic class, a few an all-encompassing religion as the desirable basis for society. But as in literature, so in all fields the trend was clear. Music became "German," "French," or "American" rather than just music—symphony or quartet, instrumental or vocal.[28] Newspapers, commercial advertising, movies, radio, television were not only increasingly "national" but they attempted to make their readers, listeners, and viewers good patriots. In spite of continued diversities of theological beliefs, religions became ever more "national." Even the foods of the various peoples tended to become uniform within the nation as well as differentiated from those of other nations. Cooking was no longer primarily known by its locality or its excellence but by whether it was "French" or "English." Every good patriot now liked his own "steak and potatoes," his own national dishes best.

Everywhere men turned, their cultures influenced them to become national minded. Within each group symbols and stereotypes arose to stir their imaginations, to arouse their loyalties. Each national group had its own national holidays, its own symbolic animal, flower, or tree, its own saint, and its own mythical half-human character which somehow personified it. John Bull, Marianne, Uncle Sam, and Michel equaled England, France, the United States, and Germany. A shamrock was Ireland, a bear Russia. These symbols somehow took on mystical qualities. For each people their own flag, its colors and its designs came to represent all that was heroic and good, beautiful and true, what was highest in civilization, something never to be desecrated, something always to be worshiped.[29]

At different times peoples attributed different meanings to these symbols as did the French to Marianne. Usually they incorporated for each group what each thought were its finest characteristics: John Bull is dogged and Uncle Sam honest. By so doing individuals within each group could "appropriate the complimentary adjectives" for their "own countrymen," and by "reflection of virtue" for themselves.[30] Thus they could describe themselves as hard-working, intelligent, generous, brave, and peace-loving. On the other hand each people tended to see other national groups through stereotypes given quite opposite meanings. "John Bull, for Germany, becomes a caddish, insolent ogre-like figure: Uncle Sam, for Europe, a desiccated, heartless Shylock, and German Michel, for France, a sly double-crossing fool; in the same way Marianne is all too easily transformed into a flighty harum-scarum."[31] Reinforced by literature, history, and the movies these stereotypes for each people, both the "good" for themselves and the "bad" for other nationalities, tended to become fixed. After Hollywood had portrayed and twentieth-century American children had viewed Americans as handsome heroes and German, Japanese, and Russians as brutal beasts for years, it would be difficult for most Americans to see them as individuals who, like Americans, varied widely both physically and mentally.

To be certain that individuals were shaped by the nationalist pattern, patriots in each nation formed societies to bring pressure upon governments and to propagandize for "right ideals." Early in the nineteenth century these societies, like the *Hetairia Philike* in Greece, the Carbonari and "Young Italy" in the Italies, the *Burschenschaft* in the Germanies, the *Selspabet for Norges vel* in Norway, and the Philomathians in Poland strove to create national consciousness, to unify their peoples and to obtain national independence. Once these objectives were obtained, similar if less conspiratorial societies were formed to intensify national loyalty, to strengthen the national military forces, and to guard and to extend (particularly in the case of the British and Germans) the nation's possessions. From the 1880's these patriotic organizations sprang up rapidly. Composed usually of respectable, middle-class, and conservative citizens, many of them with some military background, they had a stake in the established order, liked it, and wanted to keep "superior" people like themselves on top. To do so as well as to stimulate patriotism they prodded governments to indoctrinate national ideals through the schools, to push national interests exclusively by whatever methods seemed necessary, and to nationalize (or eliminate) the "alien" groups within the nation.[32]

To attempt to list all these patriotic societies would take too much space. In a brief examination of the American records the present writer found fifty-odd such groups established in the United States before 1917, and one count revealed eighty-four in Germany in 1914.[33] Among the most prominent societies were the Royal Empire Society and the Primrose League of Britain, the Daughters of the American Revolution and the Grand Army of the Republic in the United States, the League of Patriots and the National Alliance for the Increase of French Population in France, and the Pan-German League and the Navy League in Germany.

These groups and the many like them held meetings to hear inspirational patriotic talks. They published magazines, occasionally newspapers, and handed out propaganda in pamphlets and news stories. They brought pressure upon their governments to increase military appropriations and adopt "strong" foreign policies. They demanded the teaching of patriotism and tried to weed out unpatriotic teachers and teachings. They exhibited the national flags and relics and publicly celebrated national holidays. They attempted to "Americanize" or "Germanize" the foreigners within their gates, and to "purify" the national languages. They were vociferously for any and all policies which in their view enhanced the prestige of their nation. They were just as vociferously against anything they thought foreign or international.

Their memberships were usually not large, the better-known organizations numbering 40,000 to 300,000 and only occasionally, like the American GAR and the British Primrose League, exceeding a million. But they spoke loudly and with self-assurance. While a few, like the Pan-German League, would be unpopular with their governments, while most of them were filled with old gentlemen and ladies, they served to make national patriotism respectable. Not infrequently as in the case of the various Navy and Security Leagues they influenced political leaders who wished to be re-elected, and thereby were successful in increasing the size of the military establishments. If they were not effective in any other way, they spread fear of other nations, caused many of their compatriots to "view with alarm," hence accentuated distrust of foreigners and sharpened feelings of national exclusiveness.

While there was no society that might be termed "typical" among them, the early activities of one, the Daughters of the American Revolution, is not unrepresentative.[34] The Daughters held patriotic assemblies to inspire themselves and their communities. They presented copies of national songs and documents to schools, convinced boards of education and legislatures that the American flag should be flown on every school, decried any "misuse" of the flag, and asked that men (not women) doff their hats when it passed. They reviewed the national history, especially its glorious moments, made pilgrimages to historical spots, gave entertainments in historical costumes, and erected national monuments. They gave prizes to children for patriotic essays and made certain that the "right" books were in the libraries. "In every way" the Daughters desired to "cherish, maintain and extend the institutions of American freedom, to foster true patriotism and love of country," [35] which, of course, meant they wanted other Americans to be loyal to their kind of nation. While like most of the patriotic societies they shunned politics (on paper), they were always on the side of the national authorities, particularly the conservative ones. They were always fearful of the "foreigner"; they were always against any "radical" doctrines like socialism; and they were always for "adequate" defense which in practice meant the biggest army and navy the country could afford without heavy taxes upon the well-to-do.

With all these social pressures upon them, few men could be anything but national patriots. As David Hume observed in the eighteenth century, "the human mind is of a very imitative nature; nor is it possible for any set of men to converse often together, without acquiring a similitude of manners, and communicating to each other their vices as well as virtues. . . ." [36] Men were forced into national molds by their cultures. Their initial impulses, whatever they might be, were thus conditioned and directed toward national loyalties, national goals until it might almost be said they acquired a patriotic reflex. If the language of psychoanalysis may be borrowed, their unconscious ("super-ego") controls and their conscious ("ego") thinking were both shaped by patriotic pressures and these in turn enabled their biological drives ("id") to find satisfaction in national goals, in striving for national power and security. If they did not choose this way they lost the respect of their fellows, they might lose their livelihoods or at least their chance for economic advancement, and they would become socially uncomfortable and frustrated. If they did choose this way, they could win fame, career, and one escape from frustration.

Chapter XI

THE NATION-STATE BECOMES
MEANS AND END

ɔ| c

In response to these nationalizing pressures the national states and their governments constantly expanded, and, in turn, exercised a strong national force of their own. The effect of these economic, social, and psychological pressures must remain somewhat conjectural both because the evidence is scanty and because the conclusions that can be drawn from it cannot be experimentally tested. But in the nineteenth and twentieth centuries in much of Europe, the nation in a sense created the nation-state, and the latter in turn shaped the nation.[1] Or to put the same idea in another way the cultural needs and economic and social problems became so vast and complex that only an institution to which men were loyal and which possessed great power could meet them. This institution, in the fullest sense, became the nation-state. It became the "organized expression" of the nation.[2] It, in the words of Max Weber, alone came to have "the monopoly of legitimate physical force." Functioning in government, it became in Hobbes's words, a "Mortall God," a Leviathan, promoting its own expansion and nationalism. The nation-state which the romantics of the early nineteenth century regarded as an object of poetry and adoration, became the hard pervasive reality of twentieth-century political society.

Whether newly created or old, the national governments extended and consolidated their power within their respective nations while attempting to expand their interests and dominions abroad. For a while during the nineteenth century when liberalism was at its height, it appeared that the national states would follow policies of *laissez faire* and that their governments would therefore become weak. In Britain, France, and the United States, according to theory, the governments should have governed very little, should have been no more than policemen. In practice this was not to be the case, except for a few years around the mid-century and then only in a few countries like Britain and the United States. Importuned by this or that economic class, social group, or political clique the governments steadily expanded the scope, legal and functional, of their activities and hence made their peoples ever more nationally conscious.

So strong did these governments become that the basic tenets of liberalism were often denied, particularly during and after the twentieth century's great wars. But during the nineteenth century particularly in western Europe and the United States liberalism and nationalism grew together, liberalism, especially in its democratic aspects, contributing to the growth of nationalism. For it was within and through the nation-state, not a church or an international organization, that the individual obtained his freedom and the vote.[3] In obtaining these he felt he belonged; when he became a citizen he became, in fact, part of the nation, part of its government. When there was a *plébiscite de tous les jours,* he could speak upon and influence the national decisions and destinies. What was then good for the nation was good for him, for his security, his family, his business, his job, and in turn what was good for him was good for the nation.

For most of the nineteenth century only the upper and middle classes participated in the national affairs and were strongly nationalist. Later, as pointed out above, all classes

began to participate, to receive or expect benefits. Then,
they too became nationalist, even most of the socialist
workers and intellectuals who preached class rather than
national solidarity. Thus, in general, individual interests
came to be almost completely identified with the national
interest as this was represented by the national government.[4]

When the dictators arose in the twentieth century they
denied men both liberty and effective voice in government.
They did *not* deprive them of the sense of belonging to
the nation. Rather just the opposite.[5] Their success arose
in large part out of the shrewd use of symbols and propaganda through which they identified themselves, the nation,
and the people. When Louis XIV acted as if he were the
state, he did not trouble himself with the people. When
Hitler and Mussolini spoke, they shouted to and in the
name of the entire nation. The difference between the
absolute monarchs of the seventeenth century and the authoritarian dictators of the twentieth lies partly in the fact
that the first were dynastic heads of states and the second
were leaders of peoples united by national feeling into a
political and cultural, a national state they believed their
own.

When the state and nation were identified, the governments were called upon to govern for all special and general interests.[6] Economists like the Germans Georg Friedrich List and Max Weber and the Frenchman Paul Louis
Cauwès first, and later many other economists like Herbert
Croly in the United States, argued for strong national governments to promote the national economy. And many
radical theorists such as the nineteenth-century Edward
Bellamy and William Dean Howells in America as well as
twentieth-century fascists like Alfredo Rocco and Alfred
Rosenberg advocated national control of all forms of economic activity.

If their economic proposals often were fought, their
nationalist arguments found ready acceptance. The na-

tional governments, more often than not, acted as they had advocated. These governments stressed national economic production, for production meant wealth and wealth meant power.[7] This meant, first of all, assistance to business at home and abroad. But as all men became part of the nation, the governments had to care for all. This meant that these governments had to act for agriculture and labor as well. From the 1880's they did precisely this and went beyond. Increasingly they were held responsible for a minimum subsistence for all, for the provision of education and opportunity for all. During the depression beginning in 1929 they supplied jobs and basic necessities for millions.

Now protection for and assistance to domestic capital, agriculture, and labor in the prevailing scheme of things required national legislation concerning tariffs and trade quotas, banking and currency, wages, hours, and working conditions, and agricultural production and prices. Aid for the unemployed, the old, the disabled, the sick meant national social security laws such as Bismarck established in the 1880's in Germany. Most of these entailed huge national expenditures. The expenditures, in turn, necessitated huge national taxes.[8] All of the governmental measures necessitated still more national laws and these in turn required more national courts. Even individual liberty had to be guaranteed by national constitutions, parliaments, and courts.

When the great twentieth-century wars and the acute economic depression of 1929 hit Western societies, only the national governments were able to offer security and assistance to frightened and confused men. Then, everywhere, these governments directly controlled and supported production, set minimum prices for businessmen and farmers, minimum wages and maximum hours for industrial workers, provided jobs for the unemployed and benefits of all kinds for those who, like some of the aged, could not take care of themselves. National governments, like the English, became the managers of national welfare states. Each time they extended their activities they encouraged the tendency to look to them for all things, for the realization of all hopes, for existence itself. The nation-state thus became the institution through which everything was to be accomplished and all conflicts resolved. Within it all sorts of diverse groups, from financiers to day laborers, could find a way of attaining their diverse aims.

If, however, the nation-state were to afford the strongest bulwark, it had to nationalize all groups within it, make certain that the people formed a united whole and were firmly loyal. Somehow the "alien" elements had to be rooted out to prevent disunity, to eliminate any potential weakness. The governments, therefore, promoted the common language, tried with some success, as did the French and Germans, to impose the same language upon all inhabitants.[9] More important, the national governments built their own power through control of opinion. In some nations, especially the more democratic like France, they achieved this end largely through the public schools. Many, such as the totalitarian governments at all times and the democratic in time of war, not only censored the news but created it and were its only source. All established "public relations" offices and instituted official agencies, like the World War II Office of War Information in the United States, to publicize and win favor for the national policies.[10]

When the national governments expanded their functions they directly employed more and more people. In the peacetime years of the 1920's the French government employed one out of every twenty of its citizens, if school and military personnel were counted.[11] In the United States in 1950 over 2,500,000 civilians worked for the federal government and about the same number were in the armed forces. In wartime, democratic and capitalist governments such as the United States directly paid and controlled the livelihood of more than a tenth of their population, indirectly employed 30 to 40 per cent of their people through

nationally subsidized war industry, and, in addition, chan-
neled the energies of the entire populace toward the end
of national survival and expansion. For the totalitarian
states, in peace and war, the percentages of those directly
employed ran higher. In the minds of some patriots, evidently, the better a national government did its job, the
more citizens it employed and brought into direct dependence upon the state.

The national governments in these ways turned the eyes
of more and more of their citizens toward the nation. At the
same time forces encroaching upon the nation-state from
without had a similar effect. As each state grew stronger, it,
with the prevailing conditions of international anarchy,
seemed to threaten every other nation. For its own security
each national government believed it must create a solid
and strong national front against every other nation. Each
nation in consequence had to build its military forces,
make alliances, expand its trade and its colonial empire.
That this solution ultimately brought disaster, not security,
proved nothing. No nation could afford to stop building
land forces, sea forces, air forces, no nation could withdraw
from its colonies and tear down its trade walls—unless all
the others did. All felt obligated, on the contrary, to build,
build, build. When a committee of three British admirals
in 1888 gave it as their opinion that the British navy should
be larger than "that of any two powers," [12] they were simply
leading the way to a tremendous naval race in which all the
great powers had to take part. The Germans led by Admiral
von Tirpitz and their Navy League and the Americans
under the influence of Admiral Mahan, President Theodore Roosevelt, and their steel manufacturers indulged in
the same kind of fantasy—to be safe each nation had to have
a navy capable of "defending" (expanding) the national
interests against all possible opponents anywhere at any
time. The result could not be anything but fear and eventual war and these in turn accentuated nationalism. Each
national official felt bound to forward his nation's military

might, to assume an aggressive foreign policy. If he did not he was a traitor who criminally betrayed his country.[13] Palmerston, the clever and successful British foreign minister, asserted that every British minister ought to "consult the interests of the country in preference to every other consideration." [14] This is exactly what most national officials did. And the bulk of the citizens in each country would have had it no other way. For they, too, thought their own welfare and safety dependent upon the national power. When other nations threatened them, they saw no recourse but to strengthen their own.

Modern war and the fear of it forced the national states to become ever more national, their citizens to become ever more nationalist. Modern war demanded utmost effort and power if victory was to be won.[15] A vicious circle ensued. As each nation confronted each other nation, national strength and unity in each, even in peacetime, became imperative. Under the prevailing conditions of international politics each greater national effort compelled greater national efforts on the part of each other nation. This eventually necessitated the total involvement of the total nation, absolute loyalty on the part of citizens. The various governments hence believed they had to propagandize their peoples, compel them to conform and to contribute taxes for armies and navies. The British government used national fear of France and later Germany, the French government fear of Britain and later Germany, the German government fear of Britain and later Russia, and the American government fear of Germany and later Russia all for the same purpose: to build their own national unity and power.[16] And as most people believed possible defeat meant oppression, perhaps death, most men acquiesced and went further to urge their own governments to still greater efforts. When the wars actually began, when shells exploded, bombs fell, and men died, each people became still more nationalistic, more nation-conscious, more loyal, more exclusive, and they increasingly feared, distrusted,

hated other nations.[17] They, then, demanded omnipotent
national governments. These governments in turn willingly, eagerly fostered this sentiment, built their instruments of war, only to create deeper fears, a more intense
nationalism. When the wars brought inevitable frustration
and defeat for some nations, these, like Italy and Germany after World War I, reached a state of mind that
justifies the use of the word pathological.[18]

Once established as a going institution the national state
possessed a momentum of its own. One activity led to another, one success to other successes, power fed power. As
a modern Catholic critic of nationalism, Don Luigi Sturzo,
observed, "Once a country or a people has succeeded in
developing a consciousness of its own personality and in
affirming it in the struggles with which history has confronted it, there is no stopping." [19] When the national state
became large it could act and command as no other institution could. It could effectively deal with, subordinate,
or eliminate, all other competitive institutions.

As early as 1820, in the *Cohens* vs. *Virginia* decision,
the great Chief Justice of the United States Supreme Court,
John Marshall, made clear for his own government what
was to become theory and practice everywhere in the
course of the next century. "The United States," he declared, "form, for many, and for most important purposes,
a single nation. . . . In war, we are one people. In making
peace, we are one people. In all commercial regulations,
we are one and the same people . . . and the government
which is alone capable of controlling and managing their
interests in all these respects, is the government of the
union. It is their government and in that character they
have no other. America has chosen to be, in many respects,
and to many purposes, a nation; and for all these purposes,
her government is complete. . . . It can, then, in effecting
these objects, legitimately control all individuals or governments within the American territory." [20]

The national governments, of course, moved far beyond

Marshall's still limited conception of what they could and
should do. By the twentieth century no other sovereignty
was allowed within them. Each became the almost absolute master of its own people and territory. As the Nazis
had it, *Gemeinnutz geht vor Eigennutz,* and the national
state was identified with the common welfare (*Gemeinnutz*) and took charge of the individual welfare (*Eigennutz*). Adolf Hitler was but stating bluntly what was becoming the reality not only in Germany but everywhere
when he wrote in *Mein Kampf,* "It is clear that everything
else must be subordinated to the nation's interests; and in
particular, we cannot permit any single State within the
nation and the *Reich* (which represents the nation).
. . ." [21] In relation to other nation-states each was independent, able to do whatever its own power permitted. It
represented a people and territory, an efficient unit which
in the play of domestic and international politics was superior to lesser institutions within and more heterogeneous
states without.[22] The English authority on international
law, H. Lauterpacht, accurately described the law and the
fact when he wrote, "The sovereign State does not ac-
knowledge a central executive authority above itself; it
does not recognize a legislature above itself, it owes no
obedience to a judge above itself." [23]

In the system of power relationships that characterized
international politics each nation believed that to survive
it had to follow this pattern, to form an independent national government, weld itself together into an ever more
uniform, integrated, coherent whole. Here a kind of social Darwinism, a competitive struggle among nations,
seemed to operate. If the "survival of the fittest" did not
really apply to the national struggles, patriots thought that
it did and what they thought was more significant than the
truth or falsity of the doctrine. What was believed about
group survival, was equally applicable if the nation was to
forward what its members considered their interests, the
national interests.

Many large and small national groups, the Italians, the Germans, the Bulgarians, the Czechs, and later many Asiatic and African peoples, felt compelled to imitate the older nations, establish independent nation-states. This, to them, was the only way to obtain relief from oppression, to achieve "regeneration" and a better life. Once their nation-state was created they had to make their governments strong, their unity complete, create armies, educational systems, and all the other nationalizing agencies the older nations possessed. As Francis Delaisi, keenest of the French critics of nationalism, observed, "From the moment a state such as France was able [in 1793] to decree the levy in mass of all its citizens, it became necessary for all the others in the interests of the balance of power to replace their professional armies by national armies. . . ." [24] What one nation did the others had to do.

Everywhere in fear and in hope many men became willing if not eager to make of their nation a fetish, to permit their nation-state to become totalitarian, to incorporate within the national society all values and actions.[25] By the mid-twentieth century, and only to a lesser extent in the democratic countries than in the fascist, the nation for most men had become the supreme ideal and physical fact, and its government the omnipotent if not the omnicompetent arbiter of individual and social destinies.

To the most ardent patriots, the nation had become the beginning, the way, and the end. In the nineteenth century the liberal patriot Michelet saw his country "above everything, as dogma and principle." [26] Before World War I the most passionate nationalists, the Frenchman Charles Maurras, the Englishman L. J. Maxse, the German Heinrich Class, the leaders of the patriotic societies, and the professional patriots, had come to believe that everything should be integrated into the nation.[27] All efforts were to be directed toward its defense, its power, its glory. All sacrifices were to be made in its name. Many men were coming to believe what a French schoolbook explained to French children, "The Fatherland is the nation which you should love, honor and serve with all the energy and all the devotion of your soul." [28]

What the integral nationalists preached became most completely practiced in the totalitarian states that followed World War I, Fascist Italy and Nazi Germany. Though in these nations the nationalism was beclouded by individual ambitions, and in the case of Germany by racial nonsense, they became total states which totally represented the total nation and acted for the totality whether the people consented or not. The integral nationalists, the fascist totalitarians, went further, it is true, than did most patriots in peacetime. But in wartime, from 1914 to 1918, from 1939 to 1945, most other men followed the same fanatical faith. In peace and war, most Western men indeed came to regard their own nation as the greatest and best, the strongest bulwark against evil, the highest source of joy and happiness. [29] In the words of Daniel Webster arguing against Hayne in the American Senate, the nation provided "safety at home," "consideration and dignity abroad," "a copious fountain of national, social, personal happiness," and "high, exciting and gratifying prospects." In addition, as Webster did not say, it offered the way to power, to dominion over other men. Patriotism toward the nation was thus both the expression of self-interest and in Hegel's prose, "the sentiment of regarding the weal of the community as the substantial basis and final end." [30]

When men believed this, they could completely subordinate themselves to the nation. All their interests—economic, political, social—were swallowed up in it. They could apply, as Theodore Roosevelt told Americans and Maurice Barrès the French, the national solution to every problem; they could resolve every question by reference to the national interest. [31] To them the truth itself became not universal but national. They now regarded their nation as a fit object of poetry and worship, something so wonderful that it was divine. [32] The shibboleths by which they rationally and irrationally lived and perhaps died were no longer the Christian Trinity or the French Revolutionary "Liberty, Equality, and Fraternity," but embodied in the slogans, "My country, right or wrong," "America First," or "Deutschland über Alles," "The true nationalist," the French royalist newspaper *Action Française* correctly asserted, places "the fatherland above everything." [33]

Since this was true, the best man, according to a true nationalist, was really a "chauvinist," a "jingo," a "one hundred percenter" who in his fervent, blind patriotism contributed his services, his money, his life to his country, its expansion, its power, its glory. The greatest reward such a man could win was the coveted and highest honor his country could bestow, the Congressional Medal, the Croix de Guerre, the Victoria Cross, and the Iron Cross. And these were won only in military action for his nation and most often awarded posthumously.

The true nationalist was also "anti" everything not of his nation. He was antiman, believing only in particular men. He was antiforeigner, distrusting, disliking or hating men of other "breeds." [34] He was anti-Semitic since the Jews represented an international tradition. He could be anti-Christian, as were the Nazis, because Christianity, no matter how practiced, stood for the brotherhood of man. He was antisocialist because socialism was international. He was anti-world government whether in a weak League of Nations or a stronger world federation. He could even deny the principle of nationality and urge his nation to conquer other nations.[35]

Anyone who differed was "un," "uncivilized," "un-American," "un-German," that is, disloyal, subversive, a traitor. Once the words "heretic" and "sinner" were the worst epithets that could be applied to any man. With the nationalist it was "traitor." To be a traitor was to be the lowest and most despicable of criminals. A traitor committed "treason." Treason condemned a man to a fate worse than death, to being a man without a country.

208 THE AGE OF NATIONALISM

Philip Nolan, the "man without a country," spoke to the young boy and the "words rattled in his throat," "And for your country, boy, and for that flag, never dream a dream but of serving her as she bids you, though the service carry you through a thousand hells." What church, what religion, what community could demand and receive more? Nation and nationalism, though not biologically determined nor supernaturally ordained, had become the strongest force binding and dividing men in modern times.

But immediately it must be said that not for all men did the patriotic fires burn so intensely as they did for Philip Nolan, for the 100 per cent patriots, for the integral nationalists. While the national states became ever more national and their citizens ever more nationalist, not all men could be completely integrated nor could any man be all the time. The totalitarian nature of the national state and the fanatical worship of the nation which have just been described became, in fact, neither universal nor omnipresent. In a number of ways the evidence from contemporary observation revealed that nationalism, like other faiths in the past, could not completely captivate and subjugate men, and might possibly be submerged or disappear as other environmental conditions arose in the future.

During great modern wars, especially those of 1914-1918, 1939-1945, most Western men gave complete devotion to their nation, were willing, if need be, to die for it. But during the worst wartime crises some businessmen, workers, and peasants paid allegiance to other gods, whether of monetary gain, social class, or supernatural religion, and a few, like the conscientious objectors and the members of obscure religious sects, were willing to make the last sacrifice for what they thought to be higher ideals. Even in the most totalitarian states there was not absolute unity: the German mutineers of 1944 against Hitler refused to obey and conform completely and during Hitler's entire twelve years some Germans were Nazi only to protect themselves against persecution. Thus even when national feeling rose to its highest pitch in the military struggles for national survival, individuals still sought individual and social goals outside and inside the national.

In peacetime the ordinary man paid much less attention to his nation. He might and probably did profess patriotism, pay national taxes, and give two years of his early life to military service but most of his time he gave to the concerns of his personal life. Customarily he ate, slept, worked, thought, and dreamed without much heed to the flags, the oaths, the emotional outpouring of the professional patriots, or for that matter to the most pressing national problems of any kind. As child and as adult he was generally too absorbed by daily interests to care much what happened to his nation short of disaster. As a child he had his play, his little joys, his little tragedies in family and neighborhood; as an adult he had his job, his hobbies, his family, his sex drives. These seemed little related to nation or state. Set against the compulsions of the nation the folkways and folk mores established by the difficulties of individual survival and by family and neighborhood custom proved tenacious and sometimes the stronger. Moreover, particularism in the sense of provincialism persisted in all the great nations. A Yorkshire man did not consider himself the same as a Londoner. A Breton in France retained customs that set him apart. A Texan was a special breed of man in the United States. And a Bavarian German felt he was not like a Prussian. In Great Britain Englishmen, Welshmen, and Scotsmen failed to see eye to eye on many questions, and few Irishmen felt any loyalty to the government in London.

During the same period as nationalism reached its height, moreover, some intellectuals turned to other wider loyalties, to internationalism and cosmopolitanism, while older and more universal religions such as Catholicism and some Protestant faiths still claimed willing followers. Even the superpatriotic Mazzini told Italians they were men before they were citizens and a good many thoughtful men would

always agree with him.[36] After World Wars I and II fear of
new war, ideals of peace, and the realities of science caused
many thinking men to see themselves as part of "one world."
Catholic leaders persisted in viewing "exaggerated nationalism" with alarm and in denying to a people or a state an
"idolatrous worship" outside the "order of things created
and commanded by God." [37] In addition, signs of a possible
decline of nationalism appeared within some of the best
developed and oldest nations, as France, where divisions on
class and religious grounds seemed so sharp that the future
of France as a nation was in doubt. The nation as *the* social
organization, *the* social end of man's endeavors, it could
be plausibly argued, was no more permanent than were
the older feudal principalities, the older empires.[38] But
here the historian must decline the role of prophet, for he
as a historian knows that institutions and ideas have a way
of living on, defying decline, even when all the signs point
in this direction.

Few sweeping predictions were hence possible concerning the intensity, the spread, or the permanency of nationalism. Nor was it possible to generalize without reservation
upon the common character of the various nationalisms.
Everywhere peoples evinced the same sort of uniformity
and unity, the same kind of loyalty to and pride in their
nation and nation-state. But in Britain, France, and the
United States the nationalism was more rational and liberty loving than it was in much of central and eastern
Europe, where it was tied more closely to an authoritarian
state and to romantic notions of folk and race.[39] Among
the individual nations sharp distinctions could hardly be
drawn but some lesser ones were fairly obvious. German
nationalism, often so romantically idealistic, seemed more
thorough and belligerent, perhaps because Germany was a
parvenu nation, late in reaching unity and behind, therefore, in obtaining colonial possessions and great power
prestige. British nationalism, perhaps because the nation
was older and better established, appeared less assertive,

less demanding, more assured and more tolerant of difference.[40] Based upon a long historical experience in which
Britain was both isolated and a world power, British national feeling did not need so desperately to assert itself,
and was for this reason less vocal, less actively belligerent if
no less strong. Influenced greatly by eighteenth-century rationalism French nationalism was tied more closely to
a priori conceptions of the nature of man.[41] The nation
and the citizen's place in it, according to the intellectuals,
were not as much determined by historical precedent as by
natural law, and since this law established liberty the
French, more than most other peoples, customarily associated rationalistic conceptions of individual freedom with
their idea of nation. In the United States there were elements of all these different nationalisms, its citizens being
heirs chiefly of western Europe, but differences appeared
as well. The presence of an open frontier down to 1890 and
the lack of a long national past meant more hope for the
future. Where opportunity beckoned and experience tempered little, the future appealed all the more. In the
United States, too, the national aims were more closely
associated with achievement of material ends.[42] To its citizens greatness seemed to depend more upon national
productivity and wealth than in other nations. When
fundamental questions arose in the United States, they
were more likely to be answered pragmatically in terms of
utilitarian values.

Other qualifications concerning the nature of modern
nationalism must be set down. In the contemporary world
the relationship of social class to nationalism was no clearer
than it had been in earlier times. While the middle classes
displayed the most ardent nationalism, some individual
bourgeois were internationalists, and by no means all nationalists were bourgeois. For reasons of profit, if no other,
some businessmen hoped to tear down national economic
barriers. To protect their own wages some workers in economically advanced lands demanded high national tariffs

and rigorous exclusion of "foreign" labor, and hence were highly nationalist. In Scandinavia the nationalism was dominantly agrarian,[48] and in contemporary Soviet Russia the strongest nationalists were bureaucrats who professed belief in international communism. In the so-called backward countries in southeast Europe, in Asia, and in Africa, nationalism seemed to belong to no class but, fostered especially by the intellectuals, army officers, and bureaucrats, to unite all against foreign oppressors.

There are, then, no dogmatic conclusions that can be laid down at this time about the contemporary nature of nationalism or its future. Answers to questions of "why" and "what" must be pluralistic; no one categorical explanation will suffice. That modern nationalism historically developed and is not a biologically determined association no reasonable man can deny. Because it developed historically and has never been static, it could evolve in the future into some other kind of loyalty or dissolve into something quite new and unexpected. By the middle of the twentieth century the student could reasonably guess that, barring extinction of man in atomic war, the nations would either become incorporated into new great empires or unite into regional federations, possibly one world federation. For it was clear that if men were biologically of the same species, cultural differences alone divided them. And the cultural differences, not being ordained from on high, might be seen as what they were—differences which were deeply rooted in the dynamic flow of history but which future developments might modify or even cause to disappear. Nations developed out of villages, towns, feudal states. They grew by conquest, diplomacy, and out of the need of peoples for social organization. They and their governments promoted their own growth and loyalties and solidified their power. But just as they swallowed smaller social groups, so they themselves might in turn be absorbed by larger social groupings which would more closely meet the needs of men.

DELUSIONS ABOUT MAN
AND HIS GROUPINGS

Chapter XII

MEN ARE MORE ALIKE*

ɔ|ɕ

"Nature hath plac't us in the world free and unbound, wee emprison our selves into certaine streights."

Montaigne, *The Essays*, Florio translation,
Bk. 3, Ch. 9.

"And the idea of the Nation is one of the most powerful anaesthetics that man has invented. Under the influence of its fumes the whole people can carry out its systematic programme of the most virulent self-seeking without being in the least aware of its moral perversion,—in fact feeling dangerously resentful if it is pointed out."

Tagore, *Nationalism*, p. 57.

The customary method of historians in our times, and for the last two centuries, has been to write national histories, to study national institutions, to attempt solution of national problems. It is easier and more convenient, the material can be more readily collected and synthesized, they themselves are nationalists, it is politic, and it has become a tradition. They also do it because the nation has become the most important social unit and the most obvious one to study. People in our time live in nation-states and possess national consciousness; most of their vital activities are carried on within the framework of the nation-state. Moreover, as practitioners of the scientific method, scholars are bound to look for distinctions, for differences based on kind, level, and function; and nationality is the most significant contemporary group distinction. Our Western civilization, and

---

* This chapter, in a slightly different form, appeared in the *American Historical Review*, Vol. LVII, 1952, pp. 593-624.

this is one of the marks of a highly civilized society, teaches its intelligent men to look for variations from whatever seems to be the norm and to classify these within closed, schematic concepts. This, in the present case, usually means study of national thought and action, not the universal or local, study of but fragments of men particularly as they differ from other fragments. The whole scholarly orientation is thus toward the elaboration of differences rather than concentration upon commonness or similarity.

Whatever the cause, the modern historians of civilization, the Gibbons, Voltaires, Buckles, Guizots, and Andrew D. Whites [1] are few and the standard works, with few exceptions, are histories of this or that nation, national idea, or institution. This way of looking at men has validity; it is not always false; it is often the only way historians, for example, can get at anything tangible—most modern documents are produced by national institutions. But to study men as if they existed only in segments, to ignore what they have in common and how they are alike is not to approximate the whole truth. It is partial, incomplete, and in a sense false. It is also incidentally one way to court the destruction of all men. A prominent American historian, H. Morse Stephens, over a generation ago saw "written in blood, in the dying civilization of Europe, the dreadful result of exaggerated nationalism as set forth in the patriotic histories of some of the most eloquent historians of the nineteenth century." [2] He was right for his time as well as ours.

But the historians are not alone. Like them, twentieth-century diplomats, social scientists, journalists, and novelists have all been trained by their education and conditioned by their societies to seek the different, to bring out the peculiarities, and to build their policies, their theses, and their stories upon these, not upon the likenesses among men. In their sometimes well-meaning, sometimes self-seeking efforts to foster their own countries' interests, to classify types scientifically, to gain popularity (or circula-

tion) by catering to prejudice, and to bring out the novel
or esoteric, they have nearly all overlooked the simple fact
that men as individuals and men in groups are in many
ways more alike than different.

In the nature of their trade diplomats act, as Robert
Sherwood remarks in *Roosevelt and Hopkins,* not for men
but for particular men.[3] From Aristotle onward science has
been, in part, the art of observing, distinguishing, and classifying phenomena—which in most cases means the establishment of convenient resemblances which *differentiate*
specific objects from all other objects. Journalism, from
its beginning, and especially since Hearst, has been the
business of selling news, that is the odd or the new, and
their customers have bought more papers when the superiority of their own peculiarities has been confirmed by comparison with others'. Novelists beginning with Fielding
have delighted in depicting the national (not the common)
character of men, becoming therefore not just novelists
but English, French, or Russian novelists.[4] In all fields of
writing, with the possible exception of some in pure science, authors have usually attempted to describe their
subjects not only in terms of properties within the subjects
themselves but also as peculiar to a particular race, class, or
nation. Since the eighteenth century few intellectuals have
been able to see men as *man.* Even the apostles of Marxian
internationalism have succumbed to nationalism. We may
poke fun at the American schoolmarm who in France desperately desires her orange juice and Kohler plumbing.
She is evincing the same provincialism on a superficial level
as the social scientist on a deeper level who studies only
the national mind, the national problems, and sees only
these and not man.

Immediately it must be granted that differences exist
among individuals and among societies. Immediately it
must be admitted that differences of culture based upon
climate, physiology, class, nation, and possibly race war-
rant all manner of intensive scientific research. The study

of these, however, ought to be tempered by realization and study of similarities that are at least as important. Homo sapiens is a species![5] Within the species varieties occur. But as with the trees and forests the varieties ought not to obscure the view.

Someday new mutations may occur which break up the species. As yet man is a single species and there is no evidence that this kind of cleavage impends. This is true in spite of all the findings of the young sciences of man, psychology and anthropology, and of all the descriptions of men found in the older disciplines of history and political economy. It is true though the studies and writings of great students like Galton, Binet, Frazer, Childe, Marx, Sombart, and Kohn have been convincing in their conclusions about individual, tribal, class, and national differences.

Men vary; the study of their variations has given us important insights into man's actions. Nevertheless, as this volume has repeated again and again we know little about the fundamental nature of man, not to speak of nations and races. There are few truly scientific studies. While there has been extended observation there has been little experimentation. There is, consequently, little real evidence that will serve for more than tentative hypotheses. What we *know* is largely of negative nature. What we ought to realize about all men in regard to nationality and race is what Professor Otto Klineberg and his collaborators concluded from their study of the Negro: inherent differences between white and Negro may be found; our scientific methods of investigation have not yet revealed them or what they may signify.[6]

And yet we base our diplomacy and the shape of our future upon these alleged differences. We venture death because of diversities which may or may not exist. Our mental habits, nurtured by science and prejudice and dignified by Aristotelian logic as well as debased by ignorance, force us to stress unlikeness, and thence it is a short road to hate and destruction. Nowhere, save for a few rare scholars, poets, and philosophers, is there full recognition of what may be after all the plainest fact about men, that they are of man. The species may not long survive; certainly it will not if social scientists seeking the complete truth do not perceive the full importance of this fundamental fact.

What has been said about survival is also true if the species is to flourish. It is a truism (little recognized to be sure in contemporary Russia and the United States) that whatever "progress" men have achieved is the result of the common efforts of many men, nationalities, and races. Genius knows no national, racial, or any other boundary. Like imbecility it is uncommon in all groups, and at the same time common to all. When Russians or Americans claim a "first" they only reveal their naïveté. All inventions and discoveries are built upon previous ones and these in turn, as in the case of atomic energy, came from men of many nationalities and races located everywhere on the earth and living at least as long ago as the classic Greeks (Democritus).[7] The simple electric light involved among others an Italian, an Englishman, a German, a Frenchman, and an American Middle Westerner—Volta, Watt, Ohm, Ampère, and Edison. What is true here is no less true, though much less recognized, of all ideas in literature, philosophy, of all knowledge in all the arts in all civilizations.

The outward likenesses among men, often overlooked because they are commonplace, are easy to see. All men walk upright, and, unlike most other vertebrates, normally use stairs instead of branches. Nine tenths of the mature members of the species measure four feet ten inches to six feet two in height, a relatively small difference if all vertical dimensions are considered.[8] Nearly all men as adults weigh from 90 to 220 pounds, a small range compared to the variations in animal life. All of them require daily, though they may not get them, from 2,500 to 4,000 calories and a certain variety of vitamins to be gained from meat, grains, green and leafy vegetables, and fruit. Nearly all of them have facility for manipulating their thumbs, and for conceptual thought and speech as, with a few exceptions, no other animals do. More than any other living thing they can store knowledge, establish traditions. They are not forced to start from scratch but can, though this is rare enough, begin with the accumulated experience and wisdom of the species. Unlike the dog and the ape, men may use (though they rarely do) the spoken word and books to avoid the mistakes of their ancestors and thus determine the direction of human evolution.[9] Though the opposite seems most often true, man is, to a greater degree than any other form of life, teachable. He is at times, potentially at least, rational, and the ranges of his comprehension and adaptability are wider. Men, it also seems, are singular in that they can modify what were once termed their "instincts," and may, without artificial conditioning, acquire neuroses. At the same time only they find escape in laughter and tears.[10]

Precisely because men are of man and share one planet, they everywhere face the same basic problems, those concerned with food and shelter as well as those involving social relationships and creativity in the arts. Nearly all of man's food, however refined, comes from the soil and seldom has there been too much of either land or edibles. Always shelter is needed against the rain or the sun, the heat or the cold, and seldom have the caves or the houses been plentiful. Because men are gregarious they have always had to seek how best to live together, and their social problems remain basically as the *Republic* and the *Politics* stated them, freedom or authority, justice or injustice. While there are many levels of culture, man's arts have always faced similar dilemmas: material usefulness or propitiation of the gods, truth or beauty, realism or escape.

Again, though there be arctic and torrid zone, hill and valley, the ranges of climate and geography which surround men are relatively narrow. Ellsworth Huntington's books show perhaps too vividly how geography and climate condition civilizations,[11] but, in spite of his bad astronomy,

Comenius was as near the truth when he wrote, "The same sky covers us, the same sun and all the stars revolve about us, and light us in turn." [12] It is not the heat and the cold, the hills and the valleys which divide men. "Nature begins and ends everywhere and nowhere." [13] Only men set up the barriers which divide them, and this in itself is a common and peculiar disposition of man.

Men would appear to the proverbial interspatial invader, perhaps arriving these days in flying saucers from Venus, to be scarcely distinguishable from each other. Missing the tenuous distinctions set up by men themselves, he would probably think of them as one rather unimportant type of life. He would be right. Compared to a rotifer they are huge, to a whale small, to a star infinitesimal. In terms of simple magnitude they are midway between the largest material body, the giant red star, and the smallest, the electron—"the mean between macrocosm and microcosm." [14] Their likeness, then, appears readily in their differences from other forms of matter. And if the invader turned to their spiritual nature he would perceive that everywhere on the Earth, in the words of Abdala the Saracen as reported by Pico,[15] "There is nothing to be seen more wonderful than man," and in the phrase of Innocent III, "nothing more miserable."

Again, it must be reiterated, great differences exist. The moron is not a genius. An Englishman is not a Chinese. A Comanche is not a Nordic. In the total picture perspective is nevertheless absent when these differences are given first importance. Shylock was a Jew with the "same eyes, hands, organs, dimensions, senses, affections, passions" as other men and he was "fed with the same food, hurt with the same weapons, subject to the same diseases, healed by the same means, warmed and cooled by the same summer and winter" as other men.[16] The level or complexity of men's cultures condition them and influence their habits and their outlooks. But the cultures are all human, men are of man, and the Earth is common to all. The more closely one examines the evidence or the lack of it, the more clearly this becomes evident.

Men are all vertebrates and mammals. They are all multicellular animals with the same kinds of nervous, blood, respiratory, and reproductive systems.[17] The same approximate percentages of chemical elements make up their bodies. So long as there are males and females reproduction between all varieties is possible, even probable. Their females all carry their young nine months and usually produce only one offspring at a time. Maturation for all offspring is comparatively slow. Unlike all other animals the desire of their adults for sexual activity is continuous: the adult male is normally capable of reproducing at any time and the adult female of about fifteen to forty-five years of age twelve times a year. Probably none of them, Lysenko notwithstanding, can inherit acquired characteristics. All of them, regardless of race or nationality, have the same few O, A, B, and AB blood types. Though learned studies use terms like brachiocephalic and dolichocephalic their head shapes vary little, all being somewhat oblong. While their hair is round or oblong and straight or kinky, it is hair, and all usually have it in slightly varying intensities at the same points on their bodies. Their coloration runs from white to black but all gradations exist, while microscopic examination shows but slight differences in pigmentation and even these differences seem rapidly to be fading.

Where these types of differences occur, little is known of what they signify. On the basis of fact no one can say whether color, hair, head shape, or blood type have any relationship to the quality of a man, to his character, philosophy, and intelligence, or to how he will react in any circumstance. Observable differences like these may be easily classified and the classifications statistically presented in impressive, encyclopedic volumes. That is all. These particular differences occur. Nothing more can be added, no more meaning can be attached to them.

In intelligence, to be sure, the gap between moron and genius may be as wide as Galton's studies and Binet's tests have shown. But both occur in all large groupings of men, and the gap between them is not as wide as between man, moron or genius, and other forms of life. All men above the imbecilic seem to have greater facility, though they may not use it, for reflective intelligence than do the smartest chimpanzees. On the other hand all are a bit short of omniscient gods. Further, it is impossible to disentangle the environmental factors in the formation of intelligence. No one knows to what extent intelligence is a product of a good diet and to what extent it is a part of the inherited physiological structure of the individual.[18] Nor does anyone know whether any particular kinds of intelligence are universally superior. In some primitive forest situations, in contemporary American college football, or in modern warfare, success most likely comes to the physically well co-ordinated individual whom the imaginative poet might rightly consider dull and insensitive. As with intelligence so with emotions. All human creatures have the capacity for love, hate, and anger. While the depths and heights of their natures differ, capacity is common to all. The potential range and depth is greater in man than in any other animal, and which capacity is best in each situation has not been determined.

Since Darwin, men's differences have been transformed into a sliding scale for moral evaluation, a scale which somehow indicates inferiority and superiority.[19] During the latter half of the nineteenth century men calling themselves scientists, though their interpretation of "survival of the fittest" was certainly erroneous, first erected complex classifications of human characteristics with the clear purpose of showing how much fitter and therefore better were some groups of men than others. Their reasoning (read Houston Stewart Chamberlain or Madison Grant for the popular versions) [20] went something like this: (1) men are naturally different as is proved by their observable physical and mental traits; (2) some are naturally fitter, hence superior; (3) some races and nations are naturally fittest and therefore superior; and (4) nature and evolution made men this way and hence some races and nations should be masters and others servants. With this structure of illogic, differences became the ideological basis of social action. And further to prove superiority, the significance of the obvious differences has been deepened and new distinctions are fanatically sought.

No intelligent man who knows anything of science and methods of scientific research need be told of the absurdity of this unreason. Though able scholars like Julian Huxley, Franz Boas, Ashley Montagu, and Ruth Benedict [21] have torn away the fabric of prejudice to reveal the few known facts, the fallacies persist and must be attacked again and again. Men as individuals differ widely. That men differ does not indicate inferiority or superiority. If it did, that would not show that nations and races either differ or are inferior or superior. If some races and nations were superior that might not be owing to nature but to chance, cultural environment, and historical development.

Who are the "fittest"—the little, wiry men who formed the bulk of Rommel's North African army, the giants who play American football and basketball, the pale, bespectacled, physical scientists in the laboratories, the emaciated saints of the Middle Ages who surely went to Heaven soonest, or that "cream" of contemporary Western nations, the steel-nerved navigators and pilots of the long-range bombing planes? If it be agreed that the last are today's fittest, does it follow that their respective races or nations are? Are races and nations fittest just because they can destroy other races and nations most efficiently? Does, finally, fitness indicate anything about superiority unless certain prejudices are accepted as absolute values? Does, indeed, survival indicate anything but luck? The survivors in the next war, as in those of the past, will very likely be those who survive —nothing more.

Let us assume, however, that some nations survive and are therefore superior. There is no evidence to prove that this superiority, or any other, is natural. Rather what little knowledge we have reveals that the physical environment and cultural level of the society into which a man is born are at least as determinant in individual development as the gene and chromosome.[22] The younger Mill was not far wrong when he wrote, "Of all the vulgar modes of escaping from the consideration of the effect of social and moral influences on the human mind, the most vulgar is that of attributing diversities of character to inherent natural differences." [23]

What has been said above of the physiological diversities among men can be applied with greater force to the differences among the so-called races.[24] We know that intelligence, emotional capacity, and bodily structure and size vary widely *within* each race.[25] We also have solid grounds for believing that so far as we are able to measure these characteristics as well as other less obvious ones, they differ more widely within each race than they do from race to race. In all human characteristics there is overlapping among all races; the alleged differences are chiefly in statistical averages which hide the basic similarities.

That intelligent men should base any serious argument concerning the differences among men upon race is as absurd as to base diplomacy upon the consideration that one man likes his cottage cheese with garlic and another with onion.[26] As everyone who reads can know, all races have ceaselessly intermixed and have become so "impure" that almost all the peculiarities of any importance ascribed membership in these groupings are the fabrication of wish fancy.[27] Ralph Linton, the anthropologist, neatly put it: "There is no human group whose ancestry is known for even five generations in the exact terms necessary for racial determinations." [28]

In his zeal to make Christians out of heathens Paul preached that God "made of one blood all the nations of men for to dwell on all the face of the earth." His real converts at Athens may not have been many; his biology and sociology were good. Race usually cannot be distinguished because of visible, physical signs such as size, shape, or even color. Much less can it be determined by character and intelligence or any of the more esoteric classifications of dissimilarities. Conceivably, fundamental differences may be discovered. Our present scientific tools do not reveal them—even between "Slavic" Russians and "Anglo-Saxon" Americans. One may be able to tell something about a man by his shoes or by his color. One can tell something about his shoes and his color. French children of the Third Republic, like German children of the Third Reich, were sometimes told that their ancestors "were very tall, their eyes blue, and their hair was blond." [29] The only known fact is that no one can know *who his* ancestors were nor can any group determine them with any exactitude except that they were men and before that——.

Few if any of the so-called racial characteristics tell anything of importance about *a man*. Men have been encyclopedically catalogued as to hair form and color, skin pigmentation, eye color and shape, stature, head form, size and structure of bones, and the way the head sits on the shoulders. What does this all mean? Simply that in these specific physical ways individual men vary and for this or that group there is a slightly different mean or average or deviation for each of the *particular* physical parts of the body. To ascribe greater weight to these differences than this would be as wrong as to assert that all men are exactly alike because all their bodily temperatures average around 98.6 degrees.

Race theories (they are only that by the grace of inaccurate terminology) have varied widely in time and often with the race or nationality of the investigator. Moreover, racial characters, if they exist, seem to have changed quite unbelievably through the years. Once ("Nordic") England was called "merry" but that was not the England of Attlee and Cripps. Once a Venetian ambassador spoke of the "low morals and excellent cooking" of the English but that was in the sixteenth not the nineteenth century.[30] In praising folly, Erasmus spoke of the martial reputation of the ("Mediterranean") Spaniards,[31] a characteristic few would accuse them of possessing in our times. Once what we call the northern Europeans ("Nordics"?) were supposed to be "full of spirit" but unintelligent (Aristotle); [32] the modern version is quite different. None of this proves that theories based upon race are completely untrue. It shows only that there is nothing scientific or God-given about them and that they are for the most part merely a priori guesses of men about other men.

The fallacies based upon racial interpretation of human societies may be slowly crumbling. Those pertaining to na-tionalism still cling as tenaciously as only prejudices can. The human race seems united in a common desire to de-stroy itself, and nationalism happens to be the most popu-lar, contemporary method.

The true nationalist, as the *Action Française* declared, is one who "places the fatherland above everything." [33] What the nationalist does not understand is what Schiller taught: That every "remarkable occurrence" that happens "to men" is of importance to *men*.[34] Denying Bentham's axioms about self-interest seeking the happiness of the greatest number, he believes his own self-interest to lie in develop-ment of his own nation's peculiar interests, in its gaining power and prestige at the expense of other like groups.[35]

There is no more natural basis for the nationalistic in-terpretation of man and his relationships than there is for prejudices concerning race. No one can know, as Herder thought he knew,[36] that God created different nationalities just as he did different flowers and plants. Every nationality is a mixture of many peoples, races, tribes, families. The modern French are in origin of the Mediterranean, Alpine, Nordic, and a good many other "races." The modern Ital-ians are compounded of Etruscans, Ligurians, Romans,

Iberians, Greeks, Gauls, Teutons, and in recent times almost every nationality in Europe and some in Africa. Nor
are the Germans, Russians, or Americans any purer.

All modern history, as we have shown, is a document
attesting to national intermixture: migrations, invasions,
wars, conquests, marriages. In various degrees every nationality is a conglomeration of the short and tall, the round
and the long-headed, the stupid and the smart, the virtuous
and the sinful. Any one of these characteristics is singular
to no nationality, and among all nationalities the characteristics are endlessly duplicated. In fact the attempt to classify
nations according to any biological or inherent mental characteristic is only a naïve error inherited from early propa-
gandist historians like Tacitus and pseudoanthropologists
like Gobineau. Defoe could have been speaking of any nationality with his

> *Thus from a mixture of all kinds began*
> *That heterogeneous thing, an Englishman.*[37]

How little we know about national biological traits becomes clear when we consider that no nationality in Europe
or America has individuals so different that they, given
the same clothes, cannot easily be taken for members of
any of several other nationalities. In Europe, as elsewhere,
the so-called national physical characteristics do not correspond with boundary lines, with race, or even clearly
with language.[38] In fact they exist only as vague and almost
meaningless averages for particular physical features. Do
Alsatians have French or German bodies? How does the
chemical content of the French body differ from that of the
German? Can the German spermatozoa impregnate a
French egg?

Nor is there any such thing as a constant or ever-present
national character.[39] National characters if any exist are
certainly of recent origin and the nations themselves have
not been constant. Attempts to describe the national characters of the various peoples, especially in the last half-cen-

tury, are impressive in their bulk. They seldom go far beyond the random guesses of such intelligent men as the eighteenth century's David Hume. For the most part they are the prejudices of racialists like Gobineau and Houston Stewart Chamberlain, the superficialities of psychologists like Le Bon, and the entertaining guesses of shallow popularizers like Madariaga and Siegfried.[40] Available evidence from contemporary psychological and anthropological studies shows that different peoples may differ in their reactions to this or that stimulus, and that one may emphasize this or that cultural idea, value, or institution more than another. But all generalizations, even the intelligent ones, are no more than tentative, unproved hypotheses. If they have any validity it is only for a particular moment and then with so many exceptions that they are inaccurate; if they contain any truth for the whole national group, they more than likely do not apply to any individual within the group; and if they have any meaning, this is not because of anything inherent in man and nature but only because different groups have different historically evolved cultures.[41] A modern student of nationality claims that the Russian is "morose and melancholy as the steppes of his country" while the Italian is "passionate and excitable" because he is "warmed by the sun." [42] Many Russians, especially those at conferences of foreign ministers, are "morose" and one part of Russia is "steppes." Many Italians are "excitable" and certainly the sun shines in Italy. But Communists like crocodiles seem to know how to laugh and the sun shines now and then in Russia—especially, for example, in Stalin's Georgia. Leonardo da Vinci and Benedetto Croce, since they were sometimes calm and dispassionate, were of course not Italians. Only poetic license or intuition could connect steppes and sun with gloom and passion.

Of no nations has more of this kind of nonsense been written than of modern France and Germany. Possibly this is so because of the three wars since 1870 as well as because

popular science during this period lent its weight to conflicting national interests. The Germans (including the
Rhenish peoples?) are supposed to have a disciplined, military character—exactly the opposite of that they were supposed to possess during the early Napoleonic period. The
French are thought of today as logical, cultivated (*fine*),
pacifist lovers of freedom; exactly the opposite of what most
Europeans considered them during the latter part of the
Napoleonic era. What is German character, that of Goethe
or Bismarck? What is French cultivation, that of Voltaire
or Pétain?

This kind of fallacy, of course, grows not only out of
bad history. The same error is committed by contemporary
two-week tourists and society editors temporarily turned
foreign correspondents who set out to confirm all their
prejudices and to footnote with their profound platitudes
all the horrible peculiarities everyone already, of course,
knows about without having investigated. The French, to
many contemporary Americans, are a penny-pinching, im-
moral (not to say licentious) people who have good wine,
beautiful, scantily clad women, and a "mess in politics."
The Germans to the same Americans are either agreeable,
potbellied, kraut-eating, beer-drinking, and music-loving
people, or more often during recent war years tall, ramrod-
like, blond sadists who cruelly file out the gold fillings of
their victims. There are Germans and Frenchmen who fit
these stereotypes and Russians and Americans too. But how
French logic and cultivation are combined with French
licentiousness and "messy" politics is a French national
secret and a universal secret as well. A picture of the tall,
fierce Prussian soldier eating kraut is somehow unbelievable and did not appear even in Hollywood's colossal
dramas or the more realistic shots of the Signal Corps during either Great War. And it happens more kraut is eaten
in the United States than in any other country, while tall,
fierce soldiers are highly desired and generally found in the
armies of a good many countries.

Over the course of history there is no proof that any one nation is more criminal or warlike than another or that any is more moral or peaceful. Individuals in each nation have been peaceful and warlike; sometimes more in one nation are peaceful, sometimes more in another nation are warlike, but this is all. Nationalist allegations to the contrary are based upon casual observation or the citation of one or two examples and they reveal nothing except the bias or ignorance of those who utter them.[43] The national character of any people is in point of fact "so complex, seemingly so contradictory and so largely determined by intangibles that almost anything can be read into it." [44] And almost everything and anything has been read into the character of each people by themselves, their friends, their enemies. The enemy has always been barbarous while one's own nation and its friends have always been civilized.[45]

Oliver Goldsmith's comment to a half-dozen patriotic Englishmen of the eighteenth century could be instructive even to modern social scientists.[46] He heard one of them declare "that the Dutch were a parcel of avaricious wretches; that the French were a set of flattering sycophants; that the Germans were drunken sots and beastly gluttons; and the Spaniards proud, haughty and surly tyrants: but that, in bravery, generosity, clemency, and in every other virtue, the English excelled all the other world." Goldsmith's reply was, "For my own part, I should not have ventured to talk in such a peremptory strain, unless I had made the tour of Europe, and examined the manners of these several nations with great care and accuracy: that perhaps, a more impartial judge would not scruple to affirm that the Dutch were more frugal and industrious, the French more temperate and polite, the Germans more hardy and patient of labour and fatigue, and the Spaniards more staid and sedate, than the English; who, though undoubtedly brave and generous, were at the same time rash, headstrong and impetuous. . . ." But of course,

Goldsmith lived in the eighteenth century, which occasionally looked beyond national boundaries at man. And even then Goldsmith was asked why he stayed in England if he didn't like it.

The limited view of the nationalist stems from either blindness or vanity, probably both. As David Hume wrote in the eighteenth century, "The vulgar are apt to carry all national characters to extremes; and having once established it as a principle that any people are knavish, or cowardly, or ignorant, they will admit of no exception, but comprehend every individual under the same censure." [47]

The faulty reasoning is simple to demonstrate, though its effects are tragic. A group, be it nation- or city-state, cannot be described, though many a wise theorist like Socrates or good modern historian like C. D. Burns has done so, as if it were a single man, an individual with very special qualities. [48] Reasoning by analogy is often helpful; it is never accurate. Does Gide, Pissarro, De Gaulle, or a Breton fisherman represent France? Does Mann, Kathe Kollewitz, Streicher, or a Moselle vineyardist stand for Germany? Every nationality has many, not just, as it is now popular to say of the Germans, two sides. Every nation has so many sides that it becomes almost impossible to classify any of them as exclusively or even primarily national. Every nation is composed of individuals not stereotypes. "Mind and consciousness," character, "are found only in the individual, and even if all . . . individuals in a community think the same . . . or are accustomed to react in a like manner . . . we still do not get a 'folk-mind' . . . but many minds which resemble one another." [49] When Thomas Mann has his Deutschlin announce, "The Russians have profundity but no form. And in the West they have form but no profundity. Only we Germans have both," [50] one can only hope that the present "Field Marshal of Literature" is himself completely clear on the matter.

As with physical traits the mental and spiritual charactertistics of the individuals in any one nation overlap those of individuals of other nations. Individuals within nations differ; at the same time they are much like individuals in other nations and the characteristics of any one nation are strangely enough found in individuals of other nations. If there are exclusive national traits, those English, French, and Spanish ones, for instance, so persuasively described by Madariaga, we still know so little about them that we cannot base any intelligent action upon them. "You can always tell an American by his shoes," goes an old tourist axiom. The point that you can't tell anything about *the* American usually escapes.

Languages have most often been thought to denote sharp differences between nations. No one can deny that languages are different, that one or another may be better for any one purpose, or that their differences impede international understanding. But the old story about the American pointing at a French menu at five different places and getting *pois* five times has a point; it is not that the French are queer but that language may hide the fact that all men seem to dislike monotony. It is quite possible that the English language is best for novelists and German for scientists. It is also possible that were their languages the same the Russians and Americans might occasionally agree. Yet Fichte's dictum that the elasticity and precision of German made the German superior is precisely as unfounded as Bentham's fancy that English was superior because of its simplicity and force or Dostoevski's insistence that only the Russian could understand all humanity.[51] The fact is we don't know and probably can't know.

The superstructure of fantastic nonsense built upon the real differences in language might be dismissed by a hearty laugh were not its consequences so dangerous. The well-known English authority on early man, V. Gordon Childe, once pontificated, "The Nordics' superiority in physique fitted them to be vehicles of the superior [the Aryan] language." [52] In this short sentence only five fallacies appear:

(1) the Nordics are not superior unless certain quite un-
certain, arbitrary criteria are accepted; (2) the Aryan languages may be considered superior only in the same way;
(3) a good many non-Nordics use an Aryan language and
some Nordics use a non-Aryan language; (4) all languages,
including one of the best developed of the Aryan family,
the English, have had a tremendous influx of foreign words
and phrases, and all languages are built upon older languages which in turn are built upon still others until each
has a "medley of origins"; and (5) in many cases, as in
France and England, peoples like the Bretons and Alsatians
and Welsh and Scots have had national languages forced
upon them by conquerors, and now may want to go back
to their old languages which they think are superior.

This is not all. As we have pointed out before, national
languages are of recent origin, dating back at most to late
medieval times. They were generally in western Europe,
where nationalism first arose, not regarded as the national
languages until the fourteenth and fifteenth centuries.
Again within any nation the nationals, as for instance the
Swiss, may not speak the same language while in other nations people of diverse "races," as the American whites and
Negroes, may speak the same language. At the same time
nationals of separate nations may speak the same language
as do the Spanish and most Latin American peoples, or the
English and the Americans. There is not, then, any exact
correlation between language groups and nationalities, and
language differences do not clearly divide nationalities.[53]

No objective criteria are available for the determination
of superiority in language. All developed human languages,
no matter how widely divergent, seem to be more alike
than different, and have much more potential capacity for
significant and specific meaning than do the sounds emitted
by any other living thing. "With all their diversities," as
one of the great authorities on language, Otto Jespersen,
has declared, they "disclose the existence of a great common factor in men's trend of thought and in men's craving

for expression." [54] No matter how beautiful the language of Shakespeare or Goethe or Turgenev, there is no proof that language differences are of great importance except as barriers to understanding. The purely subjective and self-seeking fancies of nationalists like Fichte and Dostoevski are just that, fancies, and they are fancies apparently common to all nationalities.

If we know little of significance about physiological, racial, and language differences among nations, this does not prove that all nations are alike. To understand that nations differ in many minor ways takes as much thought as to read "Lil' Abner." They are all and each the result of the myriad, cultural influences that have helped mold them in historical time, especially the last five hundred years of historical time. They differ, too, because their peoples have been trained and propagandized to feel and believe that they are peculiar, because, by way of illustration, their historians like Treitschke, Michelet, Green, and Bancroft have often provided each of them with a common and peculiar history, at times quite out of whole cloth. But that they differ here or there does not mean that they are more different than they are alike.

The fundamental import of their real historical differences, except that they lead to war, we do not know. And the little we do know points to similarities both as striking and as important. Our little knowledge indeed reveals that nations most often differ precisely because they have conflicting aims for similar ends—prestige, power, and security.

Schiller asked, "What is the greatest of nations but a fragment?"—A fragment of humanity, one might add, which the Jew Jesus, the Frenchman Montesquieu, the German Goethe [55] held to be above the arbitrary divisions into which petty patriots, narrow scholars, sadistic dictators, cheap journalists, and popular novelists have divided mankind.

Men are physiologically, racially, nationally at least as much alike as they are different. That is not surprising.

Homo sapiens is a species. The individuals of the species are not only much alike but so are their problems and their institutions. This is not so strange either. They have inhabited one globe in a comparatively short period of whatever is universal time. They all have had to provide for sustenance and protection against the elements. They have all had to seek the best circumstances for reproduction and the rearing of their children. They all have had a common desire for some kind of creative activity, for a "noble employment of their leisure" if not an "instinct for workmanship." Now they have the common problem of controlling science so that they may survive. As Lawrence K. Frank recently wrote, "all men, everywhere, face the same life tasks, share the same anxieties and perplexities, bereavements and tragedies, seek the same goals in their cultures." [56] And what is true now may have always been true. It has been the common error of men not to see this.

As men have set about to solve their similar problems, they have naturally evolved similar institutions.[57] The family with its ceremony of marriage is almost universal, though there may be plural husbands or plural wives and some societies are exogamous and some endogamous, and some are conjugal and some consanguine. Government, though there may be Aristotle's 158 varieties of constitutions of which some provide justice and others injustice, is common to all. A class system of some kind has evolved in all, even in Soviet Russia. A church with one or several heads to administer a religion that provides some kind of explanation of the unknown has always grown, though it may be mono- or polytheistic, anthropomorphic or supernatural. Since man in the plural is men and since men inhabit a common Earth, they have met common problems and erected common institutional answers. They are not, whatever they may have thought, so unlike each other, and their cultures have as much in common as in difference.

Of the individual differences among men, of their national and racial dissimilarities, the studies are many and some profound. They err chiefly in that they are based upon partial observation. They are incomplete because they are so exclusively histories of nations and of national heroes, analyses of national problems, and descriptions of national institutions. All that is argued here is that the whole truth be sought, not just the national truth. If men are to survive and the species to flourish, the historian must pay at least as much attention to the species as to its varieties. Men are, as Josiah Royce remarked, apparently all a little lower than the angels.[58] We can hope that they will remain a bit above other animals only if their experts write histories and make studies that go beyond the national stories and analyses, only if they see Germans, Russians, Chinese, Japanese, Englishmen, and Americans as part of a common breed called men. It may be that in their search for truth scholars will find differences not now apparent, and that these will lead to the extinction of man. Our present knowledge does not reveal these differences. Scholars who stress the differences to the exclusion of the known similarities do so at the expense of truth and to their own and mankind's great peril.

If men are not brothers, it is not because they inherently differ. That sentiment of unity and exclusiveness which we have defined as nationalism now keeps them apart. This nationalism, however, does not mean that men could not be brothers, could not live in peace. For there is no basis, historical, biological, psychological, for believing this nationalism must be or will be permanent. Below the surface of their national peculiarities, men remain, so far as we know, more alike than different.

NOTES
BIBLIOGRAPHY
INDEX

NOTES

The notes in this volume are worth attention if readers wish (1) further authority for a statement or the source of a quotation, (2) further amplification of meaning especially if there are differences of opinion, (3) a guide for additional reading.

CHAPTER I (Pages 3-11)

1. In 1851 at Turin Professor Pasquale Mancini's good nineteenth-century definition of nationality was, *"Una società naturelle di uomini, da unità di territoria, di origini, di costumi, di lingua conformata a communanza di vita e di cosienza sociale,"* *Della Nazionalità come fondamento de diritto delle Genti,* reprinted in *Saggi sulla nazionalità* as part of *Pensiero politico italiano,* no. 3, Sestante, 1944, p. 39. Francis Lieber's 1868 definition of nation also came close to modern concepts. *Fragments of Political Science on Nationalism and Internationalism,* New York, 1868, pp. 7-8.

2. Definitions from different points of view of basic terms, nation, nationality, nationalism, in twentieth-century studies like those of Hayes, Kohn, Johannet, Meinecke, Hertz, the Royal Institute of International Affairs, and Weill all differ. Definitions are studied in, for example, the thorough analysis of Louis Snyder, *The Meaning of Nationalism,* New Brunswick, 1954; and in Karl Deutsch, *Nationalism and Social Communication: An Inquiry into the Foundations of Nationality,* New York, 1953, where much needed spadework is done; Paul Henry, *Le problème de nationalités,* Paris, 1937; and Earle Hunter, *A Sociological Analysis of Certain Types of Patriotism,* New York, 1932. Most systematic studies appeared after World War I. One good earlier volume is *Deutsche Gesellschaft für Soziologie,* Schriften, ser. I, *Verhandlungen der deutschen Soziologentage,* Vol. II, Tübingen, 1913,

with essays by, among others, Paul Barth and Roberto Michels, and discussions by Max Weber and Werner Sombart.

3. See Guido Zernatto, "Nation, the History of a Word," *Review of Politics,* Vol. VI, 1944, pp. 351 ff. *Natio* meant a group of men belonging together because of similarity of birth but the contemporary word nation is similar only in that most people of a nationality are usually born within the wide confines of the territory of the actual or desired political state. Nationality may be acquired quite apart from place of birth by naturalization, treaty, or conquest, or perhaps just the will of the individual, as in Macedonia. A member of a nation may not belong to the same state or be born in the same territory as his fellow nationals; further, as was true of the Jews until recently, he may not have a state to which he may aspire or belong; finally a state, like Switzerland, may contain several culturally different peoples who juridically, nevertheless, are one nationality and who possess a national consciousness.

4. Four definitions of nation and nationality which in stressing different elements clearly show the root difficulty are John Stuart Mill, *Representative Government,* Everyman's edition, chap. XVI; J. K. Bluntschli, *Theory of the State,* Oxford, 1885, p. 90; Joseph Stalin, *Marxism and the National and Colonial Question,* New York, n.d., p. 8; and René Johannet, *Le principe de nationalités,* Paris, 1923, p. 7.

5. Charles Cole, "The Heavy Hand of Hegel," in E. M. Earle, ed., *Nationalism and Internationalism,* New York, 1950, pp. 65-78, neatly demonstrates this.

6. Good history is Carlton Hayes's, "Nationalism is a modern emotional fusion and exaggeration of two very old phenomena— nationality and patriotism." *Essays on Nationalism,* New York, 1926, p. 6.

7. See chap. VI.

8. The French distinction between patriotism as peaceful and based on "natural" attachments and benefits, and nationalism as ambitious, passionate, desirous of conquest is useful but seldom followed even by French writers. For a discussion see Maurice Vaussard, *Enquête sur le nationalisme,* Paris, 1924, p. 179.

9. For an example see Julien Benda, *Esquisse d'une histoire des Français dans leur volonté d'être une nation,* Paris, 1932, but a great number of patriotic historians and political scientists are likewise guilty. Some anthropological studies such as those of Boas, Benedict, Linton, Huxley, and Herskovits on early societies and their loyalties have, on the other hand, much to offer the student of nationalism, if the connection between early and modern societies is not seen as a developing continuum.

10. Rough but suggestive distinctions were made by Martin Buber, *Kampf um Israel, Reden und Schriften,* Berlin, 1933, p. 232. "To

be a people is like having eyes in one's head which are capable of seeing . . . to be a nationality is like having learned to comprehend their use . . . nationalism is like having diseased eyes and being constantly preoccupied with them. A people is a phenomenon of life, nationality . . . is one of consciousness, nationalism one of superconsciousness." But these distinctions are scarcely applicable today when nearly all peoples have become nationalistic.

11. Misapplied Darwinism, "survival of the fittest," is often associated with this. James Bryce described the intensification of national pride which led to the "struggle for life" in his "The Principle of Nationality," *Essays and Addresses in Wartime*, New York, 1918, pp. 146-48.

12. The classic statement is Renan's: "A nation is a soul, a spiritual principle. Two things, which in reality are one, make up that soul, that spiritual principle. One is the possession in common of a rich inheritance of memories, the other is the actual desire of living together, the will to turn to account together the inheritance bequeathed individuals." His famous discourse, "Qu'est-ce qu'une nation?" first given at the Sorbonne, is in his *Discours et conférences*, Paris, 1887, 2nd ed. Renan's definition is close to that formulated by Fustel de Coulanges in his well-known debate with Mommsen in 1870 over Alsace-Lorraine.

13. This is also the dominant Catholic view. To Don Luigi Sturzo the nation was not a spirit or soul "beyond the single individuals who compose it." *Nationalism and Internationalism*, New York, 1946, p. 17.

14. J. S. Huxley and A. C. Haddon, *We Europeans*, Oxford, 1940, p. 16.

15. Compare Royal Institute of International Affairs, *Nationalism*, London, 1939, pp. 249 ff.; Johannet, pp. 378 ff. The latter's definition of nationality is pertinent here: ". . . *une nationalité est l'idée d'une personnalité collective, variable d'inspiration, de conscience, d'intensité et de grandeur, relative à l'État, soit qu'elle représente un État unifié disparu, soit qu'elle coincide avec un État unifié existant, soit qu'elle aspire ou se prête à former un État unifié futur, et qui cherche dans ses caractéristiques naturelles d'origine la justification de son identité comme de ses prétentions.*" See also the essays of Hertz, Steinmitz, Boehm, and others in G. Salomen, ed., *Nation und Nationalität, Jahrbuch für Soziologie*, Vol. I, Karlsruhe, 1927.

16. Emphasis on race is most evident in German studies but Meinecke's definition (in *Weltbürgertum und Nationalstaat*, Munich, 1928, p. 1) was also scholarly: "*Gemeinsamer Wohnsitz, gemeinsame Abstammung—oder genauer gesagt, da es keine im anthropologischen Sinne rassenreinen Nationen gibt—, gemeinsame oder ähnliche Blutmischung, gemeinsame Sprache, gemeinsames geistiges Leben, gemeinsamer Staatsverband oder*

*Föderation mehrerer gleichartiger Staaten—alles das können
wichtige und wesentliche Grundlagen oder Merkmale einer Nation
sein, aber damit ist nicht gesagt, dasz jede Nation sie alle zusammen
besitzen muszte, um eine Nation zu sein. Unbedingt vorhanden
sein musz in ihr wohl ein naturhaften Kern, der durch Blutsver-
wandtschaft enstanden ist."*

17. "The Spirit of Whiggism," 1836, reprinted in *Whigs and Whiggism, Political Writings of Benjamin Disraeli,* London, 1913, p.
343.

18. Stalinist and Marxian views which stress only the economic are
like Disraeli's, too simple. Stalin's definition (*Marxism and the
National and Colonial Question,* p. 8) was "A nation is a historically evolved, stable community of language, territory, economic
life, and psychological make-up manifested in a community of
culture," but his explanation of the rise of the nation was exclusively economic.

19. Ferdinand Brunot, *Histoire de la langue française,* Vols. IV, VI,
VII, and IX, enlightens both on communication and education
in relation to the spread of national patriotism. But see below
for amplification.

20. See the devastating analysis of Francis Delaisi, *Political Myths
and Economic Realities,* New York, 1927; the frontal attacks of
Harold Laski, *Nationalism and the Future of Civilization,* London, 1932; and Julius Braunthal, *The Paradox of Nationalism,*
London, 1946.

CHAPTER II (Pages 15-28)

1. J. Novicow, *Conscience et volontés sociales,* Paris, 1897, p. 313.
2. Carlton J. H. Hayes, "Philosopher Turned Patriot," in James
Shotwell, ed., *Essays in Intellectual History,* New York, 1929,
p. 194.
3. Robert R. Ergang, *Herder and the Foundations of German
Nationalism,* New York, 1931, p. 97. Schleiermacher (1768-1834),
the German Protestant theologian, held a like view. See George
Sabine, *History of Political Theory,* New York, 1950, p. 630;
and Koppel Pinson, *Pietism as a Factor in the Rise of German
Nationalism,* New York, 1934, pp. 75, 195.
4. *Addresses to the German Nation,* tr. by R. F. Jones and G. H.
Turnbull, Chicago, 1922, p. 232.
5. In Frederick Page, ed., *Anthology of Patriotic Prose,* London, 1915,
pp. 124-26.
6. Quoted by Samuel Flagg Bemis, *John Quincy Adams and the
Foundations of American Foreign Policy,* New York, 1949, p. 182.
7. This is a constant theme of his *The Duties of Man* (1862). It is
often reiterated in his other writings. The Oath of Young Italy
began "In the name of God" and the young initiate swore to
perform the duties which bound him to the land where God

had placed him. To Mazzini each nation had a God-given mission. See especially his letter to Melegari, October 2, 1833, in *Mazzini's Letters*, tr. by Jervis, introd. and notes by Bolton King, London, 1930, p. 3.

8. A variation of this theme was the British patriot J. A. Cramb's belief that empires, including the British, were successive incarnations of the divine idea. *The Origins and Destiny of Imperial Britain and Nineteenth Century Europe*, New York, 1915, pp. 230-31.

9. Deuteronomy 14:2.

10. Cromwell, for example, thought the English "had a stamp upon them from God. . . ." S. C. Lomas, ed., *Letters and Speeches of Oliver Cromwell, with Elucidations by Thomas Carlyle*, London, 1904, Vol. II, pp. 404 ff. The theories of Cromwell and his followers are thoroughly outlined in George Lanyi, *Oliver Cromwell and His Age, a Study in Nationalism*, Ph.D. dissertation, Harvard, 1949, typescript. On Russian messianic hopes see Hans Kohn, *Prophets and Peoples*, New York, 1946, pp. 142 ff., and on American, Albert Weinberg, *Manifest Destiny*, Baltimore, 1935, *passim*.

11. Georges Weill, *L'Europe du XIXᵉ siècle et l'idée de nationalité*, Paris, 1938, p. 144. Walter Sulzbach, *National Consciousness*, Washington, 1943, p. 138. In France the nationalist Maurice Barrès in 1917 quoted Pope Urban II (1088-99), "People of France, nation elect of God. . . ." *The Undying Spirit of France*, New Haven, 1917 p. 49.

12. *Nationalism and Internationalism*, New York, 1930, p. 270.

13. *Realism and Nationalism, 1852-1871*, New York, 1935, p. 304.

14. *The Leviathan*, ed. by J.A.R. Waller, Cambridge, 1904, pt. I, p. 84. This view of human nature and the desire for a strong national government were, in different context of course, those of Machiavelli 150 years before in *The Prince*.

15. *The Social Contract*, New York, 1946, p. 17. A detailed analysis is Alexandre Choulguine, "Les origines de l'esprit national moderne et Jean-Jacques Rousseau," *Annales de la Société Jean-Jacques Rousseau*, Vol. XXVI, 1937, pp. 9-283.

16. *Considérations sur le gouvernement de Pologne . . .*, *Oeuvres complètes*, Paris 1826, Vol. VI, pp. 229-376.

17. *The Theory of Moral Sentiments*, in H. W. Schneider, ed., *Adam Smith's Moral and Political Philosophy*, New York, 1948, pp. 240-42. The book was first published in 1759.

18. Beatrice Hyslop, *French Nationalism in 1789 according to the General Cahiers*, New York, 1934; Boyd C. Shafer, "Bourgeois Nationalism in the Pamphlets on the Eve of the French Revolution," *Journal of Modern History*, Vol. X, 1938, pp. 31-50.

19. On Carnot see René Johannet, *Le principe des nationalités*, Paris, 1918, pp. 97-98. Fichte's famous *Reden* given 1807-1808 are translated as *Addresses to the German Nation*, cited above, note

4. To Görres it was *"reiner Naturtrieb, dass ein Volk, also scharf und deutlich in seine natürlichen Grenzen eingeschlossen, aus der Zerstreuung in die Einheit sich zu sammeln sucht."* Quoted in Lord Acton, "Nationality," in *Essays on Freedom and Power,* Boston, 1948, p. 178.

20. *Realism and Nationalism,* p. 303.

21. Peter Manniche, *Denmark, a Social Laboratory,* New York, 1939, pp. 87-88 n., citing Ernst Borup.

22. Robert Ergang, *Herder,* pp. 85-86.

23. *Theory of the State,* Oxford, 1887, p. 91.

24. *Nationalism and the Communal Mind,* London, 1937, *passim.*

25. Joseph de Maistre, the French conservative philosopher of Burke's time, employed almost the same ideas in his *Considérations sur la France* (1796), and his *Essai sur le principe générateur des constitutions politiques* (1809).

26. See particularly Burke's *Reflections on the French Revolution* (many editions), and his *Reform of Representation in the House of Commons* (1782), *Works,* Bohn ed., London, 1861, Vol. VI, pp. 146 ff. For discussion see Friedrich Hertz, *Nationality in History and Politics,* London, 1944, pp. 325-29.

27. Tr. by S. W. Dyde, London, 1896, esp. pp. 257-58, 273, 331. His plan for Germany is in *Die Verfassung Deutschlands, Werke,* ed. by Lasson, Vol. VII. A good summary of Hegel's significance is Charles Cole, "The Heavy Hand of Hegel," in E. M. Earle, ed., *Nationalism and Internationalism,* New York, 1950, pp. 65-78. Two attacks on Hegel's concept of the state and nation are J. T. Delos, *La nation,* Vol. II, *Le nationalisme et l'ordre de droit,* Montreal, 1944, pp. 64-88; and L. T. Hobhouse, *The Metaphysical Theory of the State,* New York, 1918.

28. The organism theory with many variations has been held by Müller, Royer-Collard, De Maistre, Durkheim, Bosanquet, and many others, including modern fascists like Rocco of Italy. To the last named the nation was "not merely the sum total of living individuals, nor the instrument of parties for their own ends, but an organism comprising the unlimited series of generations, of which individuals are merely transient elements; it is the synthesis of all the material and non-material values of the race." See Howard Marraro, *Nationalism in Italian Education,* New York, 1927, p. 2, but the best source is Mussolini's article on the doctrines of Fascism in the *Enciclopedia Italiana.*

29. The late unlamented Nazi, Ernst Roehm, in a speech *Warum SA?,* pamphlet, Berlin, 1933, p. 14, told the diplomatic corps, *"Der nationalsozialistische Staat ist endgültig, unwiderruflich— damit müssen sich seine Feinde drinnen und drauszen abfinden. Denn der Staat ist das Volk! Und das Volk ist der Staat."*

30. Here the quoted phrases are taken from his *"Qu'est-ce qu'une Nation?"* and the preface to his *Pages françaises,* Paris, 1921, pp. 4-5, 68-69, 72. Two fine English historians have held views

something like Renan's. G. P. Gooch wrote (*Nationalism,* London, 1920, p. 6), a nation is an "organism, a spiritual entity. All attempts to penetrate its secrets by the light of mechanical interpretations break down before the test of experience." See also J. Holland Rose, *Nationality in Modern History,* New York, 1916, p. 147.

31. *Scènes et doctrines du nationalisme,* Paris, n.d., particularly pp. 10-13 and 84-96. A thorough discussion of Barrès and Charles Maurras, who usually shared Barrès' views, is William Buthman, *The Rise of Integral Nationalism, with Special Reference to the Ideas and Activities of Charles Maurras,* New York, 1939, *passim.*

32. A devastating attack on this view is that of Arnold Van Gennep, *Traité comparitif des nationalités,* Vol. I, Paris, 1922, pp. 27-30.

33. Contrary to Hegel's dictum that "each particular National genius is to be treated as only one Individual in the process of Universal History." *Philosophy of History,* tr. by Sibree, rev. ed., New York, 1900, p. 53.

CHAPTER III (Pages 29-39)

1. Salo Baron, *Modern Nationalism and Religion,* New York, 1947, p. 12.

2. Quoted by Julian Huxley and A. C. Haddon, *We Europeans,* Oxford, 1940, p. 46.

3. *La politique tirée des propres paroles de l'écriture sainte, Oeuvres complètes de Bossuet,* ed. by the Abbé Migne, Vol. XI, Liv. I, Art. II, Prop. III, p. 486. A later great English Catholic historian, Lord Acton, cited Bossuet approvingly in his essay, "Nationality," in *Essays on Freedom and Power,* Boston, 1948, p. 190.

4. Carnot and the French revolutionaries of '93 made much of the natural boundary argument. Albert Sorel, *L'Europe et la Révolution française,* Paris, 1946, used this as the key to French Revolutionary diplomatic history.

5. Robert R. Ergang, *Herder and the Foundations of German Nationalism,* New York, 1931, p. 89. C. J. H. Hayes, "Contributions of Herder to the Doctrine of Nationalism," *American Historical Review,* Vol. XXXII, 1927, p. 723.

6. *History of Civilization in England,* 2nd ed., New York, 1883, p. 29. First published 1857 and 1861.

7. *Lectures on the Early History of Institutions,* New York, 1875, pp. 72-74. This was also the view of the contemporary American ethnologist, Lewis H. Morgan, in his *Ancient Society,* New York, 1878. The German jurist Rudolf von Ihering felt that the soil and the habitat formed the nation, and geography gave a people its national character which was thereafter transmitted by history. *The Evolution of the Aryan,* tr. by A. Drucker, London, 1897, esp. pp. 69-77.

8. Among their books might be cited respectively *Anthropogeo-graphie,* 2 vols., Stuttgart, 1882-91; *Influences of Geographic Environment,* New York, 1911; *Human Geography,* New York, 1920; and *Civilization and Climate,* New Haven, 3rd ed., 1924.

9. But cf. J. T. Delos, *La nation,* Vol. I, *Sociologie de la nation,* Montreal, 1944, pp. 103-11.

10. *Political Myths and Economic Realities,* New York, 1927, pp. 152-53.

11. A brief account of the "myth of common descent and racial unity" is in Florjan Znaniecki, *Modern Nationalities: A Sociological Study,* Urbana, 1952, pp. 86-93.

12. Jacques Barzun, *Race: A Study in Modern Superstition,* New York, 1937; Louis Snyder, *Race, a History of Modern Ethnic Theories,* New York, 1939.

13. Johann F. Blumenbach's *De generis humani varietate,* Göttingen, 1775, was the first serious scientific study. He measured skulls but his classification into five races was based on color.

14. E. G. Murphy, *The Basis of Ascendancy,* New York, 1909, pp. 78-80.

15. Perhaps the most fanatical racist before the Nazis, Houston Stewart Chamberlain, on the other hand, saw the Teutonic race as the basis of all modern civilization and at the same time the nation as creating the conditions for the formation of race. *The Foundations of the Nineteenth Century,* tr. by Lees, London, 1913, Vol. I, p. 292. Another racist, the American H. F. Osborn, thought race far more important "than language or nationality in moulding the destinies of man." Preface to Madison Grant, *The Passing of the Great Race,* New York, 1922. The Germans are usually blamed most for "race" thinking but Englishmen and Americans, and to a lesser extent Frenchmen, are hardly less guilty, as the Englishmen, Americans, and Frenchmen cited in this section prove.

16. Hannah Arendt, "Race-Thinking before Racism," *Review of Politics,* Vol. VI, 1944, p. 49. Herder had a contrary view, that all men were of one race. Ergang, p. 89.

17. Quoted by Walter Langsam, *The Napoleonic Wars and German Nationalism in Austria,* New York, 1930, pp. 65-66.

18. *Histoire de France,* Paris, 1869, édition définitive, Vol. I, pp. 105-09. The Thierrys, Augustin and Amedée, and the Comte de Montlosier in his *De la monarchie française depuis son établissement jusqu'à nos jours,* 3 vols., Paris, 1814, continued the old theme of the Comte de Boulainvilliers (1658-1722) that France was composed of two races, a view which was to become that of the best known of the racists, Gobineau.

19. *Lectures on Early English History,* London, 1906, pp. 3-75.

20. *Ancient Law,* New York, 1883, p. 124. Edward A. Freeman and J. R. Green likewise based some of their conclusions upon race. A later prominent English historian, J. Holland Rose, in his

Nationality in Modern History, New York, 1916, p. 12, attributed England to "the union of Norman energy and Anglo-Saxon stubbornness." A sound anthropological attack on "kinship in blood" as "the sole possible ground of community" is R. H. Lowie, *The Origin of the State,* New York, 1927, pp. 51 ff.

21. *Op. cit.,* Vol. I, p. xv, Vol. II, pp. 149, 187.

22. *Politics,* London, 1916, p. 271.

23. Barzun, *Race,* p. 203.

24. *The Psychology of Peoples,* London, 1899, pp. 19-20. Le Bon frequently used such nonsensical terms as "national soul."

25. *Nationality and Race,* London, 1919, p. 33; and *The Place of Prejudice in Modern Civilization,* New York, 1931. Alfred Zimmern, an English internationalist, in his *Nationality and Government, and Other War-Time Essays,* London, 1918, p. 74, also thought nationality "an instinct."

26. *The Group Mind,* New York, 1928, p. 283. See also his *National Welfare and Decay,* London, 1921. The American geographer Ellsworth Huntington during the same years was advocating a somewhat like view in books dealing with climate and race, particularly *The Character of Races,* New York, 1924.

27. *Nationality, Its Nature and Problems,* New Haven, 1929, preface and p. 246.

28. *Weltbürgertum und Nationalstaat,* Munich, 1928, p. 1.

29. The Nazi view was most fully developed not in *Mein Kampf* but in Alfred Rosenberg's *Der Mythus des 20 Jahrhunderts,* Munich, 1930. But the German Nazis were only the loudest of the modern racists. Cf. the popular writings of Madison Grant and Lothrop Stoddard in the United States.

30. *History of Civilization in England,* World Classics ed., Vol. I, p. 30 n.

31. Of all the definitions of race that by Melville Herskovits (*Man and His Works: The Science of Cultural Anthropology,* New York, 1949, p. 133) seems closest to what is basic: "A race is a principal division of mankind marked by physical characteristics which breed true."

32. G. M. Morant's conclusion is sound: "The differences in body characters which distinguish the races of Europe are only small differences between the *averages* for the groups. There are no characters which distinguish all members of race A from all members of race B, and, indeed, no approach to this condition is ever found." *The Races of Central Europe: A Footnote to History,* London, 1939, pp. 51, 142. For what outstanding anthropologists and geneticists think, see the UNESCO booklet, *The Race Concept,* Paris, 1952.

33. A. L. Kroeber's classification is used here. *Anthropology: Race, Language, Culture, Psychology, Prehistory,* New York, rev. ed., 1948, p. 144. See also Huxley and Haddon, *We Europeans,* p. 14 and *passim.*

34. *The Study of Man: An Introduction,* New York, 1936, pp. 34-35.
35. *Genetics and the Races of Man,* Boston, 1950, p. 202.
36. H. J. Fleure, *The Peoples of Europe,* London, 1925, p. 42.
37. Kroeber, p. 135.
38. G. M. Morant, p. 150.
39. Kroeber, p. 135; O. D. von Engeln put it succinctly, "There is no correspondence between the distribution [in Europe] of the three racial types and the various developments of nationality." *Inheriting the Earth,* New York, 1922, p. 14.

CHAPTER IV (Pages 40-56)

1. On child training see the pioneering study of Lloyd Allport, "The Psychology of Nationalism," *Harpers Magazine,* Vol. CLV, 1927, pp. 291-301; and chap. X below; on health Ellsworth Huntington, *Mainsprings of Civilization,* New York, 1945, pp. 250-62; on diet Robert McCarriston, "Nutrition and National Health," *Journal of the Royal Society of Arts,* Vol. LXXXIV, August 28, September 4, 11, 1936, pp. 1047-1110; on environment Kroeber, *Anthropology: Race, Language, Culture, Psychology, Prehistory,* New York, 1948, p. 127.
2. The kind of generalities with which we must be at present satisfied are phrased by the psychologist-psychiatrist Norman Cameron: Human nature is a "dynamic organization of interlocking behavior systems that each of us develops through learning processes, as he grows from a biological newborn to a biosocial adult in an environment of other individuals and cultural products. . . . It is always this interplay of biology and society." *The Psychology of Behavior Disorders: A Biosocial Interpretation,* Boston, 1947, p. 16.
3. Ralph Linton, *The Cultural Background of Personality,* New York, 1945, p. 151.
4. *Capital,* Everyman's ed., Vol. II, p. 848. Marxian ideas concerning nationality are expertly discussed by John Maynard in *The Russian Peasant and Other Studies,* London, 1942, the chapter on Marxian nationalism.
5. *Selected Works,* Vol. IV, London, 1936, "On the Right of Nations to Self-determination," p. 250. See also his *Critical Remarks on the National Question,* Moscow, 1951.
6. *Marxism and the National and Colonial Question,* New York, n.d., pp. 13, 14-15. A further elaboration of the Stalin "line" is M. D. Kammari, *The Development by J. V. Stalin of the Marxist-Leninist Theory of the National Question,* Moscow, 1951.
7. For a fuller description of the view see Boyd C. Shafer, "Bourgeois Nationalism in the Pamphlets on the Eve of the French Revolution," *Journal of Modern History,* Vol. X, 1938, pp. 31-50. Basic interpretations are Albert Mathiez, *La Révolution française,* Paris,

1948, Vol. I, pp. 114-15; and Alphonse Aulard, *The French Revolution*, tr. by Miall, New York, 1910, Vol. I, p. 127.

8. The Social Democrat Otto Bauer formulated a "concentric" theory in which the aristocracy commenced the nation and then the national spirit spread through the rich bourgeoisie and finally the masses. This theory, except that it is too simple, is not completely unhistorical. But see his *Die Nationalitätenfrage und die Sozialdemokratie*, Vienna, 1924.

9. *Politics*, tr. by Dugdale and DeBille, London, 1916, Vol. I, pp. 3-18, 54-55, 77. He saw, however, "two strong forces working in history; firstly the tendency of every State to amalgamate its population in speech and manners into one single mould, and secondly, the impulse of every vigorous nationality to construct a State of its own" (p. 272).

10. *Ibid.*, Vol. I, p. 51. Not only Germans like Treitschke, Clausewitz, and Bernhardi but men of widely diverse views of many nations like Theodore Roosevelt, Admiral Mahan, Tennyson, Cramb, Proudhon, and many of the popularizers of science who came after Darwin praised war as a great creative force.

11. François P. G. Guizot, *History of European Civilization*, tr. by W. Hazlitt, Bohn ed., 1846, Vol. I, p. 138.

12. *The Valor of Ignorance*, New York, 1909, pp. 8 ff.

13. *Physics and Politics*, New York, 1881, pp. 17, 81-111.

14. *National Life from the Standpoint of Science*, London, 1901, pp. 19, 34, and *passim*.

15. *Le principe des nationalités*, Paris, 1916, pp. 12-13.

16. See the recent writings of Ashley Montagu, especially *On Being Human*, New York, 1951, for the argument that co-operation is the basic law.

17. The keenest study of the development of national languages is Otto Jespersen, *Mankind, Nation and Individual from a Linguistic Point of View*, Oslo, 1925, which shows that language itself is a result of social forces in history. But cf. Carl D. Buck, "Language and the Sentiment of Nationality," *Political Science Review*, Vol. X, 1916, pp. 44-69.

18. Rundle, *Language as a Social and Economic Factor in Europe*, London, 1946, pp. 46-47, citing G. M. Morant, *The Races of Central Europe*, London, 1939. A more detailed discussion is in Morant, esp. pp. 132-43.

19. Ralph Linton, *The Study of Man*, New York, 1936, p. 390, points out that language distributions everywhere "are only superficially related to those of any other element of culture."

20. Francis Delaisi, *Political Myths and Economic Realities*, New York, 1927, p. 202.

21. The most monumental historical study of a language, Ferdinand Brunot's multivolumed *Histoire de la langue française*, Paris, 1905-47, is a record of change and growth and clearly reveals how uncommon French was for many Frenchmen down to the eight-

eenth century. Among other pertinent studies of the relation of
language and nationalism are Karl W. Deutsch, "The Trend of
European Nationalism—The Language Aspect," *American Political Science Review,* Vol. XXXVI, 1942, pp. 533-41; and Leon
Dominian, *The Frontiers of Language and Nationality in Europe,* New York, 1917.

22. On English, see C. T. Onion, for example, "The English Language," in Ernest Barker, ed., *The Character of England,* Oxford,
1947, p. 281; and A. C. Baugh, *A History of the English Language,*
New York, 1935.

23. Ernest Barker, *National Character and the Factors in Its Formation,* London, 1927, p. 146; and Delaisi, pp. 156-65.

24. To Jespersen, "the language of a nation" was no more than "the
set of habits by which the members of the nation are accustomed
to communicate with one another," *op. cit.,* p. 23.

25. In Herbert W. Schneider, ed., *Adam Smith's Moral and Political
Philosophy,* New York, 1948, pp. 240-41.

26. Quoted by J. M. Thompson, *The French Revolution,* New York,
1945, p. 14. The word "family" was often used in place of the
word "nationality" by patriots of the early Revolution. Possibly the
writer of the article "Patrie" in Diderot's *Encyclopédie,* Vol.
XXIV (1780 ed.), pp. 472-73, popularized this concept when he
likened the *Patrie* to both a mother and a father.

27. Koppel S. Pinson, *Pietism as a Factor in the Rise of German
Nationalism,* New York, 1934, p. 199.

28. Maurice Barrès, *Scènes et doctrines du nationalisme,* Paris, n.d.,
pp. 98-99.

29. *Nationality and Government,* London, 1918, pp. 52, 67, 77.

30. See the *Lectures on the Principles of Political Obligation,* in Vol.
II of the *Works of Thomas Hill Green,* edited by R. L. Nettleship, London, 1911, particularly lectures G and K.

31. *Anthropology and Modern Life,* 2nd ed., New York, 1932, p. 92.

32. As Michelet eloquently had it, *"La nationalité, la patrie, c'est
toujours la vie du monde. Elle morte, tout serait mort," Le
peuple,* Paris, 1946, p. 235.

33. Robert R. Ergang, *Herder and the Foundations of German Nationalism,* New York, 1931, p. 96. Herder might have taken the
idea from Rousseau's *Considérations sur le gouvernement de
Pologne,* where Rousseau argued there were no longer Frenchmen or even Englishmen, only Europeans at home wherever
there was money to steal or women to seduce. Carlton Hayes
described Herder's views in the *American Historical Review,*
"Contributions of Herder to the Doctrine of Nationalism," Vol.
XXXII, 1927, pp. 719-36.

34. *Sermons,* 1809, "On the Love of Country," in Frederick Page,
An Anthology of Patriotic Prose, London, 1915, p. 127. A like
opinion was held by the Russian contemporary historian
Karamzin, who thought "the true cosmopolitan . . . either a

metaphysical conception or a phenomenon so unusual that it is not worthwhile to mention him. . . ." Quoted by Royal Institute of International Affairs, *Nationalism,* Oxford, 1939, p. 67.

35. Michelet's was the greatest voice and some French writers, perhaps in reaction to their own cosmopolitan intellectuals, the most ardent advocates. For illustration there is Augustin Cochin, "Le patriotisme humanitaire," *La revue universelle,* April, 1920; and Georges Goyau, *L'idée de patrie et l'humanitarisme: Essai d'histoire française, 1866-1901,* Paris, 1913.

36. Quoted by Albert Guerard, "The Quick and the Dead," "English or Literature," *Chap Book,* College English Association, 1951, p. 5.

37. With a good deal of insight J. A. Hobson diagnosed extreme nationalism as the "neurotic temperament generated by town life." *The Psychology of Jingoism,* London, 1901, p. 8.

38. *Utilitarianism, Liberty, Representative Government,* Everyman's ed., p. 360. See also Ernest Seillière in M. Vaussard, *Enquête sur le nationalisme,* Paris, 1924, p. 106.

39. If the date 1789 seems too late, then the time might be moved back to the period of the Hundred Years' War, before which even many of the inhabitants of the center of what is now France had little in common except an often disputed monarchy.

40. The Royal Institute of International Affairs, *Nationalism,* p. 274, makes this observation of all peasants.

41. In 1758 a Dr. J. G. Zimmerman of Zurich remarked, "The vanity of mankind has ever filled the immense vacuity beyond the authentic memorials of the origin of every nation with fabulous history, at pleasing removing their antiquity in the remotest ages, in order to proportionately increase its luster." Quoted from his *Essay on National Pride,* tr. by Samuel Wilcocke, New York, 1797, in Harold Lasswell, *World Politics and Personal Insecurity,* New York, 1935, p. 40.

42. "The Development of Modern European Historiography," *Atlantic Monthly,* Vol. LXVI, 1890, p. 325.

43. J. W. Thompson, *A History of Historical Writing,* New York, 1942, Vol. I, pp. 492, 626. A good many of the legends of early England were apparently started by Geoffrey of Monmouth. But see Halvdan Koht, "The Dawn of Nationalism in Europe," *American Historical Review,* Vol. LII, 1947, p. 271.

44. Whether or not they have generally been more sophisticated is debatable. For an absurd attempt to give Germany a long history see Kurt Pastenaci, *Das viertausendjährige Reich der Deutschen,* Berlin, 1940.

45. *Politics,* Vol. I, p. 272.

46. *Nationality, Its Nature and Problems,* London, 1929, p. 313.

47. *Esquisse d'une histoire des Français dans leur volonté d'être une nation,* Paris, 1932.

48. This was also the opinion of G. Monod, *Du role d'opposition des races et des nationalités dans la dissolution de l'Empire Carolingien, Annuaire de l'École pratique des hautes études,* 1896. For a discussion of when French historians "started" French nationality see René Johannet, *Le principe des nationalités,* Paris, 1923, pp. 27 ff.

49. *A Short History of the English People,* New York, n.d., p. 7. A popularized version of the Anglo-Saxon early origins of Britain was Grant Allen's *Anglo-Saxon Britain,* London, 1884.

50. As Arnold Toynbee stated, "It is impossible to urge *a priori* from the presence of one or even several of the factors [as language] to the existence of a nationality; they may have been there for ages and kindled no response." *Nationality and the War,* London, 1915, p. 14.

51. Actually little is known of Jeanne d'Arc's ideas. But cf. Delaisi, pp. 180-81.

52. *Regards sur le monde actuel,* Paris, 1931, p. 63.

CHAPTER V (Pages 59-96)

1. A. F. Pollard, for example, makes the point that nationality is very modern though he finds the origins of the British in the fourteenth century. But every student differs. *Factors in Modern History,* London, 1926, chap. I, "Nationality."

2. E. Westermarck (*The Origin and Development of Moral Ideas,* New York, 2nd ed., 1912, Vol. II, pp. 167 ff.) declared that patriotism was widespread among uncultured peoples and elements of it among the lowest savages. James Harvey Robinson agreed in his "What Is National Spirit," *The Century Magazine,* Vol. XCIII, 1916, pp. 57-64. F. E. Williams (*Orokaia Society,* London, 1930, pp. 156, 325) shows that this tribe, for example, has a common territory, distinctive customs and dialect, and common enemies. Fred Voget ("Acculturation at Caughnawaga," *American Anthropologist,* Vol. LIII, 1952, pp. 220-31) describes the feeling of separateness, of being a "chosen people" among some American Indians.

3. Socrates, arguing with Crito concerning his right to evade execution, asked, "Has a philosopher like you failed to discover that our country [city] is more to be valued and higher and holier far than mother or father or any ancestor, and more to be regarded in the eyes of the gods and of men of understanding?—to be obeyed, suffered for in silence even when punished, to die for?" *The Dialogues of Plato,* tr. by Jowett, New York, 1937, Vol. I, p. 435. Whether there was nationalism among ancient peoples has been the subject of much dispute. Compare Theodore Haarhoff, *The Stranger at the Gate; Aspects of Exclusiveness and Cooperation in Ancient Greece and Rome . . . ,* Oxford, 1948;

M. T. Walek-Czernecki, "Le rôle de la nationalité dans l'histoire de l'Antiquité," *Bulletin of the International Committee of Historical Sciences,* Vol. II, pt. II, 1929, pp. 303-20; Moses Hadas, "Aspects of Nationalist Survival under Hellenistic and Roman Imperialism," *Journal of the History of Ideas,* Vol. XI, 1950, pp. 131-39; and M. Rostovtzeff, *A History of the Ancient World,* 2nd ed., Oxford, 1930, Vol. I, pp. 229-37.

4. The modern use of the word state as a body politic occurred first in Italy in the early sixteenth century. It was not so used in England until 1635. George Sabine, "State," *Encyclopedia of the Social Sciences,* Vol. XIV, pp. 328 ff.

5. See chap. I.

6. René Johannet, *Le principe des nationalités,* Paris, 1918, pp. 61-62. Ernesto Sestan, in *Stato e Nazione nell 'alto Medioevo: Ricerche sulle origini nazionali in Francia, Italia, Germania,* Naples, 1952, reviewed by Catherine Boyd, *American Historical Review,* Vol. LVIII, 1953, pp. 890-91, shows nascent nations but not nationalism as early as the eighth century.

7. "The Laicization of French and English Society in the Thirteenth Century," *Speculum,* Vol. XV, 1940, pp. 77-78.

8. The great Norwegian historian Halvdan Koht saw the "beginnings of actual nationalism" in France, England, Poland, Denmark, the Germanies, and the Italies as early as the twelfth century. "The Dawn of Nationalism in Europe," *American Historical Review,* Vol. LII, 1947, p. 279.

9. Johannet, p. 400. Many conservative French historians have taken this view, for example, Auguste Lognon, *Origines et formation de la nationalité française,* Paris, 1912, but it is widely held that the state preceded the nation. A succinct statement is that of Ernest Barker, *National Character and the Factors in Its Formation,* London, 1927, pp. 15-16.

10. Suggestive is the argument of R. H. Lowie, in *The Origin of the State,* New York, 1927, that administrative ability and war in addition to kinship and territorial association contributed to the origin of the state. He believed: "A coercive force . . . whether vested in a person or a group seems the short cut to intensifying and bringing into consciousness the incipient feeling of neighborliness that has been found a universal trait of human society. Once established and sanctified, the sentiment may well flourish, without compulsion, glorified as loyalty to a sovereign being or to a national flag" (pp. 116-17).

11. Here the pertinent volumes of the Ernest Lavisse, ed., *Histoire de France* and of the fine Halphen and Sagnac, eds., *Peuples et civilisations* series are basic and authoritative. The best short history of France is that of Charles Seignobos, *A History of the French People,* tr. by Phillips, London, 1933. See also the compact little volume by Régine Perroud, *L'unité française,* Paris, 1949.

12. Albert Sorel argued cogently that the "politics of the Capetians, considered by their consequences and tradition, had two principal objects: internally to build a homogeneous and coherent nation; externally to assure the best frontiers, the independence of the nation and the power of the state." *L'Europe et la Révolution française,* Paris, 1946 ed., Vol. I, p. 189. But he was using hindsight as we are here.

13. These points are made in Derwent Whittlesey, *Environmental Foundations of European History,* New York, 1949, p. 83.

14. Where many nationalist historians err is in assuming that the historical development that came was inevitable, that the nations which did evolve were the only ones that could. It is quite conceivable that Burgundy, Provence, Wales, Scotland, Bavaria, Prussia could have developed into and remained separate nations.

15. Subsequently the monarchy lost and won these lands several times. Definite dates for the acquisition of these and other territories can scarcely be established. Rulers and their lawyers began to try to establish "precise frontiers" rather than spheres of influence in the thirteenth century. Strayer, p. 81. But they were seldom successful.

16. John had stolen the betrothed of one of Philip's vassals.

17. The significance of these territorial acquisitions for the modern nation is nowhere shown more clearly than in the thirteenth-century change in the royal title from *Rex Francorum* to *Rex Franciae,* a fact which indicated that, unlike the Roman practice, the state was beginning to be associated with a definite territory. Ernst Kantorowicz, "Pro Patria Mori in Medieval Political Thought," *American Historical Review,* Vol. LVI, 1951, p. 487 n.

18. The actual conquest of Languedoc began with Philip Augustus and the Albigensian Crusade.

19. This is a paraphrase of Seignobos, p. 106. In England the Norman, Plantagenet, Lancaster, and Tudor dynasties, in Russia the Romanov, in Germany the Hohenzollern, in Italy the House of Savoy each sought aggrandizement of their family holdings. As late as the nineteenth century, when nationalism was reaching its height, the kings of Piedmont and Prussia were not so much national-minded as desirous of more personal power through enlargement of their kingdoms.

20. Strayer, pp. 76-86.

21. Philippe Sagnac, *La fin de l'ancien régime et la Révolution américaine,* Vol. XII of Halphen and Sagnac, *Peuples et civilisations,* Paris, 1947, pp. 22-23, 565-66. In Spain the monarchy was not as successful. It left the country until quite recent times "a congeries of separate states, differing from one another in race, in traditions, in language, and in government . . . a loose-jointed, heterogeneous empire, the fundamental principle of whose administration was that of decentralized despotism." Roger

Bigelow Merriman, *The Rise of the Spanish Empire in the Old World and the New,* New York, 1918, Vol. II, p. 74.

22. Myron Gilmore has a good chapter on "Dynastic Consolidation" in his *The World of Humanism, 1453-1517,* New York, 1952.

23. The pertinent chapters of the *Cambridge Medieval History* and the *Cambridge Modern History* provide good detailed analyses of the growth of monarchical power in England, but there is a wealth of studies. A good, short description is in G. M. Trevelyan, *History of England,* New York, 1926, esp. pp. 133-357. For a detailed account of thirteenth-century England there is F. M. Powicke, *King Henry III and the Lord Edward: The Community of the Realm in the Thirteenth Century,* 2 vols., Oxford, 1947.

24. The first systematic study of English law was made by Ranulf de Glanvil (d. 1190) during the last decade of Henry II's reign in his *Tractatus de legibus et consuetudinibus regni Angliae.* Bracton wrote his more important work, comprising nearly 2,000 cases, a work which became a cornerstone of English law, in the 1250's.

25. Trevelyan, pp. 140-41.

26. According to Esmé Wingfield-Stratford, *The History of English Patriotism,* London, 1913, Vol. I, pp. 57-58, Edward I was perhaps the first great English patriot king. But in his own patriotism Wingfield-Stratford saw the English brand arising much earlier than would the cautious student.

27. Strayer (p. 84) believed the governments of France and Britain had as early as 1300 begun "to see that nationalism could be useful to them," and that the "concentration of political authority . . . encouraged the growth of nationalism by decreasing the differences between provinces and increasing the differences between countries."

28. Henry V (1413-1422) started the navy but it had since been neglected. Conyers Read's comment on Henry VIII is pertinent, "In short, by the beginning of the year 1537 Henry had established his kingdom, established his church, established his line." *The Tudors,* New York, 1936, p. 83.

29. During the thirteenth century the French kings gradually gained the power to impose a tax *pro defensione regni* which went beyond the old feudal aids. "In other words, by the end of the thirteenth century the national monarchy of France was strong enough and sufficiently advanced to proclaim itself as *patria* and to impose taxes, including church taxes, *ad defensionem natalis patriae.*" Kantorowicz, p. 479. Joseph R. Strayer, "Consent to Taxation under Philip the Fair," in Strayer and Charles H. Taylor, *Studies in Early French Taxation,* Cambridge, Mass., 1939.

30. Pierre Dubois in his *De Recuperatione Terrae Sanctae* (1305-1307) went so far as to assert, "it would be expedient for the whole world to be subject to the realm of the French." G. G.

Coulton, "Nationalism in the Middle Ages," *Cambridge Historical Journal*, Vol. V, 1935, p. 36.

31. *The Seventeenth Century*, Oxford, 1950, pp. 125, 140, 219. See also the essays of Paul L. Léon on ideas concerning the sovereignty of the monarchs before Rousseau in the *Archives de philosophie du droit et de sociologie juridique*, 4 and 7 années, 1934 and 1937, pp. 197-237 and 152-185.

32. *History of Germany in the Nineteenth Century*, tr. by Eden and Cedar Paul, New York, 1915, Vol. I, p. 46. Guy Stanton Ford discussed Prussian military training in "Boyen's Military Law," *American Historical Review*, Vol. XX, 1914-15, pp. 528-38.

33. Bossuet in his *Politique tirée de l'Ecriture sainte* was the theorist of this view. But see Carl J. Friedrich, *The Age of the Baroque*, New York, 1952, pp. 14-30. The opinion of Sir Thomas Smith was common, "To be short the prince is the life, the head and the authoritie of all thinges that be doone in the realme of England." Quoted in Hans Kohn, "The Genesis and Character of English Nationalism," *Journal of the History of Ideas*, Vol. I, 1940, p. 72, from *De Republica Anglorum, The Manner of Government or Policie of the Realme of England* (1583). This was the view also of James I and, for different reasons, of Bodin and Hobbes. Althusius, the German jurist of the same period, asserted the superiority of the nation in more democratic fashion.

34. J. A. Williamson, "England and the Sea," in Ernest Barker, ed., *The Character of England*, Oxford, 1947, p. 509.

35. *The Principall Navigations . . .* , London, 1927, Vol. I, p. 19.

36. Charles W. Cole (*Colbert and a Century of French Mercantilism*, New York, 1939, Vol. I, p. 25) believed, "Mercantilism represented the economic counterpart of *étatism*. In practice it sought to bring all phases of economic life under royal control." Robert Livingston Schuyler, on the other hand, thought mercantilism was the "economic phase of nationalism." *Political Science Quarterly*, Vol. 37, 1922, p. 445. Perhaps it was both.

37. Eli Hecksher, *Mercantilism*, tr. by Schapiro, London, 1935, Vol. I, pp. 22-23.

38. H. Munro Chadwick (*The Nationalities of Europe and the Growth of National Ideologies*, Cambridge, 1945, pp. 69-70) argues that "the linguistic map of western and west central Europe had assumed more or less its present form" by the end of the sixth century but that great changes continued much longer in the north, east, and southeast. But much depends upon the interpretation of what is a distinct and developed language.

39. The discussion in Edward P. Cheyney, *The Dawn of a New Era, 1250-1453*, New York, 1936, pp. 247 ff., is a good introduction. As V. H. Galbraith has pointed out in the case of fourteenth-century England, however, the growth of a vernacular is not necessarily connected with national feeling and any contrived relation could be anachronistic, "Nationality and Language in

Medieval England," *Transactions of the Royal Historical Society,*
Vol. XXIII, 1941, pp. 113-28.

40. Dante denied even to Tuscan the honor of "illustrious Italian
vulgar tongue" in his *De Vulgare Eloquentia.*

41. The "Sequence de Sainte Eulalie," a formless rhapsody of the
ninth century, is possibly the first literary effort in recognizable
French.

42. Villehardouin's work has been called "the first work of importance and sustained dignity in the French tongue. . . ." See James
Westfall Thompson, *A History of Historical Writing,* New York,
1942, Vol. I, p. 322.

43. The earliest-known history in French, however, was the *Histoire
des Engles* written about mid-twelfth century by the Norman
Geoffrey Gaimar. Charles Haskins, *The Normans in European
History,* Boston, 1915, pp. 183-84. The Latin text of famous
Grand Chronique de France or *Grands Chroniques de St. Denis,*
which more or less officially record the events of the French
monarchy from 1247, terminated in 1340.

44. The time of the first translation of the Bible into the vernacular
is significant because so much life centered upon religion. On
Wyclif see H. B. Workman, *John Wyclif, a Study of the English
Medieval Church,* 2 vols., Oxford, 1926.

45. Quoted in Trevelyan, p. 235 n.

46. Trevissa's observation is a modification of a like earlier one in
Ranulf Higden, *Polychronicon,* ed. by Churchill Babington
and Joseph R. Lumby, 9 vols., London, 1865-86, Rolls series no.
41. *Piers Plowman,* XV, 1, 368, notes the change from learning
in French to learning in English eight years earlier.

47. Royal Institute of International Affairs, *Nationalism,* London,
1939, p. 14; Froissart, *Chronicles,* ed. by Kervynde de Lettenhove,
Brussels, 1867-77, Vol. II, p. 236.

48. In *Deux dialogues du nouveau langage français italianizé* (1578)
and *La précellence du langage français* (1579).

49. R. Carew in Camden's *Remaines concerning Britaine* (1614), 6th
impression, London, 1657, p. 43, maintained that English had
all the beauties and none of the ugliness of each of the other
tongues. "Now we [English] in borrowing from them, give the
strength of consonants to the Italian, the full sound of words to
the French, the variety of terminations to the Spanish, and the
mollifying of more vowels to the Dutch; and so (like bees)
gather the honey of their good properties, and leave the dregs
to themselves. And thus when substantialness combineth with
delightfulness, fullness with fineness, seemliness with portliness
and correctness with staidness, how can the language which con-
sisteth of all these sound other than most full of sweetness."

50. Quoted in Brunot, *Histoire de la langue française,* Vol. VI, pt. II,
by Alex François, p. 870.

51. In J. Novicow, *Conscience et volontés sociales,* Paris, 1897, p. 313. Walter Sulzbach, *National Consciousness,* Washington, D. C., 1943, pp. 12-13. The statement was first attributed to Henry IV by Pierre Mathieu, in his *Histoire de Henry IV,* published in Paris in 1631.

52. See the informed discussion in Otto Jespersen, *Mankind, Nation and Individual from a Linguistic Point of View,* Oslo, 1925.

53. Kohn, *The Idea of Nationalism,* New York, 1953, p. 606 n.

54. W. H. V. Reade ("Political Theory to c. 1300," *Cambridge Medieval History,* Vol. VI, New York, 1929, p. 633) held "the irregular boundary between the medieval and the modern is crossed as soon as the conception of Christendom, embodied for Dante in the Roman Empire, gives way to the belief that the largest autonomous community should be the territorial or national state."

55. For illustrations of this see Koppel Pinson, *Pietism as a Factor in the Rise of German Nationalism,* New York, 1934.

56. Salo Baron, *Modern Nationalism and Religion,* New York, 1947, p. 14, and Marcel Handelsman, "Le role de la nationalité dans l'histoire du Moyen Age," *Bulletin of the International Committee of Historical Sciences,* Vol. II, pt. II, pp. 244-45.

57. Though a direct connection cannot be shown, it is possible that love of one's nation or fellow nationals is an outgrowth of Christian charity as Tolomeo of Lucca in his continuation of Aquinas' *De regimine principum* directly states, "Love of the fatherland is founded in the root of charity which puts, not one's own things before those common, but the common things before one's own. . . ." Kantorowicz, p. 488.

58. *Protestantism and Progress: A Historical Study of the Relation of Protestantism to the Modern World,* tr. by W. Montgomery, London, 1912, p. 127.

59. As Marsiglio of Padua earlier in the *Defensor Pacis* (1324) and as Machiavelli in the *Prince* in Luther's time.

60. What Ernest Barker wrote of English Protestantism is valid for much early Protestantism: "There is what I should call Étatism, as well as nationalism in our English Reformation, and in the beginnings there is more Étatism than nationalism, though there was always some nationalism there. In other words the English Church began as a State Church rather than a national Church; but in the course of time the position was gradually changed and inverted. I should say that it became a national Church . . . in 1660." "The Reformation and Nationality," *Modern Churchman,* Vol. XXII, 1932, p. 340.

61. F. J. C. Hearnshaw, ed., *The Social and Political Ideas of Some Great Medieval Thinkers,* London, 1923, pp. 216 ff.

62. Quoted in Baron, p. 11.

63. The Old Testament, as H. G. Wells aptly remarked, is something of a nationalist history. *The Anatomy of Frustration,* London,

1936, pp. 181-82. For an illustration of nationalist opinion in this respect see J. Martineau, *National Duties and Other Sermons*, London, 1903.

64. *The Letters and Speeches of Oliver Cromwell, with Elucidations by Thomas Carlyle*, ed. by S. C. Lomas, London, 1904, Vol. II, pp. 404 ff. Hans Kohn brilliantly sums up the relation of Puritanism to nationalism in his *The Idea of Nationalism*, pp. 165 ff., and his previously published article, "Genesis and Character of English Nationalism," *Journal of the History of Ideas*, Vol. I, 1940, pp. 84-89. See also Ernest Barker, *Cromwell and the English People*, Cambridge, 1937, pp. 24, 82, 104. A detailed study is George Lanyi, "Oliver Cromwell and His Age, a Study in Nationalism," Ph.D. dissertation, Harvard, 1949, typescript.

65. Probably religious and nationalist motivations were indissolubly mixed. The Hussites went to war in 1420 "to liberate the truth of the Law of God and the Saints and to protect the faithful believers of the Church, and the Czech and Slavonic language." Kohn, *Idea of Nationalism*, p. 111.

66. *Op. cit.,* p. 136.

67. Charles Maurras, the French nationalist, was not as wrong as usual when he wrote, *"L'humanité avait alors pour garantie la chrétienté. Depuis que la Réforme a coupé en deux notre Europe, la chrétienté n'existe plus. Où est le genre humain, pour chaque homme? Dans sa patrie."* Quoted in Johannet, p. 61.

68. This was particularly true of the enthusiastic religious groups of the seventeenth and eighteenth centuries like the Pietists in Germany. Pinson, *passim*.

69. Claus Petri translated the Old and New Testaments into Swedish in 1540-41. Christiern Petersen published the first Danish Bible in 1543. There was a Finnish translation of the New Testament in 1548. The Statenbybil, published in 1626-37, was instrumental in making the dialect of Holland accepted in the northern Lowlands.

70. George C. Powers showed some was present at the Council of Constance but as at medieval universities the word "nation" was not used in the same sense as it is today. *Nationalism at the Council of Constance (1414-1418)*, Washington, 1927. See also Louise Loomis, "Nationality at the Council of Constance," *American Historical Review*, Vol. XLIV, 1939, pp. 508-27, where it is pointed out that the "nations" showed "touchy conceit," "unscrupulous assertiveness," at the Council.

71. René Johannet (p. 27) probably overemphasizes Roland's national patriotism as he does most nationalism before the eighteenth century.

72. Pange, Comte de Jean, *Le roi trés chrétien*, Paris, 1949, p. 439. Dorothy Kirkland, an able student, gives other specific illustrations for France. She concludes, "articulate patriotism must be sought in vain before the fifteenth century, although certain

aspects of the national sentiment can be seen here and there, stronger at one time than another, present in one place and absent in the next, but on the whole gaining ground. . . ." "The Growth of the National Sentiment in France before the 15th Century," *History,* Vol. XXIII, 1938, p. 24.

73. *Matthew Paris's English History from the Year 1234 to 1273,* tr. by Giles, London, 1854, Vol. I, p. 312, Vol. III, p. 84. For original see the Luard (Rolls Series) edition of the *Chronica Majorca,* Vol. V, p. 450. His descriptions of the Tatars remind one of present-day Western attitudes toward the Russians.

74. Quoted by G. G. Coulton, "Nationalism in the Middle Ages," *Cambridge Historical Journal,* Vol. V, 1935, p. 19. A little earlier Guibert de Nogent (1053-1124) in his *Gesta Dei per Francos* refuted the German archdeacon of Mainz, who thought the French weak and cowardly, with, "If the French had not by their strength and courage opposed a barrier to the Turks, not all you Germans, whose name is not even known in the East, would have been of use." Thompson, *History of Historical Writing,* Vol. I, p. 233. For other illustrations, particularly between east and west, see E. N. Johnson, "American Medievalists and Today," *Speculum,* Vol. XXVIII, 1953, pp. 849-50.

75. Quoted in Thompson, Vol. I, p. 516.

76. The poem, a part of the *Grand Testament,* is translated in D. B. Wyndham Lewis, *François Villon: a Documentary Survey,* New York, 1928, pp. 295-96.

77. Kantorowicz, pp. 482-91.

78. Petrarch, *Sonnets and Songs,* tr. by Anna Maria Armi, New York, 1946, pp. 203, 209.

79. Quoted by Wingfield-Stratford, *History of English Patriotism,* Vol. I, p. 72.

80. Quoted in H. F. Stewart and Paul Desjardins, eds., *French Patriotism in the Nineteenth Century (1814-1833),* Cambridge, 1923, introd.

81. Quoted in Johannet, p. 26.

82. *The Prince,* tr. by W. K. Marriott, Everyman's ed., p. 213. In the sixteenth, seventeenth, and early eighteenth centuries Muzio, Boccalini, and Muratori as well as a few others spoke of the glories of Italy and in some cases pleaded for national sovereignty. Emiliana Pasca Noether, *Seeds of Italian Nationalism, 1700-1815,* New York, 1951, *passim.*

83. Though he liked Italy he hated and disliked Frenchmen and ridiculed the Spaniards. But see Cumberland Clark, *Shakespeare and National Character,* London, 1928; and R. V. Lindabury, *A Study of Patriotism in the Elizabethan Drama,* Princeton, 1931. A little earlier, one of the fathers of the English Church, Thomas Becon, was declaring that men ought to love their native country more than "parents, kinsfolk, friends." "Our parents only give us this gross, rude and mortal body. Our country doth not only

receive and joyfully sustenate it, but also most opulently adorn
and garnish both that and the mind with most goodly and godly
virtues." Quoted from "The Policy of War," by Wingfield-Stratford, Vol. I, pp. 144-45.

84. Marquess of Halifax (George Savile), "The Character of a Trimmer," *Complete Works of George Savile*, ed. by Walter Raleigh,
Oxford, 1912, p. 97. "The Character of a Trimmer" was first
published in 1688.

85. Trevelyan, p. 233.

86. Hans Kohn, *The Idea of Nationalism*, pp. 139-42.

87. Hajo Holborn, *Ulrich von Hutten and the German Reformation*, New York, 1937, p. 42.

88. J. Malye, "Leibniz, theoricien du nationalisme allemand,"
L'Acropole, Vol. I, 1920, pp. 442-58.

89. Chief reliance in this section is upon Thompson, *History of Historical Writing*, whenever original research has not been done.

90. That the last chapter of Bede's (673-735) much earlier *Ecclesiastical History* is titled "Of the Present Stage of the English Nation"
should not be overlooked. But for several centuries after Bede
little that is pertinent here was written.

91. Geoffrey probably started the legend that the Trojan wanderer,
Brutus, established Britain. He also worked at the Arthurian
legend.

92. See the quotation from Voiture in Johannet, p. 20. The comment
of Charles Homer Haskins, *Renaissance of the Twelfth Century*,
Cambridge, 1928, p. 275, is relevant: "By 1200 vernacular history
had come to stay, and this fact is one of more than linguistic or
literary significance, since it involved ultimately the secularization and popularization of history."

93. Thompson, Vol. I, p. 608.

94. At the time he died, 1508, the German humanist Konrad Celtis
was planning a *Germania illustrata*, probably in imitation of
Flavio Biondo's *Roma illustrata*.

95. Johannet, p. 39.

96. Of course a great many other sixteenth-century national histories
could be mentioned like Peutinger's (1465-1547) *Sermones con-
viviales de mirandis Germaniae antiquitabus* where it was "discovered" that the Rhine's left bank was German before Caesar.

97. Kantorowicz, p. 475.

98. E. Littré, *Dictionnaire de la langue française*, "patrie." A. Aulard
thought *patrie* was first used in 1539 in the *Songe de Scipion
traduit nouvellement du Latin en Français*. See his *Le patriotisme
française* . . . , Paris, 1916, p. 14.

99. Quoted in Martin Buber, "The Beginning of the National Idea,"
Review of Religion, Vol. X, 1946, p. 254.

CHAPTER VI (Pages 97-117)

1. This analysis is suggested by the social psychologist Hadley Cantril who wrote, "People are not gangsters or law-abiding citizens, Fascists or Communists, agnostics or believers, good or bad, because of innate dispositions. . . . People's actions take the directions they do because a certain set of conditions have provided status, meaning satisfaction. . . ." "Don't Blame It on Human Nature," *New York Times Magazine*, July 6, 1947. A fuller treatment of the whole question is Cantril's *The Psychology of Social Movements*, New York, 1941. See T. W. Adorno and others, *The Authoritarian Personality*, New York, 1950, for experimental evidence upon related subjects.

2. On distinctions in the type of nationalism see Friedrich Meinecke, *Weltbürgertum und Nationalstaat*, 2nd ed., Munich, 1911, pp. 13-16.

3. These last points were provocatively developed in 1922 by Ernst Troeltsch, "The Ideas of Natural Law and Humanity in World Politics," in Otto Gierke, *Natural Law and the Theory of Society*, ed. and tr. by Ernest Barker, Cambridge, 1934, Vol. I, Appendix I, pp. 201-22.

4. A good history of eighteenth-century cosmopolitanism is needed. Albert Mathiez's last published essay is a good introduction, "Pacifisme et nationalisme au dix-huitième siècle," *Annales historiques de la Révolution française*, Vol. XIII, 1936, pp. 1-17; a brief treatment is Elizabeth Souleyman, *The Vision of Peace in 17th-18th Century France*, New York, 1941; and John Stevens examines the death of the idea in "Anacharsis Cloots and French Cosmopolitanism," Ph.D. dissertation, Arkansas, 1954, typescript.

5. From "Annus Mirabilis," *Dryden's Poetical Works*, Oxford ed., London, 1948, p. 36.

6. Or as G. M. Trevelyan pointed out for England, the national monarchy increased its power by an "alliance of the strongest forces of the coming age—London, the middle classes, the sea-going population, the Protestant preachers, the squirearchy bribed and reinforced by the abbey lands. . . ." And he adds "together they proved more than a match for the forces of the old world,—the monks and friars, the remnant of the feudal nobility and gentry . . . and popular Catholic piety. . . ." *History of England*, London, 1926, p. 270.

7. Cf. J. B. Condliffe, *The Commerce of Nations*, New York, 1950, p. 29; and W. R. Scott, *The Constitution and Finance of English, Scottish and Irish Joint-Stock Companies to 1720*, Cambridge, 1912, Vol. I, pp. 440-41.

8. Carlton Hayes (*Essays on Nationalism*, New York, 1926, p. 163) applies this same reasoning to the "masses in every national

state." See also the keen remarks of Crane Brinton, *Political Ideas of the Romanticists,* New York, 1926, p. 59.

9. At the beginning of the French Revolution a sizable proportion of the clergy and nobility revealed considerable nationalism in their cahiers. Beatrice Hyslop, *French Nationalism in 1789 according to the General Cahiers,* New York, 1934, pp. 208-13.

10. The fact, too, that the aristocracy sometimes spoke as if it were the nation requires noting. Georges Lefebvre, *Quatre-vingt-neuf,* Paris, 1939, pp. 41-42.

11. See, for example, Robert R. Palmer, "The National Idea in France before the Revolution," *Journal of the History of Ideas,* Vol. I, 1940, pp. 95 ff.; and Frances Acomb, *Anglophobia in France, 1763-1789: An Essay in the History of Constitutionalism and Nationalism,* Durham, 1950, *passim;* Beatrice Hyslop, *passim;* and Boyd C. Shafer, "Bourgeois Nationalism in the Pamphlets on the Eve of the French Revolution," *Journal of Modern History,* Vol. X, 1938, pp. 31-50, *passim.*

12. Max Savelle, *Seeds of Liberty,* New York, 1948, pp. 556 ff.; cf. Merle Curti, *The Roots of American Loyalty,* New York, 1946, pp. 3-29. Joseph Tucker, an English observer about 1760, denied any unity in America. C. H. Van Tyne, *The War of Independence: American Phase,* Boston, 1929, p. 301.

13. Robert Redslob, a keen student, saw the origins of the *"principe des nationalités"* in *"le mouvement d'emancipation qui, depuis les temps de la Renaissance, agite les peuples, leur inspire la conscience d'eux-mêmes et la résolution de prendre en main les rênes de leurs destinées." Le principe des nationalités; leur origines, les fondements psychologiques, les forces adverses, les solutions possibles,* Paris, 1930, p. 1.

14. Ferdinand Brunot, *Histoire de la langue française des origines à 1900,* Vol. VI, pt. 1, p. 135. A valuable analysis is Halvdan Koht's, "L'esprit national et l'idée de la souveraineté du peuple," *Bulletin of the International Committee of the Historical Sciences,* Vol. II, pt. II, 1929, pp. 217-24.

15. For examples see Daniel Mornet, *Les origines intellectuelles de la Révolution française, 1715-1787,* 4th ed., Paris, 1947, pp. 263-64; and Palmer, pp. 98-99. Part of Coyer's work constituted the article of the *Encyclopédie* on "Patrie."

16. Carlton J. H. Hayes, "The Philosopher Turned Patriot," *Essays in Intellectual History Dedicated to James Harvey Robinson,* ed. by James Shotwell, New York, 1929, pp. 189-206.

17. Robert R. Ergang, *Herder and the Foundations of German Nationalism,* New York, 1931, p. 43.

18. Mornet, pp. 260-64.

19. *Mercure de France,* Vol. I, April, 1765, p. 50. Quoted in Acomb, p. 54. The *Dictionnaire social et patriotique,* Amsterdam, 1770, by Lefèvre de Beauvray was both pious and monarchist, but he wrote, *"C'est à vous, ô ma Patrie, que je suis redevable de mon*

existence, de mon éducation, de mes sentimens, de mes idées; c'est donc à vous que j'en suis comptable."

20. H. F. Stewart and Paul Desjardins, eds., *French Patriotism in the Nineteenth Century (1814-1833)*, Cambridge, 1923, p. xvi.

21. *L'amour de la patrie: 19ᵉ Mercuriale prononcée à la Saint Martin*, 1715, in Stewart and Desjardins, p. xxi. Probably Aulard made too much of this panegyric in his *Le patriotisme français de la Renaissance à la Révolution*, Paris, 1916.

22. Tr. by Nugent, New York, 1900, Vol. I, p. 34, and the *avertissement* in some French editions.

23. Quoted in René Johannet, *Le principe des nationalités*, Paris, 1923, p. 78.

24. Bolingbroke's works have been published many times. I have used here the London 1775 edition of T. Davies. The above essays are paged together in this edition in Vol. I. The similar contemporary ideas of the Earl of Shaftesbury and Berkeley could also be cited here. Shaftesbury believed, "Of all human affections the noblest and most becoming to human nature is love of one's country."

25. Pp. 148-49.

26. P. 191. Cf. Carlton Hayes, *The Historical Evolution of Modern Nationalism*, New York, 1931, pp. 17-21; and Hans Kohn, *The Idea of Nationalism*, New York, 1943, pp. 212-15.

27. *Correspondence littéraire*, ed. by Tourneux, Vol. II, December 15, 1754, p. 445.

28. *Encyclopédie*, 1780 ed., Vol. XXIV, p. 472, "Patrie."

29. Leon Duguit, *Law in the Modern State*, tr. by Frida and Harold Laski, New York, 1919, p. 11, put it this way: "The king was a person, a subject of right, the holder of sovereign power; like him, the nation will be a person, the subject of right, the holder of sovereign power."

30. Brunot, Vol. VI, pt. 1, p. 137.

31. The French Constitution of 1791, though it established property qualifications for voting, declared that virtually everyone born in France, born of French parents anywhere, or who born anywhere took the civic oath, was or could become a French citizen.

32. *De la convocation de la prochaine tenue des états-généraux*, n.p., 1789, p. 20.

33. Quoted in Aulard, n. 6.

34. Michelet was not only poetic when he declared, *"La Révolution française, matérialiste en apparence dans sa division départmentale qui nomme les contrées par les fleuves, n'en efface pas moins les nationalités des provinces qui jusque-là, perpetuaient les fatalités locales au nom de la liberté . . . ,"* Introduction à *l'histoire universelle*, édition définitif, Paris, n.d., p. 460.

35. Johannet made clear the intimate relationship between internal right and external sovereignty in discussing the Rights of Man and Citizen of the French Constitution of 1791: *"Ce sont ceux où*

il est proclamé que la souveraineté reside dans la nation et que la loi est l'expression de la volonté générale. Il s'ensuit que la volonté générale, seule détentrice de la loi, a compétence pour définir sa souveraineté" (p. 85).

36. See his almost classic report "sur la réunion au territoire de la République de la ci-devant principauté de Monaco," *Archives Parlementaires*, Vol. LVIII, February 14, 1793, pp. 546-51.

37. Rousseau again and again had reiterated the point that only when the people had rights and responsibilities would they love their country, perform great deeds. *The Political Writings of Jean-Jacques Rousseau*, ed. by C. E. Vaughan, Cambridge, 1915, Vol. II, pp. 427, 492, 512. For discussion see Paul L. Léon, "Études critiques: Rousseau et les fondements de l'État moderne," "L'evolution de l'idée de la souveraineté avant Rousseau," "La notion de souveraineté dans la doctrine de Rousseau," *Archives de philosophie du droit et de sociologie juridique*, 4th, 7th, 8th années, 1934, 1937, 1938, pp. 197-237, 152-85, 231-69. In Léon's words (8th année, p. 269), Rousseau *"monopolisait tout le dynamisme du droit au profit d'une seule communauté nationale."*

38. Alexis de Tocqueville, *The State of Society in France . . .* , tr. by Reeve, London, 1888, pp. 92-93.

39. *Democracy in America,* tr. by Reeve, ed. by Bowen and Bradley, New York, 1945, pp. 242 ff. He added: "The most powerful, and perhaps the only means of interesting men in the welfare of their country . . . is to make them partakers in the government . . . civic zeal seems to me to be inseparable from the exercise of political rights."

40. The leading present-day authority on the French Revolution, Georges Lefebvre, perhaps exaggerated when he declared that the National Assembly "accomplished the juridical unity of the nation" in a few hours on the night of August 4, 1789, when it wiped out the feudal regime, the domination of the aristocracy, and started financial, legal, and ecclesiastical reform. *Quatre Vingt Neuf*, Paris, 1939, p. 189. The exaggeration, however, is chiefly one of time.

41. According to Brunot, Vol. VI, p. 140, *"Dans l'usage, en France, au nom de citoyen s'attachait de plus en plus l'idée de certains droits, mais surtout de certains devoirs envers la collectivité."*

42. Mirabeau remarked in 1782, "when the *patrie* is nothing, a man owes it nothing, because duties are mutual." Palmer, "National Idea in France before the Revolution," p. 108.

43. Sydney Smith in his sermon "On the Love of Country," *Sermons,* 1809, in Frederick Page, ed., *An Anthology of Patriotic Prose*, London, 1915, p. 127, directly identified Greek "virtue," the desire to do public service, with patriotism.

44. *Oeuvres complètes de Voltaire,* 1785, Vol. XLII, pp. 263-64.

CHAPTER VII (Pages 118-133)

1. *Oeuvres complètes de J. J. Rousseau*, Baudoin, 2nd ed., Paris, 1826, Vol. VI, pp. 240-41. Complaining of the then prevalent cosmopolitanism, he advised, "*Donnez une autre pente aux passions des Polonois, vous donnerez à leurs âmes une physionomie nationale qui les distinguera des autre peuples, qui les empêchera de se fondre, de se plaire, de s'allier avec eux; une vigueur qui remplacera le jeu abusif des vains preceptes, qui leur fera faire par gôut et par passion ce qu'on ne fait jamais assez bien quand on ne le fait que par devoir ou par intérêt*" (pp. 241-42). Rousseau claimed that men were dehumanized by cosmopolitanism. See Alexandre Choulguine, "Les origines de l'esprit national moderne et Jean-Jacques Rousseau," *Annales de la Société Jean-Jacques Rousseau*, Vol. XXVI, 1937, pp. 9-283, for development of Rousseau's thought.

2. *The Federalist*, rev. ed., New York, 1901, no. 16, p. 83.

3. Koppel S. Pinson, *Pietism as a Factor in the Rise of German Nationalism*, New York, 1934, p. 201.

4. *Archives parlementaires*, Vol. IV, p. 213. See also Beatrice Hyslop, *French Nationalism in 1789 according to the General Cahiers*, New York, 1934, p. 101.

5. The Catholic Church in France, as pointed out above, had already become partly national, *ecclesia gallicana*, instead of Roman Catholic.

6. These are the words of Count Nikolaus Ludwig von Zinzendorf, the Pietist leader who closely associated religion with the national climate. Pinson, p. 91.

7. The militia became national in France in 1789 and in the United States the name was first given them in 1824 when Lafayette visited the States. As early as 1781 Joseph Servan, or perhaps one Guibert, published a book called *Soldat Citoyen*.

8. *Moniteur universelle*, August 25, 1793, p. 1008. On Barère see Leo Gershoy, "Barère, Champion of Nationalism in the French Revolution," *Political Science Quarterly*, Vol. XLII, 1927, pp. 419-30.

9. The quoted words are Robespierre's from James Eagan, *Maximilien Robespierre, Nationalist Dictator*, New York, 1938, p. 185.

10. Voltaire made this point in his *Essai sur les moeurs*.

11. August Neithardt von Gneisenau, German general and patriot, discovered the importance and superiority of patriotic troops when he joined the British forces in North America in 1782, and he helped transform the Prussian Army after its defeats in 1806. See below, pp. 138-39, and Kohn, *Idea of Nationalism*, p. 379. In their published doctoral dissertations, students of Carlton Hayes like Ergang, Langsam, Pundt, and Engelbrecht have well described, though perhaps overemphasized, the patriotism of the

Germans of this period. See also Eugene Anderson, *Nationalism and the Cultural Crisis in Prussia, 1806-1815,* New York, 1939.

12. See Herder, *Ideen zur Philosophie der Geschichte der Menschheit,* in *Sämmtliche Werke,* ed. by Suphan, Vol. XIII, p. 350, for his well-known analogy.

13. This is a paraphrase of a 1790 letter from Limoges to Bishop Grégoire of the National Assembly in Ferdinand Brunot, *Histoire de la langue française,* Vol. IX, pt. I, Paris, 1927, p. 10. On the desire for and development of French the volumes of Brunot, particularly pt. I of Vol. VII and pts. I and II of Vol. IX, are exhaustive and indispensable. Germans, like Herder and Fichte especially, made much of the last argument but it was held quite generally.

14. Quoted in Brunot, Vol. VII, pt. I, p. 91. A like view was the Abbé Coyer's in his *Plan d'éducation* (1785), *"Du Latin. Qu'apprend on en sixième? Du Latin. En cinquième? Du Latin. En quatrième? Du Latin. En troisième? Du Latin. En seconde? Du Latin. Nulle connaissance de la Nature, des Arts, des Sciences utiles. Point de choses, mais des mots; et encore quels mots? Pas même la langue nationale, rien de ce qui convient le plus à l'homme."*

15. Johann Christoph Gottsched (1700-1766) went as far as any patriotic man could when he made his future wife, Louise Kulmus, use German instead of French in her letters.

16. Most of the above facts are taken from Kohn, *Idea of Nationalism,* and the volumes of Chaconas, Chadwick, Ergang, Megaro, and Pinson cited elsewhere. The number of patriots like Galeani-Napione, Piedmontese noble, who were demanding a national tongue to be used by all inhabitants in their respective nations steadily mounted. Emiliana Noether, *Seeds of Italian Nationalism, 1700-1815,* New York, 1951, pp. 127-29.

17. Or as Brunot, Vol. IX, p. 421, had it, *"La langue elle-même, sans être sous l'autorité de l'État, a gagné à la Révolution de devenir chose d'État."* See also his superb summary of the relation between the spread of the French language and patriotism (pp. 407-08).

18. *Moniteur,* January 28, 1794, pp. 519-20. The earlier National Assembly had sent out its laws and decrees in *"tous les idiomes."*

19. Quoted by Brunot, Vol. IX, p. 8.

20. *Moniteur,* January 28, 1794, pp. 519-20.

21. Mirabeau's plea for "perfectly intelligible laws" in French was only half realized. The laws were written in French but the gothic style was not buried with the remains of feudalism as he recommended. *Courrier de Provence,* Vol. CXII, 1790.

22. In Brunot, Vol. IX, p. 412.

23. *Ibid.,* Vol. VII, pt. I, pp. 3 and 228-30.

24. *The Spirit of Laws,* tr. by Nugent, New York, 1900, Bk. IV, par. 5, p. 34. Montesquieu thought parental example the best teacher

but in the preface to his great study he declared that he would think himself the happiest of mortals if he succeeded in giving "new reasons to every man to love his prince, his country, his laws. . . ."

25. Brunot, Vol. VII, pp. 141-42. Dupont de Nemours actually wrote what Turgot here suggested. About the same time President Rolland, a director of secondary education, also was looking for a plan of education able to bring *"cette révolution . . . faire renaître l'amour de la patrie."*

26. *Considérations sur le gouvernement de Pologne et sur sa réformation projettée en Avril 1772* is in Vol. VI and the *Letter to d'Alembert* is in Vol. II of *Oeuvres complètes de J. J. Rousseau.*

27. *Oeuvres,* Vol. VI, p. 256.

28. *Oeuvres,* Vol. II, pp. 190-91, 205-07.

29. *Ibid.,* p. 28.

30. Barère quoted Rousseau at length in a successful proposal for an Ecole de Mars. *Moniteur,* June 3, 1794, pp. 1038-39.

31. Frank Maloy Anderson, *Constitutions and Other Documents Illustrative of French History,* New York, 1904, pp. 62-63.

32. Following Barère's speech the Convention decreed the establishment of the École de Mars, *Moniteur,* June 3, 1794, pp. 1038-39. See discussion in Carlton Hayes, *Historical Evolution of Modern Nationalism,* New York, 1931, p. 62.

33. Boyd C. Shafer, "When Patriotism Became Popular," *Historian,* Spring, 1943, pp. 77-96, treats the whole federation movement. The good early German nationalist Herder called the celebration "a divine and sacred festival."

34. An outdated but handy summary is Edward Reisner, *Nationalism and Education since 1789,* New York, 1922. See the footnote on educational attempts to inculcate patriotism, p. 281.

35. On the United States see Harry Warfel, *Noah Webster, Schoolmaster to America,* New York, 1936, pp. 56-60, 88, 93-94; Allen O. Hansen, *Liberalism and American Education in the Eighteenth Century,* New York, 1926, pp. 48 ff., where there are described nine plans for an American national system of education put forward between 1785 and 1800; and Charles Cole "Jeremy Belknap: Pioneer Nationalist," *New England Quarterly,* Vol. X, 1937, pp. 743-51.

36. Herder published folksongs of the Norse, Spanish, Serbs, and English, among others, in *Alte Volkslieder* and *Volkslieder* in 1778-79.

37. Robert Ergang, "Klopstock's Odes and Bardiete," in Edward M. Earle, ed., *Nationalism and Internationalism,* New York, 1950, pp. 124-26.

38. Walter Langsam, *The Napoleonic Wars and German Nationalism in Austria,* New York, 1930, p. 184.

39. In his Farewell Address Washington saw the "most commanding motives" for the union in the economic advantages of trade

and commerce between the North and South, the East and West. *Messages and Papers,* ed. by Richardson, Vol. I, pp. 213 ff.

40. Everyman's ed., Vol. I, bk. 4, chap. 2, p. 408. About the same time David Hume, no narrow patriot, made a nationalist argument for *laissez faire* when he prayed for "the flourishing commerce of Germany, Spain, Italy and even France itself"—for he was certain "that Great Britain and all other nations would flourish more" were this policy adopted. "Of the Jealousy of Trade," *Essays, Moral, Political and Literary,* ed. by T. H. Green and T. H. Grose, London, 1898, p. 348. See also Eli Hecksher, *Mercantilism,* London, 1935, Vol. II, p. 14.

41. "Report on Manufactures," to House of Representatives, December 5, 1791, *The Works of Alexander Hamilton,* ed. by Henry Cabot Lodge, Vol. IV, p. 135.

42. Fichte's *The Closed Commercial State* pointedly asked for national intervention in economic affairs for the welfare of the citizen. The classic argument of List came forty years later. In mid-eighteenth-century Italy the Abbé Genovesi lectured at Naples on the elimination of economic and political divisions in order to increase Italian prosperity. Noether, *Seeds of Italian Nationalism,* pp. 89 ff.

43. *Moniteur,* May 13, 1794, pp. 949-52.

44. See the discussion of the effect of crises on liberal democratic states in the Royal Institute of International Affairs, *Nationalism,* London, 1939, p. 39.

45. On eighteenth-century French opinion of the English, for example, see Frances Acomb, *Anglophobia in France, 1763-1769,* Durham, 1950. Prejudices went deep, even among the intelligent. Minnie Muller, in *Modern Philology,* Vol. XXXIV, 1937, pp. 365-76, analyzed in French journals for the years 1703-1762 to find that French observers believed the English, while honest and liberty loving, lacked taste and exhibited excessive pride. The French often spoke of the English as unstable, vacillating, and too prone to disorder.

46. Quoted in Johannet, pp. 18-19.

47. Quoted in F. Baldensperger, *La Révolution française,* Vol. XLIX, 1905, pp. 263-64.

48. Hans Kohn, like a good many recent historians, dates the nationalist quickening in the Germanies somewhat later, "The Eve of German Nationalism," *Journal of the History of Ideas,* Vol. XII, 1951, pp. 256-84. Most earlier writers have chosen 1807-08.

CHAPTER VIII (Pages 134-151)

1. *L'Europe et la Révolution française,* Paris, 1946, Vol. I, pp. 419-20.
2. *Archives parlementaires,* Vol. XXXVII, pp. 493-94. See *ibid.,* Vol. LII, pp. 468, 472, for other examples.

3. Alfred Cobban, ed., *The Debate on the French Revolution,*
London, 1950, is a collection of excerpts from major British
sources. See also Crane Brinton, *A Decade of Revolution, 1789-
1799,* New York, 1934, pp. 167-74.

4. Quoted by John Gazley, "Arthur Young, British Patriot," in
Edward M. Earle, ed., *Nationalism and Internationalism,* New
York, 1950, pp. 170-72. By 1793, after the fall of Louis XVI,
Young in the typical fashion of the modern patriot, saw Britain's
war against France as the "war of humanity" against "ravagers
and destroyers."

5. *Reflections . . . ,* Bohn ed., London, 1864, Vol. II, p. 306.

6. *Ibid.,* Vol. II, p. 368.

7. Louis L. Snyder (*German Nationalism: The Tragedy of a People,*
Harrisburg, 1952, introd.) sums up the German reaction thus,
"The attempt of the Corsican to spread the ideals of the French
Revolution, as interpreted by himself, into the Germanies by
force of arms provided the exterior spark which ignited the fires
of German nationalism."

8. The literature on the German nationalist awakening is volu-
minous. The following studies, of those in English, were chiefly
used here. Eugene N. Anderson, *Nationalism and the Cultural
Crisis in Prussia, 1806-1815,* New York, 1939; H. C. Engelbrecht,
*Johann Gottlieb Fichte: A Study of His Writings with Special
Reference to His Nationalism,* New York, 1933; Robert R.
Ergang, *Herder and the Foundations of German Nationalism,*
New York, 1931; the three articles by Hans Kohn on Arndt,
Fichte, and Jahn in the *American Historical Review,* Vol. LIV,
1949, pp. 787-803, the *Journal of the History of Ideas,* Vol.
X, 1949, pp. 319-43, and the *Review of Politics,* Vol. XI, 1949,
pp. 419-32; Koppel S. Pinson, *Pietism as a Factor in the Rise
of German Nationalism,* New York, 1934; Alfred G. Pundt,
Arndt and the Nationalist Awakening in Germany, New York,
1935; and Snyder, *German Nationalism.* The effect of Fichte's
Addresses to the German Nation has probably been overrated;
they were not popular in his day. The over-all picture is solidly
painted in Alfred Stern and others, *Die Französische Revolution,
Napoleon und die Restauration, 1789-1848,* Berlin, 1929, esp. pp.
1-248.

9. Quoted in Eugene Anderson, p. 183. This is exactly what the
Boyen military training law establishing universal military training attempted in 1814. Friedrich Meinecke, *The German Catastrophe,* tr. by S. B. Fay, Cambridge, Mass., 1950, p. 105.

10. Quoted by Walter C. Langsam, *The Napoleonic Wars and German Nationalism in Austria,* New York, 1930, pp. 67-68.

11. Pinson, p. 193.

12. Pundt, p. 80. In his *Kurzer Katechismus für den teutschen Kriegs-
und Wehrmann,* Arndt taught, "*Und ihr sollet euch wieder
brüderlich gesellen zu einander, alle, die ihr Deutsche heisset und*

in deutscher Zunge redet, und den Trug bejammern, der euch so lange entzweit hat."

13. Even by those who emigrated like Francis Lieber, who learned the nationalism he later evinced in the United States from Napoleon's conquest of Prussia, especially Jena. Merle Curti, "Francis Lieber and Nationalism," reprint from *Huntington Library Quarterly,* Vol. IV, 1941.

14. Charles Schmidt, in "Notes et Lectures," *La Révolution française,* Vol. XLVI, 1904, pp. 244-45.

15. Gaudens Megaro, *Vittorio Alfieri, Forerunner of Italian Nationalism,* New York, 1930, esp. pp. 94-105.

16. See, for example, Hans Kohn, *Idea of Nationalism,* New York, 1943, pp. 524-26; Stephen George Chaconas, *Adamantios Korais: A Study in Greek Nationalism,* New York, 1942; H. Munro Chadwick, *The Nationalities of Europe and the Growth of National Ideologies,* Cambridge, 1945; Wesley M. Gewehr, *The Rise of Nationalism in the Balkans, 1800-1930,* New York, 1931; and Arnold J. Toynbee, *The Balkans, a History of Bulgaria, Serbia, Greece, Rumania, Turkey,* Oxford, 1915, p. 247.

17. Kohn, *Idea of Nationalism,* p. 524.

18. Quoted by Chaconas, p. 96.

19. See especially chapter one of *Nationalism and the Cultural Crisis in Prussia.* A recent psychological study, T. W. Adorno and others, *The Authoritarian Personality,* New York, 1950, throws doubt on this hypothesis.

20. Professor Anderson's thesis is illustrated by his account of the Prussian aristocrat Heinrich von Kleist (1777-1811): "Nationalism offered a solution to almost all the problems which beset Kleist's life. The defeat and elimination of the French and the conclusion of peace would restore conditions in which he could earn a satisfactory living from his writing and thereby fulfill his destiny. Nationalism provided him with the opportunity and the incentive for achieving a great deed. It would enable him to recover his prestige with his family, to reestablish and maintain intimacy with society. . . . Above all, nationalism gave Kleist absolute assurance as to what he should do. . . . The crisis of 1808 revealed to him with perfect clarity his mission to save the nation" (p. 135).

21. See the discussion in Frederick Schuman, *International Politics,* 4th ed., New York, 1948, pp. 422 ff.

22. *Archives parlementaires,* Vol. LXXVIII, November 5, 1793, pp. 373-75. See also A. Aulard, *Le culte de la Raison et le culte de l'Être Suprême,* Paris, 1892, p. 35.

23. Pinson, p. 184.

24. J. M. Thompson, *The French Revolution,* New York, 1945, p. 258.

25. Pinson, p. 98.

26. Quoted in Carlton Hayes, *Historical Evolution of Modern Nationalism*, New York, 1931, p. 68.
27. In H. F. Stewart and Paul Desjardins, eds., *French Patriotism in the Nineteenth Century (1814-1833)*, Cambridge, 1923, p. 5. Carlton Hayes quotes a revolutionary as saying, "In 1794 we believed in no supernatural religion; our serious interior sentiments were all summed up in one idea, how to be useful to the fatherland. Everything else,—raiment, food, advancement,—was in our eyes only trivial detail. . . . For us, who knew no other large assemblies, there were numerous fetes and rites which nourished the dominant sentiment in our hearts. It was our only religion" (p. 55).
28. B. J. Buchez and P. C. Roux, *Histoire parlementaire de la Révolution française*, Vol. XV, Paris, 1835, p. 42.
29. See the discussion in Royal Institute of International Affairs, *Nationalism*, pp. 33-34; and Pinson, pp. 201 and 204.
30. Ferdinand Brunot, *Histoire de la langue française*, Vol. IX, pt. I, Paris, 1927, p. 625.
31. On July 9, 1789, the priest Grégoire spoke in the National Assembly of the crime of *lèse-Majesté Nationale*. The Assembly then provided for the crime of *lèse-Nation* and established a special court for it at Orleans. Brunot, Vol. IX, pt. I, p. 637. Very soon the term "nationomicide" was also invented.
32. Fichte gave the ultimate justification for this conformity when he declared that the state had a "higher object than the usual one of maintaining internal peace, property, personal freedom, and the life and well-being of all. . . . What spirit has an undisputed right to summon and to order everyone concerned, whether he himself be willing or not, and to compel anyone who resists, to risk everything including his life? Not the spirit of the peaceful citizen's love for the constitution and the laws, but the devouring flame of higher patriotism, which embraces the nation as the vesture of the eternal, for which the noble-minded man joyfully sacrifices himself, and the ignoble man, who only exists for the sake of the other, must likewise sacrifice himself." *Addresses to the German Nation*, tr. by Jones and Turnbull, pp. 140-41.
33. *Archives parlementaires*, Vol. LV, Thuriot speech, p. 79.
34. *L'Ami des Patriotes ou le défenseur de constitution*, Vol. II, p. 89, cited in Brunot, p. 635 n.
35. To a Swiss professor, Johann Füssli, in his 1775 *Catechetische Anleitung zu den gesellschaftlichen Pflichten*, the chief duty of every citizen toward his fatherland was "To sacrifice willingly and joyfully his property and life to it." Kohn, *Idea of Nationalism*, p. 385.
36. From F. X. Joliclerc, *Volontaire aux armées de la Révolution: ses lettres 1793-1796*, ed. by Etienne Joliclerc, 1905, pp. 141-43. Cited by Hayes, *op. cit.*, pp. 55-56.

37. See, for example, Sorel, *L'Europe et la Révolution française*, Vol. I, p. 419, for a young peasant who believed and eagerly sought to assume personal responsibility.
38. Albert Mathiez, *Les origines des cultes révolutionnaires*, Paris, 1904, p. 31.
39. *Moniteur*, August 25, 1793, p. 1008. He was arguing for the *levée en masse*.
40. The first altars to the *patrie* were erected during the Federation movement in 1790.
41. Brunot, Vol. IX, pp. 664-66. The comment of the contemporary newspaper *Journal des clubs ou sociétés patriotes* is pertinent here: "*Mon énergumène monte sur l'impériale, harangue le peuple, fait sonner les mots d'accaparement, de* sang *du peuple . . . et surtout de patriotisme. Les têtes se tournent. Le moyen de l'empêcher. Aujourd'hui c'est tout dire: le patriotisme! Soyez mauvais fils, mauvais père, mauvais mari, mauvais ami, mauvais citoyen aux yeux de la loi; soyez sans foi, sans honneur, sans vertus, sans talents; soyez sans état, banqueroutier, flétri; si vous avez du patriotisme . . . vous êtes le type et le prototype des bons citoyens.*" In Sigismond Lacroix, *Actes de la Commune de Paris*, Paris, 1906–, 2d series, Vol. II, p. 582.
42. As is well known the song was originally written to inspire love for the emperor. All of these songs would only later become officially the national songs.
43. Quoted in Brunot, Vol. IX, p. 73.
44. This oath in part was "*je m'unis de corps, de biens, de volonté et de toute ma puissance, à la nation corse, pour lui appartenir en toute propriété, moi et tout ce qui dépend de moi. Je jure de vivre et mourir pour elle, d'observer toute ses lois et d'obéir à ses chefs et magistrats légitimes en tout ce qui sera conforme aux lois.*" In *The Political Writings of Jean-Jacques Rousseau*, ed. by C. E. Vaughn, Cambridge, 1915, Vol. II, p. 350.
45. Created by John Arbuthnot in 1712 to represent the doggedness of the Whigs fighting Louis XIV.
46. Albert Mathiez, p. 27.
47. Gazley, "Arthur Young, British Patriot," in Earle, ed., *Nationalism and Internationalism*, p. 150.
48. These excerpts of the decrees are from John Hall Stewart, *A Documentary Survey of the French Revolution*, New York, 1951, pp. 381-83.
49. As the National Convention stated in its proclamation to Savoy, October 6, 1792, *Archives parlementaires*, Vol. LII, p. 472.

CHAPTER IX (Pages 155-181)

1. *Mémoire adressé au Roi en juillet 1814*, Brussels, 1814. See Carlton Hayes, *France: A Nation of Patriots*, New York, 1930, p. 12; Huntley Dupre, *Lazare Carnot, Republican Patriot*, Oxford

(Ohio), 1940, pp. 272-73, and his article, "Carnot's Nationalism," *South Atlantic Quarterly*, Vol. XXXVIII, 1938, pp. 291-306.
2. Quoted in Carlton Hayes, *The Historical Evolution of Modern Nationalism*, New York, 1931, p. 115.
3. C. H. Van Tyne, *The War of Independence: American Phase*, Boston, 1929, p. 271.
4. The best guide to Metternich's views are his historically unreliable memoirs, which few read and still fewer can enjoy.
5. An informed survey of nineteenth-century national ideas is Georges Weill, *L'Europe du XIXᵉ siècle et l'idée de nationalité*, Paris, 1938.
6. Max Boehm (*Das eigenständige Volk: Volkstheoretische Grundlagen der Ethnopolitik und Geisteswissenschaften*, Göttingen, 1932) and H. L. Featherstone (*A Century of Nationalism*, London, 1939) discuss the relationship of liberalism and nationalism in the nineteenth century, but, in the Germanies and central and eastern Europe where conservatism persisted and usually dominated, nationalism of different types was not any the weaker. But compare for the Germanies, Walter M. Simon, "Variations in Nationalism during the Great Reform Period in Prussia," *American Historical Review*, Vol. LIX, 1954, pp. 305-21.
7. Joseph de Maistre argued in 1797 that the French Revolutionary constitutions, made for man, were fit for none because there were only particular men. *Considérations sur la France*, in *Oeuvres complètes*, Vol. I, Paris, 1924, p. 74.
8. Robert C. Binkley, *Realism and Nationalism, 1852-71*, New York, 1935, *passim*, esp. pp. 230, 263.
9. He went so far as to include the doubtfully German Alsace-Lorraine, thus providing nationalist France with a cause for a half-century.
10. In addition to the works cited in the previous chapter, p. 273, see R. W. Seton-Watson, *The Rise of Nationality in the Balkans*, London, 1917.
11. See his "The Principle of Nationality and Its Applications," in *Essays and Addresses in War Time*, New York, 1918, pp. 141-75. The argument for self-determination was concisely put by Theodore Ruyssen, *The Principle of Nationality*, International Conciliation Pamphlet no. 109, December, 1916.
12. Georg Schwarzenberger, *Power Politics. An Introduction to the Study of International Relations and Post-War Planning*, London, 1941, p. 67.
13. Depending upon the definition of a language. H. Munro Chadwick, *The Nationalities of Europe and the Growth of National Ideologies*, Cambridge, 1945, p. 14.
14. For facts and figures see the Fish, Cole, Nevins, and Schlesinger volumes in the "History of American Life" series.
15. Eugene Staley quite conclusively proved that this economic imperialism did not pay, that the nation-state, not the private

investor, usually lost. *War and the Private Investor,* New York, 1935. But this was a scholarly conclusion reached in hindsight and changed few opinions.

16. J. Bowring (British representative), *Report on the Prussian Customs Union,* p. 17, quoted by W. L. Ashley, *Modern Tariff History,* London, 1904, p. 14.

17. On national economic policies see particularly Shepard Clough, *France: A History of National Economics, 1789-1939,* New York, 1939; J. H. Clapham, *The Economic Development of France and Germany, 1815-1914,* Cambridge, 1921; and Herbert Heaton, *Economic History of Europe,* New York, 1936.

18. *An Inquiry into the Nature of Peace and the Terms of Its Perpetration,* New York, 1919, p. 292.

19. *Socialism National or International,* London, 1942, pp. 57-58. See also D. W. Brogan, *The Price of Revolution,* New York, 1952, p. 264.

20. Shepard Clough (pp. 222 and 453) reveals how the great French socialist Jean Jaurès put national interests first. On the French socialists see Harold Weinstein, *Jean Jaurès: A Study of Patriotism in the French Socialist Movement,* New York, 1936; and Alexandre Choulguine, "Les origines de l'esprit national moderne et Jean-Jacques Rousseau," *Annales de la Société Jean-Jacques Rousseau,* Vol. XXVI, 1937, p. 273. On the German socialists see C. J. H. Hayes, "Influence of Political Tactics on Socialist Theory in Germany," in *A History of Political Theories, Recent Times,* ed. by Charles Merriam and Harry Elmer Barnes, New York, 1924; William Maehl, "The Triumph of Nationalism in the German Socialist Party on the Eve of the First World War," *Journal of Modern History,* Vol. XXIV, March, 1952; and Richard Hostetter, "The S.P.D. and the General Strike as an Anti-war Weapon, 1905-1914," *Historian,* Autumn, 1950.

21. *Marxism and the National and Colonial Question,* New York, 1935, pp. 18, 52-53, 56.

22. Cf. Hans Kohn, *Nationalism in the Soviet Union,* New York, 1933, *passim.*

23. *Manifesto of the Communist Party,* New York, 1938, p. 19. Marx, it should be noted, also argued that the struggle of the proletariat against the bourgeoisie had to be first of all carried on nationally, that the proletariat must first "raise itself to the position of the national class, must constitute itself the nation." But Communists, depending upon exigencies, have been able to read into Marx's ideas many different courses of action.

24. See Friedrich Meinecke, *The German Catastrophe,* tr. by S. B. Fay, New York, 1950, for an analysis of German experience.

25. In Tsarist Russia and possibly other nations in 1914 some political leaders were for war because it would arouse patriotism which would prevent social revolution. Sidney B. Fay, *Origins of the World War,* New York, 1928, Vol. II, p. 305; and Joseph

Swain, *Beginning the Twentieth Century,* New York, 1933, p. 346.

26. Maurras believed the absence of strikes in the Stinnes, Thyssen, and Krupp establishments was owing to the "German national spirit" and therefore he thought "popular education oriented in the national sense . . . more and more indispensable." William C. Buthman, *The Rise of Integral Nationalism in France, with Special Reference to the Ideas and Activities of Charles Maurras,* New York, 1939, p. 328.

27. An extreme view on the effect of this anxiety is Sebastian de Grazia, *The Political Community: A Study of Anomie,* Chicago, 1948. J. Coatman calls nationalism "a frightened response of the specie-making, segregating impulse against the resistless-imperious demand of the ever-widening evolutionary process toward internationalism." *Magna Britannia,* London, 1936, p. 92.

28. On the Greeks cf. C. W. Crawley, *The Question of Greek Independence,* Cambridge, 1930, p. 10, where it is said that the Greeks were not motivated by Western political ideals but by "a sense of injustice, a growing measure of prosperity and power, combined with religious zeal. . . ." But this is exactly what led to the growing nationalism.

29. J. L. Comstock, *History of the Greek Revolution,* New York, 1828, p. 143 n.

30. The passionate Mazzinian Oath of Young Italy reveals the feeling of shame, oppression, and hope that drove so many men to nationalism. It ends, "By the sufferings of the millions—I swear to dedicate myself wholly and forever to strive to constitute Italy one free, independent, republican nation." J. H. Rose, *Nationality in Modern History,* New York, 1916, pp. 81-82. Examples could easily be multiplied but let one more suffice. Kollar, the impassioned Czech poet, blamed the Germans for suffocating Czech culture, "Shame on you, Germany! Your hand is soiled with the blood of this crime." E. Denis, *La Bohême depuis la Montagne Blanche,* Paris, 1903, Vol. II, pp. 149-50.

31. See particularly Schwarzenberger, *Power Politics,* p. 59.

32. Eugene Anderson's *Nationalism and the Cultural Crisis in Prussia, 1806-1815,* New York, 1939, as indicated earlier, supports this thesis, but it should be pointed out that the psychologists T. W. Adorno and others, authors of *The Authoritarian Personality,* New York, 1950, find no certain relationship between abnormal mental states and fascism, believe that the social and economic patterns are more significant, that the authoritarian personality is frequently the better "adjusted."

33. The Frenchman Gambetta was of Italian descent, the Hungarian Kossuth of Slovak, the Irish Parnell of English, the Rumanian Codreanu of Polish, Hungarian, and German. Walter Sulzbach, *National Consciousness,* Washington, 1943, pp. 106-17. Among the most patriotic of the post-World War I Hungarians were

Jews and Germans. Rustem Vambery, "Nationalism in Hungary," *Annals of the American Academy of Political and Social Science,* Vol. CCXXXII, 1944, p. 82.

34. E. F. Durbin and John Bowlby point to a necessary qualification: "The phenomena of the identification of the individual with the group is far from simple. . . . Persons hate the State as well as love it. . . . In general, it may be affirmed that the vast majority of human beings feel themselves strongly identified with the fortunes of some group outside themselves." *Personal Aggressiveness and War,* New York, 1939, pp. 37-39.

35. As Lord Bryce remarked, of no people has hope been more characteristic than the Americans. *The American Commonwealth,* New York, 1924, Vol. II, p. 290. For general discussion see A. A. Ekirch, Jr., *The Idea of Progress in America, 1815-1860,* New York, 1944; and Boyd C. Shafer, "The American Heritage of Hope," *Mississippi Valley Historical Review,* Vol. XXXVII, 1950, pp. 427-51. The last two list significant sources.

36. This is clearest in the writings of the poets. Paul Déroulède sang, "*Mon premier frère est le frère français.*"

37. Mazzini's writings all exude this personal involvement, this realization of personal aims in national ideals. See especially *Mazzini's Letters,* tr. by Jervis, London, 1930; and the sparkling essay by Hans Kohn in his *Prophets and Peoples,* New York, 1946.

38. For the United States see Albert Weinberg, *Manifest Destiny. A Study of Nationalist Expansion in American History,* Baltimore, 1935. Of Pan-Slavism Hans Kohn has written the best account, *Pan Slavism: Its History and Ideology,* Notre Dame, 1953. Pan-Germanism can be sampled in Mildred Wertheimer, *The Pan-German League, 1890-1914,* New York, 1924. Comparable studies do not exist for other countries but for examples of the French and British messianic zeal see Georges Goyau, *L'idée de patrie et l'humanitarisme: Essai d'histoire française, 1866-1901,* Paris, 1913; Lucien Romier, *Nation et civilisation,* Paris, 1926; Louis Réau, *L'Europe française,* Paris, 1930; Sir Charles Dilke, *Greater Britain,* New York, 1869; John Cramb, *The Origins and Destiny of Imperial Britain and Nineteenth Century Europe,* New York, 1915; Evelyn Baring Cromer, *Ancient and Modern Imperialism,* London, 1910; and of course the various last wills and testaments of Cecil Rhodes.

39. *Le peuple,* Paris, 1946, p. 271.

40. *Mazzini's Letters,* pp. 104-05, 168-69, 188.

41. Frederick Artz, *Reaction and Revolution, 1814-1832,* New York, 1934, pp. 239-41.

42. John Wuorinen, "Scandinavia and National Consciousness," in E. M. Earle, ed., *Nationalism and Internationalism,* New York, 1950, pp. 469-70. See also his *Nationalism in Modern Finland,* New York, 1931; and Andreas Elviken, "The Genesis of Nor-

wegian Nationalism," *Journal of Modern History*, Vol. III, 1931, pp. 365-91, for other examples.

43. Frederick Page, ed., *An Anthology of Patriotic Prose*, Oxford, 1915, p. 158.

44. *An Inquiry into the Nature of Peace*, p. 31.

45. Ruth and David Stevens, *American Patriotic Prose and Verse*, Chicago, 1918, pp. 63-64.

46. Buthman, *Rise of Integral Nationalism in France*, p. 86. See also Maurice Barrès, *The Undying Spirit of France*, New Haven, 1917.

47. Ernst Kantorowicz, "Pro Patria Mori in Medieval Political Thought," *American Historical Review*, Vol. LVI, 1951, p. 472.

48. J. G. Frazer, *Totemism and Exogamy*, London, 1910, pp. 91 ff. Alexander Goldenweiser soundly criticizes Frazer's hypotheses in *History, Psychology, and Culture*, New York, 1933, pp. 213-361.

CHAPTER X   (Pages 182-195)

1. Two solid contemporary surveys are J. T. Delos, *La Nation*, Vol. I, *Sociologie de la nation*, Montreal, 1944, esp. pp. 140-53, and Florjan Znaniecki, *Modern Nationalities, a Sociological Study*, Urbana, 1952. An able earlier analysis is Charles E. Merriam, *The Making of Citizens*, Chicago, 1931, pp. 1-26; an ambitious recent study is Karl Deutsch, *Nationalism and Social Communication: An Inquiry into the Foundations of Nationality*, New York, 1953, esp. p. 146.

2. For example, Margaret Mead, Geoffrey Gorer, Ruth Benedict, Weston La Barre, and Erik Erickson give to the psychology of infant discipline the importance earlier writers have attributed to race or geography in personality development. A summary is Margaret Mead, "The Study of National Character," in Daniel Lerner, et al., eds., *The Policy Sciences: Recent Developments in Scope and Methods*, Stanford, 1951, pp. 70-85. For critiques see John Orlandsky, "Destiny in the Nursery," *Commentary*, Vol. V, 1948, pp. 563-69; and John Embree, "Standardized Error and Japanese Character," *World Politics*, Vol. III, 1950, pp. 439-43.

3. Sample studies are E. L. Horowitz, "Some Aspects of Development of Patriotism in Children," *Sociometry*, Vol. III, 1940, pp. 329-41; H. Meltzer, "Hostility and Tolerance in Children's Nationality and Race Attitudes," *American Journal of Orthopsychiatry*, Vol. XI, 1941, pp. 662-76; and Ross Stagner, "Nationalism," in P. L. Harriman, *Encyclopedia of Psychology*, New York, 1946, p. 404.

4. Gerald Pearson, "Some Early Factors in the Formation of Personality," *American Journal of Orthopsychiatry*, Vol. I, 1931, p. 290.

5. J. Piaget, "The Development in Children of the Idea of the Homeland and of Relations with Other Countries," *International Social Science Bulletin*, Vol. III, 1951, p. 561.

6. Paraphrased from a Clemenceau speech in 1907, quoted in Alexandre Choulguine, "Les origines de l'esprit national moderne et Jean-Jacques Rousseau," *Annales de la Société Jean-Jacques Rousseau,* Vol. XXVI, 1937, p. 27.

7. Floyd Allport, "The Psychology of Nationalism," *Harpers Monthly Magazine,* Vol. CLV, 1927, p. 294; and Ralph Linton, *The Cultural Background of Personality,* New York, 1945, pp. 137-43. The thesis is maintained for German nationalism in Bertram Schaffner, *Fatherland: A Study of Authoritarianism in the German Family,* New York, 1945.

8. On education and nationalism there are a wealth of studies, some of them good: Cecilia H. Bason, *Study of the Homeland and Civilization in the Elementary Schools of Germany,* New York, 1937; Walter C. Langsam, "Nationalism and History in the Prussian Elementary Schools under William II," in E. M. Earle, ed., *Nationalism and Internationalism,* New York, 1950; Howard Marraro, *Nationalism in Italian Education,* New York, 1927; Merriam, *The Making of Citizens* (best summary of early research); Ruth Miller, "Nationalism in Elementary Schoolbooks Used in the United States from 1776 to 1885," Ph.D. dissertation, Columbia University, 1952, typescript; Bessie Pierce, *Civic Attitudes in American School Textbooks,* Chicago, 1930; Edward H. Reisner, *Nationalism and Education since 1789,* New York, 1922; Jonathan Scott, *Patriots in the Making: What America Can Learn from France and Germany,* New York, 1916; Mark Starr, *Lies and Hate in Education,* London, 1929; Arthur Walworth, *School Histories at War,* Cambridge (Mass.), 1938; and Gregor Ziemer, *Education for Death: The Making of a Nazi,* New York, 1941.

9. Miller, pp. 394, 401.

10. From his speech on "La Loi sur la liberté d'enseignement supérieur," in *Discours et opinions de Jules Ferry,* edited by Paul Robiquet, Paris, 1895, Vol. III, p. 66.

11. For examples of official views see Otto Klineberg, *Tensions Affecting International Understanding: A Survey of Research,* New York, 1950, p. 88; Anatole G. Mazour and Herman Bateman, "Recent Conflicts in Soviet Historiography," *Journal of Modern History,* Vol. XXIV, 1952, pp. 57-59; Reisner, pp. 194-95; and Scott, pp. 21-26.

12. *The American Mind: An Interpretation of American Thought and Character since the 1880's,* New Haven, 1950, pp. 38-39.

13. Pierce, pp. 125-29. Possibly the English were less blatantly nationalistic. But the great public (private) schools formed English gentlemen, and the schoolbooks held up the great English heroes as models. Lord Cromer viewed these schools as the "natural nurseries of a very perfervid patriotism." *Political and Literary Essays,* London, 1916, p. 156. Imperialists like the Earl of Meath insisted that all the schools should teach the "solid foundations

of British patriotism." See his essay, "The Cultivation of Patriotism," in W. H. Dawson, ed., *After-War Problems,* London, 1917.

14. Scott, p. 41, quoting Aulard and Bayet, *Morale et instruction civique,* pt. I, p. 51.

15. The magazine *Youth's Companion* originated this pledge in 1892 as part of a patriotic publicity campaign. It was first publicly given at a National Public School celebration, October 21, 1892, at the opening of the World's Fair in Chicago, and was then repeated by 12,000,000 children, according to a letter of R. P. Joy of *Youth's Companion* to Professor Edward Mead Earle, June 29, 1925. Wallis Johnson (*The National Flag,* Boston, 1930, pp. 95-96) attributes the oath to a James B. Upham. The British more modestly claimed that only 500,000 children participated in Empire Day in 1928. Starr, p. 67.

16. *Mein Kampf,* tr. by R. Manheim, Boston, 1943, p. 426.

17. Lucy M. Salmon, "Study of History below the Secondary School," App. II of "The Study of History in the Schools, Being the Report to the American Historical Association by the Committee of Seven" (Andrew McLaughlin, chr.), *Annual Report of the American Historical Association,* 1898, p. 512 n. But see Charles Langlois and Charles Seignobos, *Introduction to the Study of History,* tr. by G. G. Perry, London, 1912, p. 331 n., who argue in the text for objectivity.

18. Pierce, pp. 125-29. H. G. Wells, British novelist and internationalist, rightly observed, "We have all been so taught and trained to patriotic attitudes, they have been drummed into us from our home, at school, in book, drama, in the common idioms of thought, they have been so built into the substance of our minds, that it is only by a considerable intellectual effort that any of us can liberate ourselves from the forms of thought to which we have been moulded." *The Common Sense of World Peace,* London, 1929, p. 29.

19. A good though dated survey of nationalist historians is H. Morse Stephens' American Historical presidential address, "Nationality and History," *American Historical Review,* Vol. XXI, 1916, which refers to his earlier essay, "Modern Historians and Their Influence on Small Nationalities," *Contemporary Review,* July, 1887. Additional illustrations are in G. P. Gooch, *History and Historians in the Nineteenth Century,* London, 1920; and R. W. Seton-Watson, *The Historian as a Political Force in Central Europe,* London, 1922. The great Lavisse is reported to have said, "If I did not give to the flag a pagan's cult for his idol, I do not know what I would do in this world." E. M. Carroll, *French Public Opinion and Foreign Affairs,* New York, 1931, p. 253.

20. Allan Nevins and Milton H. Thomas, eds., *The Diary of George Templeton Strong,* New York, 1952, pp. 196-97.

21. Louis Snyder, *German Nationalism: The Tragedy of a People,* Harrisburg, 1952, has a thoughtful chapter on the German historians.
22. Among the books on heroes are Eric Bentley, *A Century of Hero Worship,* Philadelphia, 1944; Sidney Hook, *The Hero in History,* New York, 1942; and Dixon Wecter, *The Hero in America: A Chronicle of Hero Worship,* New York, 1941. Thomas Carlyle, of course, led the way.
23. Ramsey Muir (*Nationalism and Internationalism: The Culmination of Modern History,* London, 1917, pp. 43, 48) believed these traditions the "soul of nations." Sir John Seeley called "that man uncivilized" who was "not connected with the past through the state in which he lives, and significantly with the great men that have lived in it." W. Macneille Dixon, *The Englishman,* New York, 1931, p. 10.
24. *Bismarck,* New York, 1919, p. 16.
25. A beginning American study is R. W. Bolwell, "Concerning the Study of Nationalism in American Literature," *American Literature,* Vol. X, 1939, pp. 405-16. A superficial treatment on a subject well worth investigation is Helen Martin, "Nationalism in Children's Literature," *Library Quarterly,* Vol. VI, 1936, pp. 405-16.
26. See Hans Kohn's penetrating essay, "Romanticism and the Rise of German Nationalism," *Review of Politics,* Vol. XII, 1950, pp. 443-72.
27. Among the many surveys and anthologies of patriotic writings are: John Drinkwater, *Patriotism in Literature,* London, 1924; Edmund G. Gardner, *The National Idea in Italian Literature,* Manchester, 1921; Ch. Lenient, *La poésie patriotique en France au moyen âge. La poésie patriotique en France, XVIᵉ et XVIIᵉ siècles. La poésie patriotique en France dans les temps modernes,* Paris, 1891 and 1894, 3 vols.; Frederick Page, ed., *An Anthology of Patriotic Prose,* London, 1915; David and Ruth Stevens, eds., *American Patriotic Prose and Verse,* Chicago, 1918; H. F. Stewart and Paul Desjardins, eds., *French Patriotism in the Nineteenth Century (1814-1833),* Cambridge, 1923; and Esmé Wingfield-Stratford, *The History of English Patriotism,* 2 vols., London, 1913.
28. And so students of music often wrote histories and criticism of national music. An early example is Carl Engel, *An Introduction to the Study of National Music,* London, 1866.
29. Said Paul Deschanel, president of the French Chamber of Deputies, and his was a typical eulogy of a national flag, "This flag carries in its folds, with the genius of France and the destiny of the Republic, fifteen centuries of heroism, power and glory. . . ." Quoted by Georges Goyau, *L'idée de patrie et l'humanitarisme: Essai d'histoire française, 1866-1901,* Paris, 1913, p. xi. Generally, accounts of the flags are patriotic exhortations. One that is better

history than most is Milo Quaife, *The Flag of the United States,*
New York, 1942.

30. William Buchanan, "Stereotypes and Tensions as Revealed by
the UNESCO International Poll," *International Social Science
Bulletin,* Autumn, 1951, p. 522. This is a study of stereotypes in
eight countries. See also the article of Klineberg in the same
issue. Another recent study is Siegfried Kracauer, "National
Types as Hollywood Presents Them," *Public Opinion Quarterly,*
Vol. XIII, 1949, pp. 53-72.

31. Gilbert Gadoffre, "French National Images and the Problem of
National Stereotypes," *International Social Science Bulletin,*
Vol. III, 1951, p. 584. A good summary is A. N. J. den Hollander,
"As Others See Us: A Preliminary Inquiry into Group Images,"
Synthese, Vol. VI, 1948, pp. 214-37.

32. A sampling of their activities and ideas can be found in Ernst
Curtius, *Maurice Barrès und die geistigen Grundlagen des
französischen Nationalismus,* Bonn, 1921; Avaline Folsum, *The
Royal Empire Society,* London, 1933; Bessie Pierce, *Citizen's Organizations and the Civic Training of Youth,* New York, 1933;
R. W. Tims, *Germanizing the Prussian Poles, the H-K-T Society
of the Eastern Marches, 1894-1914,* New York, 1941; Mildred
Wertheimer, *The Pan-German League, 1870-1914,* New York,
1924; Carlton Hayes, *France: A Nation of Patriots,* New York,
1930; Charles le Bâtonnier Chenu, *La Ligue des patriotes,* Paris,
1916; Reino Virtanen, "Nietzsche and the Action Française,"
Journal of the History of Ideas, Vol. XI, 1950, pp. 191-214; and
Wallace E. Davies, "A History of American Veterans' and Hereditary Patriotic Societies, 1783-1900," Ph.D. dissertation, Harvard,
1944, typescript.

33. Davies (*ibid.*) lists 106 veterans' and hereditary societies in the
United States to 1900. And on Germany see Wertheimer, pp.
237-39.

34. Proud accounts by the organization are to be found in *U. S. Senate
Documents,* as *Senate Document 164,* 55 Cong. 3rd Sess., 1899;
in the *American Monthly Magazine* beginning in 1892; and in
Mary S. Lockwood and W. H. Regan (Emily Lee Sherwood),
Story of the Records, Washington, D. C., 1906.

35. From their original Constitution and publicity literature.

36. *Essays and Treatises,* Vol. I, London, 1770, p. 251.

CHAPTER XI (Pages 196-212)

1. Ernest Barker formulated this hypothesis well if too sweepingly
when he wrote that after the French Revolution it was "the nation which makes the State, and not the State the nation; and
the principle of nationality, no longer championed by monar-
chism, espouses the cause of democracy. . . . Henceforward, in-

stead of the fact of a national existence being slowly formed and precipitated before the idea is consciously realized, the opposite seems to become the established law." *National Character and the Factors in Its Formation,* London, 1927, p. 124.

2. C. A. Macartney, *National States and National Minorities,* London, 1934, p. 102.

3. Guido de Ruggiero, *The History of European Liberalism,* Oxford, 1927, pp. 414-15. As Crane Brinton observed, nationalism became "one of the *working forms* the new doctrines of popular sovereignty, progress, the perfectibility of man took in the world of reality." *Ideas and Men,* New York, 1950, p. 419.

4. Ruggiero, pp. 410-11. Thorstein Veblen's penetrating remark was, "So that in the workaday apprehension of the common man . . . any infraction of the national integrity or any abatement of the national prestige has come to figure as an insufferable infringement on his personal liberty and on those principles of humanity that make up the catagorical articles of the secular creed of Christendom." *An Inquiry into the Nature of Peace . . . ,* New York, 1919, p. 184.

5. O. Kirchheimer, "Remarques sur la théorie de la souveraineté nationale en Allemagne et en France," in *Archives de philosophie du droit et de sociologie juridique,* 4 année, 1934, shows how German Naziism identified itself with the nation.

6. When Thorstein Veblen (*op. cit.,* p. 75) argued that the chief material use of national patriotism was by those engaged in foreign trade, he took much too limited a view.

7. See the fine survey by Shepard Clough, *France, a History of National Economics, 1789-1939,* New York, 1939, pp. 353-54.

8. Arguing for the income tax in 1909, Lloyd George declared, "the only question is whether it [money] won't do more good in the national purse than in the pocket of the individual. . . ." *Independent,* December 16, 1909, Vol. LXVII, p. 1376.

9. Otto Jespersen (*Mankind, Nation, and Individual from a Linguistic Point of View,* Oslo, 1925, p. 59) found "the greatest uniformity in language" where there was "markedly centralized government." One probably reinforced the other.

10. The pacifist Tolstoi caustically commented, "A strong governmental power is formed possessing milliards of money and an organized mechanism of administration, the postal service, telegraphs, telephones, disciplined armies, law-courts, police, submissive clergy, schools, even the press; and this power maintains in the people the public opinion which it finds necessary." "Patriotism and Christianity," *Complete Works,* Crowell edition, Vol. XXI, p. 51.

11. Carlton Hayes, *France: A Nation of Patriots,* New York, 1930, pp. 30-37.

12. Carlton Hayes, *A Generation of Materialism,* New York, 1941, p. 237. The nationalist arguments arising out of competitive im-

perialism are superbly discussed by William L. Langer in *The Diplomacy of Imperialism, 1890-1902*, New York, 1935, Vol. I, pp. 67-99.

13. Sir Arthur Salter (*World Trade and Its Future*, Philadelphia, 1936, p. 39) lucidly describes how in foreign trade each official was imprisoned by national interest. But the same was true in all fields.

14. Speech on the Treaty of Adrianople, House of Commons, March 1, 1848. *Hansard*, Vol. XCVII (Third Series), col. 120. Robert Sherwood remarked of World War II diplomats, "It was always safest for those who wrote reports to take an aggressively chauvinistic line toward all foreigners." *Roosevelt and Hopkins*, New York, 1950, p. 796.

15. On the effect of national war see Cavour's letter to the Count de Sellon, in Evelyn Martinengo Cesaresco, *Cavour*, London, 1924, p. 12; James Russell Lowell's remarks in Merle Curti, *The Roots of American Loyalty*, New York, 1946, p. 170; and G. Tabouis, *Life of Jules Cambon*, London, 1938, p. 109, for Cambon's comment on the effect of the Spanish-American War on American attitudes. The most provocative discussion is that of Julius Braunthal, *The Paradox of Nationalism*, London, 1946, pp. 72-92.

16. Richard Cobden, in his book, *The Three Panics,* published in 1862, classically portrayed how this fear was utilized in 1848 and after by the British government.

17. R. Stagner and C. E. Osgood through psychological tests measured a marked increase in patriotism among college students and some adults as the United States entered World War II in 1940-42. "Impact of War on a Nationalistic Frame of Reference . . . ," *Journal of Social Psychology*, Vol. XXIV, 1946, pp. 187-215. John Nef, in his "The Enlightenment and the Progress of War," *Measure*, Vol. I, 1950, p. 25, shows how the rise of the common man and modern war are related in nationalism.

18. L. B. Namier in a chapter entitled "Pathological Nationalism," in his *In the Margin of History*, London, 1939, demonstrates this point.

19. *Nationalism and Internationalism*, New York, 1946, p. 16.

20. *Cohens* vs. *Virginia*, 6 Wheaton 1820, 413-14; the decision is discussed by Albert Beveridge, *Life of John Marshall*, Boston, 1916-19, Vol. IV, pp. 353-56.

21. *My Battle*, abridged ed., tr. by Dugdale, Boston, 1933, pp. 247-48.

22. Georg Schwarzenberger (*Power Politics*, London, 1941, p. 56) makes this last point.

23. *The Function of Law in the International Community*, Oxford, 1933, p. 166.

24. *Political Myths and Economic Realities*, New York, 1927, pp. 200-01, 227-30.

25. Leonard Woolf has a brilliant passage on the identification of

patriotism with the omnipotent national state, in *After the Deluge*, Penguin ed., pp. 236-37.

26. *Le peuple*, Paris, 1946, p. 267.

27. Charles Maurras first used the term "integral nationalism" in an article in *Le Soleil*, March 2, 1900. W. C. Buthman, *The Rise of Integral Nationalism in France*, New York, 1936, p. 110. On Maurras see also Denis Brogan, "The Nationalist Doctrine of M. Charles Maurras," *Politica*, Vol. I, 1935, pp. 286-311.

28. Quoted by Jonathan Scott, *Patriots in the Making*, New York, 1916, p. 31, from Gabriel Compayré, *Éléments d'instruction morale et civique*, p. 56.

29. Typical would be the American view as reported by Robert and Helen Lynd, *Middletown*, New York, 1929, pp. 488-89.

30. J. Loewenberg, *Hegel: Selections*, New York, 1929, p. 445.

31. Theodore Roosevelt, "True Americanism," *American Ideals and Other Essays*, New York, 1897, pp. 15-34; and Maurice Barrès, *Scènes et doctrines du nationalisme*, Paris, n.d., p. 814 and *passim*. "Le nationalisme," wrote Barrès, "c'est de résoudre chaque question par rapport à la France."

32. Probably it was the romantics who in modern times most transferred men's worship from the universal and supernatural to the particular and national. See, for example, Hans Kohn, "Romanticism and the Rise of German Nationalism," *Review of Politics*, Vol. XII, 1950, p. 463; and Ernst Troeltsch, "The Ideas of Natural Law and Humanity," in Otto Gierke, *Natural Law and the Theory of Society, 1500 to 1800*, ed. by Ernest Barker, Cambridge, 1934, p. 211.

33. Quoted in Buthman, p. 29.

34. In his *Dictionary of International Slurs (Ethnophaulisms)*, Cambridge (Mass.), 1944, p. 11, A. A. Roback remarked that if he were asked why he collected slurs rather than compliments, he would reply "there are practically none of the latter." See also Eric Partridge, *Words! Words! Words!* London, 1933, which has a chapter entitled "Offensive Nationality."

35. J. A. Hobson (*Imperialism: A Study*, London, 1905, p. 9) believed this a perversion of nationalism.

36. *The Duties of Man*, Everyman's ed., chap. 5, esp. pp. 54-55.

37. The quoted words are those of Pius XI from a speech at the Pontifical Urban College de Propaganda Fide in 1938 and from his encyclical letter *Mit brennender Sorge*, March 14, 1937. On the Catholic attitudes see Sturzo, *Nationalism and Internationalism;* and Maurice Vaussard, *Enquête sur le nationalisme*, Paris, 1924.

38. Or as J. B. Bury wrote, "It is unreasonable to suppose that the idea of nationality . . . is an end in itself or more than a phase of evolution." *Selected Essays*, Cambridge, 1930, p. 58.

39. Georges Weill made the following still relevant distinctions between nineteenth-century French and German brands: *"Les*

*Français invoquent les droits de l'homme et disent la nation
formée par un contrat volontaire, par le libre consentement des
individus. Les penseurs allemands tout en conservant l'idéal
humanitaire du XVIII° siècle, voient dans la nation un être
vivant, qui grandit grâce à l'action inconsciente d'une force in-
térieure; cet instinct naturel, cet esprit populaire (Volksgeist) fait
la nation supérieure aux individus, indépendante de leurs decisions."* L'Europe du XIX° siècle et l'idée de nationalité, Paris,
1938, pp. 2-3.

40. Cf. Hans Kohn, "The Genesis and Character of English Nationalism," *Journal of the History of Ideas*, Vol. I, 1940, pp. 69 ff.;
and Ernest Barker, *The Character of England*, Oxford, 1947.

41. Cf. Hayes, *France: a Nation of Patriots*.

42. David Potter thoughtfully argues that abundance "exercised a
pervasive influence in the shaping of the American character."
*People of Plenty: Economic Abundance and the American Char-
acter*, Chicago, 1954, p. 208.

43. With the possible exception of Sweden. John Wuorinen, *Nationalism in Modern Finland*, New York, 1931.

CHAPTER XII (Pages 215-237)

1. See his plea as first president of the American Historical Association in his address "On Studies in General History and the
History of Civilization," 1884, *Papers American Historical Association*, Vol. I, New York, 1886, pp. 49-72. A contemporary editor,
Norman Cousins, with justification called his volume published
in 1953, *Who Speaks for Man?*

2. In his presidential address to the American Historical Association,
"Nationality and History," *American Historical Review*, Vol.
XXI, 1916, p. 236.

3. Robert Sherwood, *Roosevelt and Hopkins*, New York, 1948, p.
796.

4. Professor Albert Guerard attacked the teaching of "English"
rather than "literature" as narrow, provincial, and impossible
because literature is world literature and related by other than
national ideas. "The Quick and the Dead[,]" "English or Literature," *Chap Book*, College English Association, 1951.

5. The best recent book dealing with the subject is William C.
Boyd, *Genetics and the Races of Man*, Boston, 1950. See also
G. G. Simpson, "The Principles of Classification and a Classifi-
cation of the Mammals," *Bulletin American Museum of Natural
History*, Vol. LXXXV, 1945, pp. 1-350. Proper classification has
been a matter of vigorous dispute, often because of semantic
difficulties, between some geneticists and some morphologists.
Cf. Reginald R. Gates, *Human Ancestry*, Cambridge, 1948.

6. Otto Klineberg, ed., *Characteristics of the American Negro*, New
York, 1944. A survey of the little experimentally known concern-

ing race and national differences is Otto Klineberg's *Tensions Affecting International Understanding: A Survey of Research*, New York, 1950, pp. 1-92.

7. See, for example, Ralph Linton, *The Study of Man*, New York, 1936, pp. 326-27; and Paul Radin, *The Racial Myth*, New York, 1937, pp. 80-81.

8. Alfred L. Kroeber, *Anthropology: Race, Language, Culture, Psychology, Prehistory*, rev. ed., New York, 1948, pp. 126-27, states that no race averages less than four feet ten inches and none more than five ten, while the majority of populations do not deviate more than two inches from the general average of five feet five inches.

9. This may only be a hope. It was John Stuart Mill's belief, "Liberty," in *Utilitarianism, Liberty, Representative Government*, Everyman's ed., p. 82, and is authoritatively maintained as a possibility by George Gaylord Simpson, *The Meaning of Evolution*, New Haven, 1949. Of course, as Professor Simpson remarks, "This awesome power includes the human prerogative of self-extinction," p. 328.

10. Linton, pp. 132 ff., summarizes some of these common characteristics.

11. Especially his *Civilization and Climate*, 3rd ed., New Haven, 1924, and *Mainsprings of Civilization*, New York, 1945.

12. Quoted in Julian Huxley and A. C. Haddon, *We Europeans*, Oxford, 1940, p. 3.

13. Walter Sulzbach, *National Consciousness*, Washington, 1943, p. 52.

14. Lincoln Barnett, *The Universe of Dr. Einstein*, New York, 1948, pp. 14-15.

15. "Oration on the Dignity of Man," in Ernst Cassirer, Paul Kristeller, and John Herman Randall, eds., *The Renaissance Philosophy of Man*, Chicago, 1948, pp. 219, 223.

16. *Merchant of Venice*, Act III, sc. i.

17. For the facts in this paragraph the writer has relied upon, in addition to the works of Boyd, Kroeber, and Linton cited above, Julian Huxley, *Man Stands Alone*, New York, 1941; Ruth Benedict, *Race: Science and Politics*, New York, 1940; Franz Boas, *Anthropology and Modern Life*, 2nd ed., New York, 1932; and Melville Herskovits, *Man and His Works: The Science of Cultural Anthropology*, New York, 1949.

18. For a sampling of what is known concerning diet in relation to individual and national behavior, see Huntington, *Mainsprings of Civilization*, pp. 417-31; Sir Robert McCarrison, "Nutrition and National Health," *Journal Royal Society of Arts*, Vol. LXXXIV, August 28, September 4, 11, 1936; Sir John Orr, *Food, Health, and Income*, London, 1936.

19. Among the many advocates of this view were: Walter Bagehot, *Physics and Politics*, New York, 1881, first published 1869; Henry

Hauser, *Le principe des nationalités, ses origines,* Paris, 1916, pp. 12-13; Karl Pearson, *National Life from the Standpoint of Science,* London, 1901; and a long list of German writers of whom Heinrich von Treitschke, especially in his *Politics,* London, 1916, is outstanding.

20. Madison Grant, *The Passing of the Great Race, or the Racial Basis of European History,* New York, 1916. A half a hundred other works could be easily cited. For the United States see Richard Hofstadter, *Social Darwinism,* Philadelphia, 1944.

21. See the works cited above, and Ashley Montagu, *Man's Most Dangerous Myth: The Fallacy of Race,* New York, 1942.

22. The genetic and cultural, we must repeat, cannot be disentangled. Norman Cameron, *The Psychology of Behavior Disorders: A Biosocial Interpretation,* Boston, 1947; Ralph Linton, *The Cultural Background of Personality,* New York, 1945; Thomas Hunt Morgan, *Evolution and Genetics,* Princeton, 1925, p. 207; and especially Huxley, *Man Stands Alone,* pp. 111-12.

23. John Stuart Mill, *The Principles of Political Economy,* London, 1849, Vol. I, p. 390.

24. In addition to the books cited in chap. III and note 17 of this chapter see Earl W. Count, ed., *This Is Race,* New York, 1950, pp. xiii ff.; and William W. Howells, *Mankind So Far,* New York, 1944. Cf. Earnest Albert Hooton, *Up from the Ape,* 2d ed., New York, 1946. A fine historian's summary of what has been thought is Georges Weill, *Race et nation,* Paris, 1939.

25. See above, chap. III. "The evidence . . . demonstrates that every large human group . . . runs very close to the gamut of human capabilities. . . ." Herskovits, p. 149.

26. And probably can only be characterized as the "art of exploiting a prejudice for an ulterior purpose." George Sabine, *A History of Political Theory,* New York, 1950, p. 889.

27. See, for example, the descriptions of English mixtures in Jacquetta and Christopher Hawkes, "Land and People," in Ernest Barker, ed., *The Character of England,* Oxford, 1947; and John Oakesmith, *Race and Nationality: An Inquiry into the Origins of Patriotism,* New York, 1919, pp. 95-100. What is true of "Anglo-Saxon" England is true of all peoples. For Europe, see Huxley and Haddon, *We Europeans,* p. 221. Very probably no pure race ever existed.

28. Linton, *Study of Man,* pp. 36-37.

29. Quoted by Francis Delaisi, *Political Myths and Economic Realities,* New York, 1927, p. 186.

30. Barker, *Character of England,* p. 558.

31. Erasmus, *Praise of Folly,* tr. by Hoyt Hudson, Princeton, 1941, p. 61.

32. Aristotle, *The Politics,* tr. by H. Rackham, Loeb Classical Library, London, 1932, Vol. VII, pp. vi, 1-3.

33. Quoted in William Curt Buthman, *The Rise of Integral Nationalism, with Special Reference to the Ideas and Activities of Charles Maurras*, New York, 1939, p. 291.

34. J. Holland Rose, *Nationality in Modern History*, New York, 1916, p. 39.

35. Bentham quoted Fénelon approvingly, "I prefer my family to myself, my country to my family, and the human race to my country." "Principles of Penal Law," *Works*, ed. by John Bowring, Edinburgh, 1843, Vol. I, p. 563. He looked forward to a "period when the moral code, grounded on the greatest-happiness principle, will be the code of nations, teaching them in their vast political concerns, to create no useless misery and to make their patriotism subservient to the demands of benevolence." Hans Kohn, *Prophets and Peoples*, New York, 1946, p. 18.

36. Robert Ergang, *Herder and the Foundations of German Nationalism*, New York, 1931, pp. 97-100.

37. *The True-Born Englishman.*

38. See, for example, the studies of Stanley Rundle, *Language as a Social and Political Factor in Europe*, London, 1946; and Geoffrey M. Morant, *The Races of Central Europe*, London, 1939.

39. Hamilton Fyfe, "The Illusion of National Character," *Political Quarterly*, Vol. IX, 1938, pp. 254 ff.; Richard Müller-Freienfels, *Persönlichkeit und Weltanschauung*, Leipzig, 1919. Max Nordau scathingly attacked concepts of national character in *The Interpretation of History*, tr. by Hamilton, London, 1910, p. 130 and ff.; a later brilliant analysis is in Adam de Hegedus, *Patriotism or Peace*, New York, 1947. Sir John Seeley's comment is pertinent: "No explanation is so vague, so cheap, and so difficult to verify." Thomas P. Peardon, "Sir John Seeley Pragmatic Historian in a Nationalistic Age," in E. M. Earle, ed., *Nationalism and Internationalism*, New York, 1950, p. 291.

40. David Hume, "Of National Characters," in *Essays and Treatises . . .* , London, 1770, Vol. I; Arthur de Gobineau, *The Inequality of Human Races*, tr. by Collins, New York, 1915; Houston Stewart Chamberlain, *Foundations of the Nineteenth Century*, tr. by Lees, London, 1913; Gustave Le Bon, *The Psychology of Peoples*, London, 1899; Salvador Madariaga, *Englishmen, Frenchmen, Spaniards: An Essay in Comparative Psychology*, London, 1928; André Siegfried, *America Comes of Age: A French Analysis*, tr. by H. and D. Heming, New York, 1927, and his other books on France, England, New Zealand, and Latin America. For a sampling of other like volumes see the bibliography for works by Grant Allen, Jules d'Auriac, Emile Boutmy, Denis Brogan, Michael Demiashkevich, W. Macneille Dixon, Alfred Fouillée, William McDougall, and Esmé Wingfield-Stratford. Possibly the Germans Lazarus and Steinthal were among the first psychologists to study national character, but the little anonymous book *Essai sur le principe des nationalités par un diplomate*,

Paris, 1882, pp. 139-239, collects the aphorisms, axioms, and truisms of the late nineteenth century and earlier.

41. Among the better recent essays at specific and comparative analy-
ses are Ernest Barker, ed., *The Character of England;* Henry
Commager, *The American Mind: An Interpretation of American
Thought and Character since the 1880's,* New Haven, 1950; the
essays of Morris Ginsburg cited in the bibliography; Otto Klineberg, "A Science of National Character," *Journal of Social Psychology,* Vol. XIX, 1944, pp. 147-62; Clyde and Florence
Kluckhohn, "American Culture: Generalized Orientation and
Class Patterns," in *Conflicts of Power in Modern Culture,* New
York, 1947, pp. 106-28; Nathan Leites, "Psycho-cultural Hypotheses about Political Acts," *World Politics,* Vol. I, 1948, pp. 103 ff.;
Margaret Mead, *And Keep Your Powder Dry,* New York, 1942;
and David M. Potter, *People of Plenty: Economic Abundance
and the American Character,* Chicago, 1954.

42. Bernard Joseph, *Nationality: Its Nature and Problems,* London,
1929, p. 86.

43. Julius Braunthal sums up evidence on the warlike proclivities of
the nations in *The Paradox of Nationalism, an Epilogue to the
Nuremberg Trials; Common-sense Reflections on the Atomic Age,*
London, 1946, pp. 45-47. Among many studies of the relation of
race and nationality to crime see E. H. Stofflet, "A Study of
National and Cultural Differences in Criminal Tendency," *Archives of Psychology,* no. 185, 1935.

44. The quoted words are those of Peter Drucker, *The End of
Economic Man,* New York, 1939, pp. 113-14.

45. Montaigne has an old man say of the "Antartik" (Brazilian)
people: "I finde (as farre as I have beene informed) there is
nothing in that nation, that is either barbarous or savage, unlesse
men call that barbarisme which is not common to them. As indeed, we have no other ayme of truth and reason, than the
example and *Idea* of the opinions and customes of the countrie
we live in. There is ever perfect religion, perfect policie, perfect
and compleat use of all things." *Essays,* Everyman ed., Vol. I,
p. 219.

46. In Frederick Page, ed., *An Anthology of Patriotic Prose,* London,
1915, pp. 198-201.

47. Hume, *Essays and Treatises,* Vol. I, p. 247.

48. Cecil Delisle Burns, *Political Ideals: Their Nature and Development,* London, 1915, pp. 179-83.

49. Otto Jespersen, *Mankind, Nation and Individual from a Linguistic Point of View,* Oslo, 1925, pp. 16-17. He continues, "A
mystically assumed 'common mind' really explains nothing whatever in any department of life, any more than the assumption of
a mystical 'common stomach' would serve to explain how it is
that people react in like manner to foods and poisons."

50. Thomas Mann, *Dr. Faustus,* New York, 1948, p. 123.

51. Johann Gottlieb Fichte, *Addresses to the German Nation,* tr. by Jones and Turnbull, Chicago, 1922, pp. 69-70; Jeremy Bentham, "Essay on Languages," *Works,* Vol. VIII, p. 310. On Dostoevski see the brilliant essay of Hans Kohn, "Russia: Dostoevsky," in *Prophets and Peoples,* pp. 140-60. An interesting older (1614) example is R. Carew, "The Excellency of the English Tongue," in Page, p. 49.

52. V. Gordon Childe, *The Aryans,* New York, 1926, pp. 211-12.

53. See chap. III.

54. Jespersen, p. 221.

55. For Montesquieu see Albert Sorel, *Montesquieu,* tr. by M. and E. Anderson, Chicago, 1888, p. 52. On Goethe see Page, p. 103. The names of Bentham, J. S. Mill, Diderot, Helvétius, and Lessing could be cited also. Possibly the Stoics were among the first to believe all men brothers. Marcus Aurelius thought, "My nature is rational and social, and my city and country, so far as I am Antonius, is Rome, but so far as I am a man, it is the world." Whitney J. Oates, *The Stoic and Epicurean Philosophers,* New York, 1940, p. xxiv.

56. Lawrence K. Frank, *Society as the Patient: Essays on Culture and Personality,* New Brunswick, 1948, pp. 394-95.

57. Clyde Kluckhohn, *Mirror for Man. The Relation of Anthropology to Modern Life,* New York, 1949, p. 266, concludes, "All human societies, from the most primitive to the most advanced, constitute a continuum." Herskovits, *Man and His Works,* p. 234; Bronislaw Malinowski, *A Scientific Theory of Culture and Other Essays,* Chapel Hill, 1944, p. 92; and G. P. Murdock, "The Common Denominator of Cultures," in Ralph Linton, ed., *The Science of Man in the World Crisis,* New York, 1945, pp. 124-33.

58. Josiah Royce, *Race Questions, Provincialism, and Other American Problems,* New York, 1908, p. 53.

BIBLIOGRAPHY

This is not a list of all the writings touching upon nationalism nor of all those cited in this volume, but of about 425 of those judged significant for the study of nationalism. At least an equal number might be added if a full bibliography on the subject were the object. The best understanding comes from reading in the primary sources, in the works of men like Barère, Herder, Barrès, and Mazzini, in the documents concerning national movements such as the French Federation movement of 1790 and the various modern patriotic societies. The footnotes to the text indicate my judgment of many of the books and articles. The forty thought most important for a student to know are here marked with an asterisk. If I were to suggest only ten secondary studies to students for further reading, they would be those with an asterisk by Hayes, Hertz, Johannet, Kantorowicz, Kohn, Meinecke, the Royal Institute of International Affairs, Weill, and Znaniecki. For a good annotated bibliography of the writings to 1934 see the volume of Koppel Pinson cited below.

Acomb, Frances Dorothy, *Anglophobia in France, 1763-1789: An Essay in the History of Constitutionalism and Nationalism,* Durham, Duke U. Press, 1950.
Acton, John Emerich Edward Dalberg, *Essays on Freedom and Power,* Boston, Beacon Press, 1948.

Adorno, T. W., et al., *The Authoritarian Personality*, New York, Harper, 1950.

Aksin, B., et al., *La nationalité dans la science sociale et dans le droit contemporain*, Paris, Sirey, 1933.

Allen, Grant, *Anglo-Saxon Britain*, London, Society for Promoting Christian Knowledge, 1884.

Almond, Gabriel A., *The American People and Foreign Policy*, New York, Harcourt, Brace, 1950.

Allport, Lloyd, "The Psychology of Nationalism," *Harpers Magazine*, Vol. CLV, 1927, pp. 291-301.

Anderson, Eugene N., *Nationalism and the Cultural Crisis in Prussia, 1806-1815*, New York, Farrar and Rinehart, 1939.

Appel, K. E., "Nationalism and Sovereignty: A Psychiatric View," *Journal of Abnormal and Social Psychology*, Vol. XL, 1945, pp. 355-62.

Arendt, Hannah, "Race—Thinking before Racism," *Review of Politics*, Vol. VI, 1944, pp. 36 ff.

Artz, Frederick, *Reaction and Revolution, 1814-1832*, New York, Harper, 1934.

*Aulard, Alphonse, *Le patriotisme français*, Paris, Chiron, 1916.

Auriac, Jules d', *La nationalité française: sa formation*, Paris, 1913.

Bagehot, Walter, *Physics and Politics, or Thoughts on the Applications of the Principles of "Natural Selection" and "Inheritance" to Political Society*, New York, Appleton, 1881.

Barker, Sir Ernest, *National Character and the Factors in Its Formation*, London, Methuen, 1927.

*——, ed., *The Character of England*, Oxford, Clarendon Press, 1947.

Baron, Salo Wittmayer, *Modern Nationalism and Religion*, New York, Harper, 1947.

Barr, Stringfellow, *Mazzini, Portrait of an Exile*, New York, Holt, 1935.

Barrès, Maurice, *Scènes et doctrines du nationalisme*, Paris, Emile-Paul, n.d. (definitive ed., Plon-Nourrit, 1925).

——, *The Undying Spirit of France*, tr. by Corwin, New Haven, Yale U. Press, 1917.

Barth, Paul; Schmid, F.; Hartmann, L. M.; Oppenheimer, F.; and Michels, R.: all in *Deutsche Gesellschaft für Soziologie, Schriften*, ser. i, Verhandlungen der deutschen Soziologentage, Vol. II, Tübingen, 1913, pp. 21-48, 55-72, 80-97, 98-139, 140-84.

Barzun, Jacques, *The French Race: Theories of Its Origins and Their Social and Political Implications Prior to the Revolution*, New York, Columbia U. Press, 1932.

*——, *Race. A Study in Modern Superstition*, New York, Harcourt, Brace, 1937.

Bason, Cecilia H., *Study of the Homeland and Civilization in the Elementary Schools of Germany*, New York, Columbia U. Press, 1937.

Bauer, Otto, *Die Nationalitätenfrage und die Sozialdemokratie,* Vienna, Wiener Volksbuchhandlung, 1924.

Baugh, A. C., *A History of the English Language,* New York, Appleton-Century, 1935.

Bay, Christian; Gullvåg, Ingemund; Ofstad, Harold; and Tönnessen, Herman, *Nationalism: A Study of Identification with People and Power,* Oslo, Institute for Social Research, 1950.

Benda, Julien, *Esquisse d'une histoire des Français dans leur volonté d'être une nation,* 6th ed., Paris, Gallimard, 1932.

*——, *La trahison des clercs,* Paris, B. Grasset, 1927.

Benedict, Ruth, *The Chrysanthemum and the Sword: Patterns of Japanese Culture,* Boston, Houghton Mifflin, 1946.

——, *Race: Science and Politics,* New York, Modern Age Books, 1940.

Berger, Monroe, "Understanding 'National Character'—and War," *Commentary,* Vol. II, 1951, pp. 375-86.

Bernhard, Gen. Friedrich von, *Germany and the Next War,* tr. by Allen H. Powles, London, Longmans, Green, 1914.

Binkley, Robert C., *Realism and Nationalism, 1852-1871,* New York, Harper, 1935.

Bluntschli, J. K., *Theory of the State,* 2nd ed., Oxford, Clarendon Press, 1887.

*Boas, Franz, *Anthropology and Modern Life,* 2nd ed., New York, Norton, 1932.

Boehm, Max Hildebert, *Das eigenständige Volk: Volkstheoretische Grundlagen der Ethnopolitik und Geisteswissenschaften,* Göttingen, Vanderhoeck and Ruprecht, 1932.

——, "Nationalism. Theoretical Aspects," *Encyclopedia of Social Science,* Vol. XI, New York, Macmillan, 1933, pp. 231-40.

Bolingbroke's Works, Vol. I, "On the Spirit of Patriotism," "The Idea of a Patriotic King," London, T. Davies, 1775.

Bolwell, Robert Whitney, "Concerning the Study of Nationalism in American Literature," *American Literature,* Vol. X, 1939, pp. 405-16.

Borkenau, Franz, *Socialism, National or International,* London, Routledge, 1942.

Bossuet, *Oeuvres complètes de Bossuet,* ed. by the Abbé Migne, Paris, 1857, Vol. XI.

Boutmy, Emile, *Éléments d'une psychologie politique du peuple américain,* Paris, Colin, 1902.

*Boyd, William C., *Genetics and the Races of Man: An Introduction to Modern Physical Anthropology,* Boston, Little, Brown, 1950.

*Braunthal, Julius, *The Paradox of Nationalism: An Epilogue to the Nuremberg Trials; Common-sense Reflections on the Atomic Age,* London, St. Botolph, 1946.

Brogan, Denis W., *The American Character,* New York, Knopf, 1944.

——, "The Nationalist Doctrine of M. Charles Maurras," *Politica,* Vol. I, 1935, pp. 286-311.

Brownell, William C., *French Traits: An Essay in Comparative Criticism,* New York, The Chautauqua-century Press, 1896.

Brunot, Ferdinand, *Histoire de la langue française,* Paris, Colin, 1905, Vol. IV (4th ed., Paris, 1947); Vol. VI, pt. 1, 1930, pt. 2, 1932; Vol. VII, 1926; Vol. IX, pt. 1, 1927, pt. 2, 1937.

Bryce, Viscount James, *Race Sentiment as a Factor in History,* London, U. of London Press, 1915.

Buber, Martin, "The Beginning of the National Idea," *Review of Religion,* Vol. X, 1946, pp. 254-65.

Buck, Carl D., "Language and the Sentiment of Nationality," *Political Science Review,* Vol. X, 1916, pp. 44-69.

Burns, C. D., *Political Ideals: Their Nature and Development, an Essay,* London, Oxford U. Press, 1919.

Bury, J. B.; Gwatkin, H. M.; and Whitney, J. P., eds., *Cambridge Medieval History,* 8 vols., New York, Macmillan, 1924-36, esp. Vol. V, *Contest of Empire and Papacy.*

*Buthman, William Curt, *The Rise of Integral Nationalism in France, with Special Reference to the Ideas and Activities of Charles Maurras,* New York, Columbia U. Press, 1939.

Cantril, Hadley, *The Psychology of Social Movements,* New York, Wiley, 1941.

Chaconas, Stephen G., *Adamantios Korais: A Study in Greek Nationalism,* New York, Columbia U. Press, 1942.

Chadwick, Hector Munro, *The Nationalities of Europe and the Growth of National Ideologies,* Cambridge, Eng., Cambridge U. Press, 1945.

Chamberlain, Houston Stewart, *The Foundations of the Nineteenth Century,* 2 vols., tr. by John Lees, London, John Lane, 1913.

Chenu, M. le Bâtonnier, *La Ligue des patriotes,* Paris, Sirey, 1916.

Cheyney, Edward P., *The Dawn of a New Era, 1250-1453,* New York, Harper, 1936.

Childe, V. Gordon, *The Aryans: A Study of Indo-European Origins,* New York, Knopf, 1926.

Choulguine, Alexandre, "Les origines de l'esprit national moderne et Jean-Jacques Rousseau," *Annales de la Société Jean-Jacques Rousseau,* Vol. XXVI, 1937, pp. 9-283.

Clark, Cumberland, *Shakespeare and National Character,* London, Wass Pritchard, 1928.

Clough, Shepard B., *France: A History of National Economics, 1789-1939,* New York, Scribner, 1939.

——, *A History of the Flemish Movement in Belgium,* New York, Richard R. Smith, 1930.

Coatman, J., *Magna Britannia,* London, Cape, 1936.

Cobban, Alfred, *National Self Determination,* New York, Oxford U. Press, 1945.

Cole, Charles W., "Jeremy Belknap: Pioneer Nationalist," *New England Quarterly,* Vol. X, 1937, pp. 743-51.

Commager, Henry Steele, *The American Mind: An Interpretation of American Thought and Character since the 1880's,* New Haven, Yale U. Press, 1950.

Condliffe, John Bell, *The Commerce of Nations*, New York, Norton, 1950.

Corbett, P. E., "Future of Nationalism and the National State," *Annals American Academy of Political and Social Science*, Vol. CCXVIII, 1941, pp. 153-61.

Coulton, G. G., "Nationalism in the Middle Ages," *Cambridge Historical Journal*, Vol. V, 1935, pp. 15-40.

Count, Earl W., ed., *This Is Race: An Anthology Selected from the International Literature of the Races of Man*, New York, Henry Schuman, 1950.

*Cousins, Norman, *Who Speaks for Man?*, New York, Macmillan, 1953.

Cramb, John Adam, *Germany and England*, New York, E. P. Dutton, 1914.

——, *The Origins and Destiny of Imperial Britain and Nineteenth Century Europe*, New York, E. P. Dutton, 1915.

Cromer, Evelyn Baring, *Ancient and Modern Imperialism*, London, Murray, 1910.

——, *Political and Literary Essays*, 3rd series, London, Macmillan, 1916.

Curti, Merle E., "Francis Lieber and Nationalism," reprinted from the *Huntington Library Quarterly*, Vol. IV, 1941.

*——, *The Roots of American Loyalty*, New York, Columbia U. Press, 1946.

Curtius, Ernst Robert, *Maurice Barrès und die geistigen Grundlagen des französischen Nationalismus*, Bonn, F. Cohen, 1921.

Davidson, Donald, *The Attack on Leviathan: Regionalism and Nationalism in the United States*, Chapel Hill, U. of North Carolina Press, 1938.

Davies, Wallace Evan, "A History of American Veterans' and Hereditary Patriotic Societies, 1783-1900," Ph.D. dissertation, Harvard, 1944, typescript.

Dawson, W. H., ed., *After-War Problems*, London, Unwin, 1917 (see essays by Lord Cromer and the Earl of Meath).

Dearing, Mary R., *Veterans in Politics: The Story of the G.A.R.*, Baton Rouge, Louisiana State U. Press, 1952.

*Delaisi, Francis, *Political Myths and Economic Realities*, New York, Viking, 1927.

Delos, J. T., *La Nation*, Vol. I, *Sociologie de la nation;* Vol. II, *Le Nationalisme, et l'ordre de droit*, Montreal, Editions de l'Arbre, 1944.

Demiashkevich, Michael, *The National Mind, English-French-German*, New York, American Book Co., 1938.

Deutsch, Karl W., *Nationalism and Social Communication: An Inquiry into the Foundations of Nationality*, New York, MIT and Wiley, 1953.

——, "The Trend of European Nationalism—The Language Aspect," *American Political Science Review,* Vol. XXXVI, 1942, pp. 533-41.

Dilke, Sir Charles, *Greater Britain: A Record of Travel in English-Speaking Countries during 1866 and 1867,* New York, Harper, 1869.

Dimier, Louis, *Le nationalisme littéraire et ses méfaits chez les français,* Paris, Correa, 1935.

Dixon, W. Macneille, *The Englishman,* New York, Longmans, Green, 1931.

Dominian, Leon, *The Frontiers of Language and Nationality in Europe,* New York, Holt, 1917.

Drinkwater, John, *Patriotism in Literature,* London, Williams and Norgate, 1924.

Dupre, Huntley, "Carnot's Nationalism," *South Atlantic Quarterly,* Vol. XXXVII, 1938, pp. 291-306.

Eagan, James Michel, *Maximilien Robespierre, Nationalist Dictator,* New York, Columbia U. Press, 1938.

*Earle, Edward Mead, ed., *Nationalism and Internationalism, Essays Inscribed to Carlton J. H. Hayes,* New York, Columbia U. Press, 1950.

Eisenmann, Louis, "Quelques aspects nouveaux de l'idée de nationalité," *Bulletin of the International Committee of Historical Sciences,* Vol. II, pt. 2, 1929, pp. 225-33.

Elviken, Andreas, "The Genesis of Norwegian Nationalism," *Journal of Modern History,* Vol. III, 1931, pp. 365-91.

Engelbrecht, H. C., *Johann Gottlieb Fichte: A Study of His Writings with Special Reference to His Nationalism,* New York, Columbia U. Press, 1933.

Engeln, Oscar D. von, *Inheriting the Earth; or, The Geographical Factor in National Development,* New York, Macmillan, 1922.

Eppstein, John, *The Catholic Tradition of the Law of Nations,* London, Burns, Oatis and Washburne, 1935.

*Ergang, Robert R., *Herder and the Foundations of German Nationalism,* New York, Columbia U. Press, 1931.

———, "Möser and the Rise of National Thought in Germany," *Journal of Modern History,* Vol. V, 1933, pp. 172-96.

Essai sur le principe des nationalités par un diplomate, Paris, Plon, 1882.

Estienne, H., *La précellence du langage françois,* nouvelle édition, Léon Feugére, ed., Paris, Delalain, 1850.

Falnes, Oscar J., *National Romanticism in Norway,* New York, Columbia U. Press, 1933.

Featherstone, H. L., *A Century of Nationalism,* London, Nelson, 1939.

Fichte, Johann Gottlieb, *Addresses to the German Nation,* tr. by R. F. Jones and G. H. Turnbull, Chicago, Open Court Publishing Co., 1922.

Finkelstein, Louis, ed., *The Jews: Their History, Culture, and Religion,* 2 vols., New York, Harper, 1949.

Fleure, Herbert John, *The Peoples of Europe*, London, Oxford U. Press, 1925.

Folsum, Aveline, *The Royal Empire Society. Formative Years*, London, Allen and Unwin, 1933.

Fouillée, Alfred, *Psychologie du peuple français*, Paris, Alcan, 1898.

Frank, Lawrence K., *Society as the Patient: Essays on Culture and Personality*, New Brunswick, Rutgers U. Press, 1948.

Frank, Walter, *Nationalismus und Demokratie im Frankreich der dritten Republik (1871 bis 1918)*, Hamburg, Hanseatische Verlagsanstalt, 1933.

Frazer, J. G., *Totemism and Exogamy*, 4 vols., London, Macmillan, 1910.

Freud, Sigmund, "Totem and Taboo," *The Basic Writings of Sigmund Freud*, tr. and ed. by Dr. A. A. Brill, Modern Library edition, 1938.

Friedmann, Wolfgang, "New Nationalism," *Fortnightly*, Vol. CLXIII (NS157), 1945, pp. 27-34.

——, *The Crisis of the National State*, London, Macmillan, 1943.

Friedrich, Carl Joachim, "The Agricultural Bases of Emotional Nationalism," *Public Opinion Quarterly*, Vol. I, 1937, pp. 50-61.

——, *The Age of the Baroque, 1610-1660*, New York, Harper, 1952.

Fyfe, Hamilton, "The Illusion of National Character," *Political Quarterly*, Vol. IX, 1938, pp. 254-70.

Galbraith, V. H., "Nationality and Language in Medieval England," *Transactions of the Royal Historical Society*, Vol. XXIII, 1941, pp. 113-28.

Gardner, Edmund G., *The National Idea in Italian Literature*, Manchester, University Press, 1921.

Gates, R. R., *Human Ancestry from a Genetical Point of View*, Cambridge, Harvard U. Press, 1948.

Gaus, John, *Great Britain: A Study of Civic Loyalty*, Chicago, U. of Chicago Press, 1929.

*Gershoy, Leo, "Barère, Champion of Nationalism in the French Revolution," *Political Science Quarterly*, Vol. XLII, 1927, pp. 419-30.

——, *From Despotism to Revolution, 1763-1789*, New York, Harper, 1944.

Gewehr, Wesley M., *The Rise of Nationalism in the Balkans, 1800-1930*, New York, Holt, 1931.

Gibbons, Herbert Adams, *Nationalism and Internationalism*, New York, Frederick A. Stokes, 1930.

Gilmore, Myron P., *The World of Humanism, 1453-1517*, New York, Harper, 1952.

Ginsberg, Morris, "National Character and National Sentiments," in *Psychology and Modern Problems*, ed. by J. A. Hadfield, New York, Longmans, Green, 1936.

——, "National Character," *British Journal of Psychology*, Vol. XXXII, 1942, pp. 183-205.

Ginsberg, Morris, "National Character," in *Reason and Unreason in Society*, Cambridge, Harvard U. Press, 1948.

Gobineau, Arthur de, *The Inequality of Human Races*, tr. by Adrian Collins, New York, Putnam, 1915.

Goetz, Walter, ed., *Propyläen Weltgeschichte*, 10 vols., Berlin, Propyläen-Verlag, 1929-33, especially vols. VI-IX.

Gooch, G. P., *History and the Historians in the Nineteenth Century*, London, Longmans, Green, 1920.

——, *Nationalism*, London, Swarthmore Press, 1920.

Gorer, Geoffrey, *The American People: A Study in National Character*, New York, Norton, 1948.

Goyau, Georges, *L'idée de patrie et l'humanitarisme: Essai d'histoire française, 1866-1901*, Paris, Perrin, 1913.

Grant, Madison, *The Passing of the Great Race: or the Racial Basis of European History*, New York, Scribner, 1922.

Grazia, Sebastian de, *The Political Community: A Study of Anomie*, Chicago, U. of Chicago Press, 1948.

Green, T. H., "Lectures on the Principles of Political Obligation," *Works of Thomas Hill Green*, ed. by R. L. Nettleship, Vol. II, London, Longmans, Green, 1911.

Grotius, Hugo, *De jure belli ac pacis libri tres*, ed. by James Brown Scott, Oxford, Clarendon Press, 1925.

Haarhoff, Theodore J., *The Stranger at the Gate; Aspects of Exclusiveness and Cooperation in Ancient Greece and Rome, with Some Reference to Modern Times*, 2nd ed., Oxford, Blackwell, 1948.

Hadas, Moses, "Aspects of Nationalist Survival under Hellenistic and Roman Imperialism," *Journal of the History of Ideas*, Vol. XI, 1950, pp. 131-39.

Hall, Charles Henry, *Patriotism and National Defense*, New York, Society for Political Education, 1885.

Handelsman, Marcel, "Le role de la nationalité dans l'histoire du Moyen Age," *Bulletin of the International Committee of Historical Sciences*, Vol. II, pt. 2, 1929, pp. 235-47.

Handman, Max Sylvius, "The Sentiment of Nationalism," *Political Science Quarterly*, Vol. XXXVI, 1921, pp. 104-21.

Hankin, Ernest Hanbury, *Nationalism and the Communal Mind*, London, Watts, 1937.

Hapgood, Norman, ed., *Professional Patriots*, New York, Boni, 1927.

Hauser, Henri, *Le principe des nationalités, ses origines historiques*, Paris, Alcan, 1916.

Hawtrey, R. G., *Economic Aspects of Sovereignty*, New York, Longmans, Green, 1930.

Hayes, Carlton J. H., "The Church and Nationalism: A Plea for Further Study of a Major Issue," *Catholic Historical Review*, Vol. XXVIII, 1942, pp. 1-12.

——, "Contributions of Herder to the Doctrine of Nationalism," *American Historical Review*, Vol. XXXII, July, 1927, pp. 719-36.

*Hayes, Carlton J. H., *Essays on Nationalism,* New York, Macmillan, 1926.

——, *France: A Nation of Patriots,* New York, Columbia U. Press, 1930.

——, *A Generation of Materialism 1871-1890,* New York, Harper, 1941.

*——, *The Historical Evolution of Modern Nationalism,* New York, Richard R. Smith, 1931.

——, "Influence of Political Tactics on Socialist Theory in Germany," in *A History of Political Theories: Recent Times,* ed. by Charles E. Merriam and Harry E. Barnes, New York, Macmillan, 1924.

——, "Philosopher Turned Patriot," in *Essays in Intellectual History: Dedicated to James Harvey Robinson,* ed. by James T. Shotwell, New York, Harper, 1929.

*Heckscher, Eli F., *Mercantilism,* tr. by Mendel Schapiro, 2 vols., London, Allen and Unwin, 1935.

*Hegedus, Adam de, *Patriotism or Peace,* New York, Scribner, 1947.

Henry, Paul, *Le problème des nationalités,* Paris, Colin, 1937.

Herskovits, Melville J., *Man and His Works: The Science of Cultural Anthropology,* New York, Knopf, 1949.

——, "Who Are the Jews?" in *The Jews, Their History, Culture, and Religion,* ed. by Louis Finkelstein, New York, Harper, 1949.

*Hertz, Friedrich O., *Nationality in History and Politics, a Study of the Psychology and Sociology of National Sentiment and Character,* Oxford, Clarendon Press, 1944.

Hobhouse, Leonard Trelawney, *The Metaphysical Theory of the State,* New York, Macmillan, 1918.

Hobson, J. A., *The Psychology of Jingoism,* London, Grant Richards, 1901.

Hoffer, Eric, *The True Believer: Thoughts on the Nature of Mass Movements,* New York, Harper, 1951.

Holborn, Hajo, *Ulrich von Hutten and the German Reformation,* tr. by Roland H. Bainton, New Haven, Yale U. Press, 1937.

Hollander, A. N. J. den, "As Others See Us," *Synthese,* Vol. VI, 1947-48, pp. 214-38.

Horowitz, E. L., "Some Aspects of Development of Patriotism in Children," *Sociometry,* Vol. III, 1940, pp. 339-41.

*Hume, David, "Of National Character," in *Essays and Treatises,* Vol. I, London, Cadeil, 1770.

Humphrey, Edward Frank, *Nationalism and Religion in America, 1774-1789,* Boston, Chapman, 1924.

Hunter, Earle L., *A Sociological Analysis of Certain Types of Patriotism,* New York, Columbia U. Press, 1932.

Huntington, Ellsworth, *Civilization and Climate,* 3rd ed., New Haven, Yale U. Press, 1924.

——, *Mainsprings of Civilization,* New York, Wiley, 1945.

Huxley, Julian S., *Man Stands Alone,* New York, Harper, 1941.

Huxley, Julian S., and Haddon, A. C., *We Europeans,* Oxford, Clarendon Press, 1940.

*Hyslop, Beatrice F., *French Nationalism in 1789 according to the General Cahiers,* New York, Columbia U. Press, 1934.

Jameson, J. Franklin, "The Development of Modern European Historiography," *Atlantic Monthly,* Vol. LXVI, 1890.

*Jespersen, Otto, *Mankind, Nation and Individual from a Linguistic Point of View,* Oslo, H. Aschehoug, 1925.

*Johannet, René, *Le principe des nationalités,* Paris, Nouvelle Librarie Nationale, new ed., 1923.

Johnson, Samuel, *The Patriot,* London, 1774.

Johnson, Wallis F., *The National Flag,* Boston, Houghton Mifflin, 1930.

Joseph, Bernard, *Nationality, Its Nature and Problems,* New Haven, Yale U. Press, 1929.

Kammari, M. D., *The Development by J. V. Stalin of the Marxist-Leninist Theory of the National Question,* Moscow, Foreign Languages Publishing House, 1951.

*Kantorowicz, Ernst H., "Pro Patria Mori in Medieval Political Thought," *American Historical Review,* Vol. LVI, 1951, pp. 472-92.

Kayser, Elmer Louis, *The Grand Social Enterprise: A Study of Jeremy Bentham in His Relation to Liberal Nationalism,* New York, Columbia U. Press, 1932.

Keith, Sir Arthur, *Nationality and Race from an Anthropologist's Point of View,* London, Oxford U. Press, 1919.

——, *The Place of Prejudice in Modern Civilization,* New York, John Day, 1931.

Kirchheimer, O., "Remarques sur la théorie de la souveraineté nationale en Allemagne et en France," *Archives de philosophie du droit et de sociologie juridique,* 4 année, 1934, pp. 239-54.

Kirkland, Dorothy, "The Growth of the National Sentiment in France before the 15th Century," *History,* Vol. XXIII, 1938, pp. 12-24.

Klineberg, Otto, ed., *Characteristics of the American Negro,* New York, Harper, 1944.

——, *Race Differences,* New York, Harper, 1935.

——, "A Science of National Character," *Journal of Social Psychology,* Vol. XIX, 1944, pp. 147-62.

——, "The Scientific Study of National Stereotypes," *International Social Science Bulletin,* Vol. III, Autumn, 1951.

——, "A Study of the Psychological Differences between 'Racial' and National Groups in Europe," *Archives of Psychology,* Vol. XX, no. 132, New York, Columbia U. Press, 1931-32.

*——, *Tensions Affecting International Understanding: A Survey of Research,* New York, Social Science Research Council, 1950.

Kluckhohn, Clyde, *Mirror for Man: The Relation of Anthropology to Modern Life,* New York, McGraw-Hill, 1949.

Kohn, Hans, "Arndt and the Character of German Nationalism," *American Historical Review,* Vol. LIV, 1949, pp. 787-803.

Kohn, Hans, "The Eve of German Nationalism," *Journal of the History of Ideas,* Vol. XII, 1951, pp. 256-84.

——, "Father Jahn's Nationalism," *Review of Politics,* Vol. XI, 1949, pp. 419-32.

——, "The Genesis and Character of English Nationalism," *Journal of the History of Ideas,* Vol. I, 1940, pp. 69-94.

*——, *The Idea of Nationalism: A Study of Its Origins and Background,* New York, Macmillan, 1943.

——, *Nationalism in the Soviet Union,* New York, Columbia U. Press, 1933.

——, *Pan Slavism: Its History and Ideology,* Notre Dame, Ind., U. of Notre Dame Press, 1953.

——, "The Paradox of Fichte's Nationalism," *Journal of the History of Ideas,* Vol. X, 1949, pp. 319-43.

——, *Prophets and Peoples: Studies in Nineteenth Century Nationalism,* New York, Macmillan, 1946.

——, "Romanticism and the Rise of German Nationalism," *Review of Politics,* Vol. XII, 1950, pp. 443-72.

*Koht, Halvdan, "The Dawn of Nationalism in Europe," *American Historical Review,* Vol. LII, 1947, pp. 265-80.

——, "L'esprit national et l'idée de la souveraineté du peuple," *Bulletin of the International Committee of Historical Sciences,* Vol. II, pt. 2, 1929, pp. 217-24.

Krabbe, Hugo, *The Modern Idea of the State,* tr. by G. A. Sabine and W. J. Shepard, New York, Appleton, 1927.

Kracauer, Siegfried, "National Types as Hollywood Presents Them," *Public Opinion Quarterly,* Vol. XIII, 1949, pp. 53-72.

Krehbiel, Edward, *Nationalism, War and Society,* New York Macmillan, 1916.

——, "Nationalism," *Annual Report of the American Historical Association,* 1915, pp. 219-22.

*Kroeber, Alfred L., *Anthropology: Race, Language, Culture, Psychology, Prehistory,* new ed., revised, New York, Harcourt, Brace, 1948.

Kuhn, Joachim, and others, *Der Nationalismus in Leben der dritten Republik,* Berlin, Paetel, 1920.

*Langer, William L., *The Diplomacy of Imperialism, 1890-1902,* New York, Knopf, 1935, Vol. I.

Langsam, Walter Consuelo, *The Napoleonic Wars and German Nationalism in Austria,* New York, Columbia U. Press, 1930.

Lanyi, George Albert, "Oliver Cromwell and His Age, a Study in Nationalism," Ph.D. dissertation, Harvard, 1949, typescript.

Laprade, W. T., "Nationalism," *Annual Report of the American Historical Association,* 1915, pp. 223-29.

Laski, Harold J., *Nationalism and the Future of Civilization,* London, Watts, 1932.

Lasswell, Harold D., *World Politics and Personal Insecurity,* New York, Whittlesley House, McGraw-Hill, 1935.

Lauterpacht, H., *The Function of Law in the International Community*, Oxford, Clarendon Press, 1933.

Lavisse, Ernest, ed., *Histoire de France depuis les origines jusqu'à la révolution*, 9 vols. in 18, Paris, Hachette, 1903-10, particularly Vols. III-IX.

———, ed., *Histoire de France contemporaine depuis la Révolution jusqu'à la paix de 1919*, 10 vols., Paris, Hachette, 1920-22.

Le Bon, Gustave, *The Psychology of Peoples*, London, T. Fisher Unwin, 1899.

Le Fur, Louis, *Races, nationalités, états*, Paris, Alcan, 1922.

Lemberg, Eugene, *Geschichte des Nationalismus in Europa*, Stuttgart, Curt E. Schwab, 1950.

Lenient, Ch., *La poésie patriotique en France au moyen âge*, Paris, Hachette, 1891.

———, *La poésie patriotique en France, XVIᵉ et XVIIᵉ siècles*, Paris, Hachette, 1894.

———, *La poésie patriotique en France dans les temps modernes, XVIIIᵉ et XIXᵉ siécles*, Paris, Hachette, 1894.

Lenin, Vladimir, *Critical Remarks on the National Question*, Moscow, Foreign Languages Publishing House, 1951.

Léon, Paul L., "Études critiques: Rousseau et les fondements de l'état moderne," "L'évolution de l'idée de la souveraineté avant Rousseau," "La notion de la souveraineté dans la doctrine de Rousseau," in *Archives de philosophie du droit et de sociologie juridique*, 4, 7, 8 années, 1934, 1937, 1938, pp. 197-237, 152-85, 231-69.

Lieber, Francis, *Fragments of Political Science on Nationalism and Internationalism*, New York, Scribner, 1868.

Lindabury, R. V., *A Study of Patriotism in the Elizabethan Drama*, Princeton, Princeton U. Press, 1931.

Linton, Ralph, *The Cultural Background of Personality*, New York, Appleton-Century, 1945.

———, ed., *The Science of Man in the World Crisis*, New York, Columbia U. Press, 1945.

*———, *The Study of Man: An Introduction*, New York, Appleton-Century, 1936.

Lognon, Auguste, *Origines et formation de la nationalité française*, Paris, 1912.

Loomis, Louise R., "Nationality at the Council of Constance," *American Historical Review*, Vol. XLIV, 1939, pp. 508-27.

Lowie, R. H., *The Origin of the State*, New York, Harcourt, Brace, 1927.

Macartney, Carlile Almon, *National States and National Minorities*, London, Oxford U. Press, 1934.

Madariaga, Salvador, *Englishmen, Frenchmen, Spaniards: An Essay in Comparative Psychology*, London, Oxford U. Press, 1928.

Maehl, William, "The Triumph of Nationalism in the German Socialist Party on the Eve of the First World War," *Journal of Modern History*, Vol. XXIV, 1952, pp. 15-41.

Malye, J., "Leibniz, théoricien du nationalisme allemand," *L'Acropole*, Vol. I, 1920, pp. 442-58.

Mancini, Pasquale, *Della Nazionalità come fondamento de diritto delle Genti*, Turin, 1873, first pub. 1851, reprinted in *Saggi sulla nazionalità* as part of *Pensiero politico italiano*, no. 3, Sestante, 1944.

Manniche, Peter, *Denmark, A Social Laboratory*, New York, Oxford U. Press, 1939.

Marraro, Howard R., *Nationalism in Italian Education*, New York, Italian Digest and News Service, 1927.

Martin, Helen, "Nationalism in Children's Literature," *Library Quarterly*, Vol. VI, 1936, pp. 405-18.

Mathiez, Albert, *Les origines des cultes révolutionnaires (1789-1792)*, Paris, Société nouvelle de librairie et d'édition, 1904.

*——, "Pacifisme et nationalisme au dix-huitième siècle," *Annales historiques de la Révolution française*, Vol. XIII, 1936, pp. 1-17.

Maxse, L. J., "Germany on the brain, or the obsession of 'a crank,'" *Gleanings from the National Review, 1899-1914*, London, "The National Review" Office, 1915.

Maynard, John, *The Russian Peasant and Other Studies*, London, Gollancz, 1942.

Mazzini, Giuseppe, *The Duties of Man and Other Essays*, New York, Dutton, [1929], Everyman's ed.

Mazzini, *Mazzini's Letters*, tr. by Alice de Rosen Jervis, with an introd. by Bolton King, London, Dent, 1930.

McDougall, William, *The American Nation, Its Problems and Psychology*, London, Allen and Unwin, 1926.

——, *The Group Mind: A Sketch of the Principles of Collective Psychology with Some Attempt to Apply Them to the Interpretation of National Life and Character*, 2d ed., New York, G. P. Putnam, 1928.

Mead, Margaret, "The Study of National Character," in Daniel Lerner, et al., eds., *The Policy Sciences: Recent Developments in Scope and Method*, Stanford, Stanford U. Press, 1951, pp. 70-85.

——, ed., *Cooperation and Competition among Primitive Peoples*, New York, McGraw-Hill, 1937.

Megaro, Gaudens, *Vittorio Alfieri, Forerunner of Italian Nationalism*, New York, Columbia U. Press, 1930.

Meinecke, Friedrich, *The German Catastrophe*, tr. by Sidney B. Fay, Cambridge, Harvard U. Press, 1950.

——, *Die Idee der Staatsräson in der neueren Geschichte*, Berlin, Oldenbourg, 1924.

*——, *Weltbürgertum und Nationalstaat: Studien zur Genesis des deutschen Nationalstaates*, Munich, Oldenbourg, 1928.

Meltzer, H., "Hostility and Tolerance in Children's Nationality and Race Attitudes," *American Journal of Orthopsychiatry*, Vol. XI, 1941, pp. 662-76.

Merriam, Charles Edward, *The Making of Citizens,* Chicago, U. of Chicago Press, 1931.

Michelet, Jules, *Le peuple,* original ed., published with notes and variations by Lucien Refort, Paris, Didier, 1946.

Michels, Roberto, *Der Patriotismus: Prolegomena zu seiner soziologischen Analyse,* Munich, Duncker und Humbolt, 1929.

Mill, John S., *Considerations on Representative Government,* New York, Holt, 189?.

Miller, Ruth, "Nationalism in Elementary Schoolbooks used in the United States from 1776-1885," Ph.D. dissertation, Columbia, 1952, typescript.

Mitscherlich, Waldemar, *Der Nationalismus Westeuropas,* Leipzig, Hirschfeld, 1920. Issued again under title, *Nationalismus: Die Geschichte einer Idee,* 1929.

Morant, Geoffrey M., *The Races of Central Europe: A Footnote to History,* London, Allen and Unwin, 1939.

Morgan, Thomas Hunt, *Evolution and Genetics,* Princeton, Princeton U. Press, 1925.

Morganthau, Hans J., *Politics among Nations: The Struggle for Power and Peace,* New York, Knopf, 1949.

Mornet, Daniel, *Les origines intellectuelles de la Révolution française, 1715-1789,* 4th ed., Paris, Colin, 1947.

Muir, Ramsey, *Nationalism and Internationalism, the Culmination of Modern History,* London, Constable, 1917.

Namier, L. B., "Pathological Nationalisms," *In the Margin of History,* London, Macmillan, 1939, pp, 21-26.

Noether, Emiliana, *Seeds of Italian Nationalism, 1700-1815,* New York, Columbia U. Press, 1951.

Nordau, Max, *The Interpretation of History,* tr. by M. A. Hamilton, London, Rebman, 1910.

Novicow, J., *L'expansion de la nationalité française,* Paris, Colin, 1903.

Oakesmith, John, *Race and Nationality: An Inquiry into the Origin and Growth of Patriotism,* New York, Stokes, 1919.

Oncken, H., "Deutsche geistige Einflüsse in der europäischen Nationalbewegung des neunzehnten Jahrhunderts," in *Deutsche Vierteljahrschrift für Literaturwissenschaft und Geistesgeschichte,* Vol. VII, 1929, pp. 607-27. Same essay in *Bulletin of the International Committee of Historical Sciences,* October, 1929.

Page, Frederick, ed., *An Anthology of Patriotic Prose,* London, Oxford U. Press, 1915.

Pange, Comte de Jean, *Le roi très chrètien,* Paris, Fayard, 1949.

Palmer, Robert R., "The National Idea in France before the Revolution," *Journal of the History of Ideas,* Vol. I, 1940, pp. 95-111.

Partridge, Eric, "Offensive Nationality," in *Words, Words, Words!,* London, Methuen, 1938.

Peabody, Selim H., ed., *American Patriotism: Speeches, Letters, and Other Papers which Illustrate the Foundation, the Development,* the Preservation of the United States of America, New York, Alden, 1881.

Pearson, Charles A., *National Life and Character: A Forecast*, London, Macmillan, 1894.

Pearson, Karl, *National Life from the Standpoint of Science*, London, Adam and Charles Black, 1901.

Phillips, Sydney A., *Patriotic Societies of the United States and Their Lapel Insignia*, New York, Broadway Publishing Co., 1914.

Pierce, Bessie, *Citizen's Organizations and the Civic Training of Youth*, New York, Scribner, 1933.

——, *Civic Attitudes in American School Textbooks*, Chicago, U. of Chicago Press, 1930.

*Pinson, Koppel S., *A Bibliographical Introduction to Nationalism*, New York, Columbia U. Press, 1935.

*——, *Pietism as a Factor in the Rise of German Nationalism*, New York, Columbia U. Press, 1934.

Pollard, A. F., "Nationality and Nationalism," *Factors in American History*, New York, Macmillan, 1925.

——, "Nationality," *Factors in Modern History*, London, Constable, 1926.

Potter, David, *Economic Abundance and the American Character*, Chicago, U. of Chicago Press, 1954.

Powers, Rev. George C., *Nationalism at the Council of Constance*, (*1414-1418*), Washington, Catholic U. of America Press, 1927.

Pundt, Alfred George, *Arndt and the Nationalist Awakening in Germany*, New York, Columbia U. Press, 1935.

Radin, Paul, *The Racial Myth*, New York, Whittlesley House, 1934.

Read, Conyers, *The Tudors*, New York, Holt, 1936.

Redslob, Robert, *Le principe des nationalités; les origines, les fondements psychologiques, les forces adverses, les solutions possibles*, Paris, Sirey, 1930.

Reisner, Edward H., *Nationalism and Education since 1789: A Social and Political History of Modern Education*, New York, Macmillan, 1922.

*Renan, Ernest, "Qu'est-ce qu'une nation," in *Discours et conférences*, pp. 277-310, 2nd ed., Paris, Calmann-Levy, 1887.

Richardson, Oliver, *The National Movement in the Reign of Henry III and Its Culmination in the Barons' War*, New York, Macmillan, 1897.

Rigg, Melvin G., *Theories of the Obligations of Citizens to the State*, Philadelphia, U. of Pennsylvania Press, 1921.

Roback, A. A., *A Dictionary of International Slurs (Ethnophaulisms): With a Supplementary Essay on Aspects of Ethnic Prejudice*, Cambridge, Mass., Sci-Art Publishers, 1944.

Robinson, James Harvey, "What is National Spirit," *Century Magazine*, Vol. XCIII, 1916, pp. 57-64.

Romier, Lucien, *Nation et civilisation*, Paris, S. Kra., 1926.

Rose, Arnold, ed., *Studies in the Reduction of Prejudice*, 2nd ed., Chicago, American Council on Race Relations, 1948.

Rose, J. Holland, *Nationality in Modern History*, New York, Macmillan, 1916.

Roucek, J. S., ed., "Nationalistic Ideology and Goals," *Annals American Academy of Political and Social Science*, Vol. CCXXXII, 1944, fourteen articles, pp. 25-115.

Rousseau, J. J., *Oeuvres complètes de J. J. Rousseau avec des éclaircissements et des notes historiques*, 2nd ed., Paris, Baudoin Frères, 1826. Contains the *Lettre sur les spectacles* (Vol. II) and the writings on Poland and Corsica (Vol. VI).

*Royal Institute of International Affairs, *Nationalism: A Report by a Study Group of Members of the Royal Institute of International Affairs*, London, Oxford U. Press, 1939.

Ruggiero, Guido de, *The History of European Liberalism*, tr. by R. G. Collingwood, London, Oxford U. Press, 1927.

Rundle, Stanley, *Language as a Social and Economic Factor in Europe*, London, Faber and Faber, 1946.

Ruyssen, Theodore, *The Principle of Nationality*, tr. by John Mez, New York, American Association for International Conciliation, 1916-17.

Sabine, George, "State," *Encyclopedia of Social Sciences*, Vol. XIV, New York, Macmillan, 1933.

Sagnac, Phillipe, *La fin de l'ancien régime et la Révolution américaine (1763-1789)*, Paris, Presses universitaires, 1947 (Halphen and Sagnac, eds., *Peuples et civilisations*, Vol. XII).

——, *La formation de la société française moderne*, 2 vols., Paris, Presses universitaires, 1945-46.

Sareth, E. N., "Race and Nationalism in American Historiography, the Late Nineteenth Century," *Political Science Quarterly*, Vol. LIV, 1939, pp. 421-41.

Salomon, ed., *Nation und Nationalität: Jahrbuch für Soziologie*, Karlsruhe, Erster Ergänzungsband, 1927, includes Friedrich Hertz, "Wesen und Werden der Nation," Sebald Steinmetz, "Die Nationalität und ihr Wille," Max Boehm, "Die Nationalitätenfrage," Gaston Roffenstein, "Zur Soziologie des Nationalismus," Elemer Karman, "Psychologie des Internationalismus."

Savelle, Max, *Seeds of Liberty*, New York, Knopf, 1948.

Schaffner, Bertram, *Fatherland: a Study of Authoritarianism in the German Family*, New York, Columbia U. Press, 1948.

Schnee, Heinrich, *Nationalismus und Imperialismus*, Berlin, Hobbing, 1928.

Schneider, H. W., and Clough, S. B., *Making Fascists*, Chicago, U. of Chicago Press, 1929.

Schuman, Frederick, *The Commonwealth of Man: An Inquiry into Power Politics and World Government*, New York, Knopf, 1952.

——, *International Politics*, 4th ed., New York, McGraw-Hill, 1948.

Schwarzenberger, Georg, *Power Politics: An Introduction to the Study of International Relations and Post-war Planning,* London, Cope, 1941.

Scott, Jonathan, *Patriots in the Making: What Americans Can Learn from France and Germany,* New York, Appleton, 1916.

Seignobos, Charles, *A History of the French People,* tr. by Catherine Alison Phillips, London, Cope, 1933.

Seton-Watson, R. W., *The Historian as a Political Force in Central Europe,* London, School of Slavonic Studies, U. of London, 1922.

——, *The Rise of Nationality in the Balkans,* London, Constable, 1917.

Shafer, Boyd C., "The American Heritage of Hope," *Mississippi Valley Historical Review,* Vol. XXXVII, 1950, pp. 427-50.

——, "Bourgeois Nationalism on the Eve of the Revolution," *Journal of Modern History,* Vol. X, 1938, pp. 31-50.

——, "When Patriotism Became Popular," *Historian,* Vol. V, 1943, pp. 77-96.

Siegfried, André, *America Comes of Age: A French Analysis,* tr. by H. and D. Hemming, New York, Harcourt, Brace, 1927.

——, *France: A Study in Nationality,* New Haven, Yale U. Press, 1930.

Simon, Walter, "Variations in Nationalism during the Great Reform Period in Prussia," *American Historical Review,* Vol. LIX, 1954, pp. 305-21.

Snyder, Louis L., *From Bismarck to Hitler: The Background of Modern German Nationalism,* Williamsport, Pa., Bayard Press, 1935.

——, *German Nationalism: The Tragedy of a People. Extremism Contra Liberalism in Modern German History,* Harrisburg, Pa., Stackpole, 1952.

——, *The Meaning of Nationalism,* New Brunswick, Rutgers U. Press, 1954.

——, *Race, a History of Modern Ethnic Theories,* New York, Longmans, Green, 1939.

Sorel, Albert, *L'Europe et la Révolution française,* 8 vols., Paris, Plon, 1946.

Stagner, Ross, "Nationalism," in P. L. Harriman, ed., *Encyclopedia of Psychology,* New York, Philosophical Library, 1946, pp. 404-07.

——, and Osgood, C. E., "Impact of War on a Nationalistic Frame of Reference: I. Changes in General Approval and Qualitative Patterning of Certain Stereotypes," *Journal of Social Psychology,* Vol. XXIV, 1946, pp. 187-215.

Staley, Eugene, *War and the Private Investor: A Study in the Relations of International Politics and International Private Investment,* New York, Doubleday, Doran, 1935.

* Stalin, Joseph, *Marxism and the National and Colonial Question: A Collection of Articles and Speeches,* New York, International Publishers, n.d.

Stannard, Harold, *What Is a Nation?*, London, Royal Institute of International Affairs, 1945.

Starr, Mark, *Lies and Hate in Education*, London, Leonard and Virginia Woolf, 1929.

Seeley, Sir John Robert, *The Expansion of England*, Boston, Little, Brown, 1905.

Steinacker, Harold, "Volk, Staat, Heimat und ihr Verhaeltnis bei den romanisch—germanischen Voelkern," *Bulletin of the International Committee of Historical Sciences*, Vol. II, pt. 2, October, 1929.

Stephens, H. Morse, "Modern Historians and Their Influence on Small Nationalities," *Contemporary Review*, 1887, pp. 107-21.

———, "Nationality and History," *American Historical Review*, Vol. XXI, 1916, pp. 225-36.

Stevens, Ruth, and Stevens, David, eds., *American Patriotic Prose and Verse*, Chicago, McClurg, 1918.

Stewart, H. F., and Desjardins, Paul, eds., *French Patriotism in the Nineteenth Century (1814-1833)*, Cambridge, Cambridge U. Press, 1923.

Stocks, J. L., *Patriotism and the Super-State*, London, Swarthmore Press, 1920.

Stofflet, E. H., "A Study of National and Cultural Differences in Criminal Tendency," *Archives of Psychology*, No. 185, 1935.

Stratton, George M., *International Delusions*, London, Allen and Unwin, 1935.

*Strayer, Joseph, "The Laicization of French and English Society in the Thirteenth Century," *Speculum*, Vol. XV, 1940, pp. 76-86.

Straus, Hannah, *The Attitude of the Congress of Vienna toward Nationalism in Germany, Italy and Poland*, New York, Columbia U. Press, 1949.

*Sturzo, Don Luigi, *Nationalism and Internationalism*, New York, Roy, 1946.

Sulzbach, Walter, *National Consciousness*, Washington, American Council on Public Affairs, 1943.

Tagore, Sir Rabindranath, *Nationalism*, New York, Macmillan, 1917.

Tansill, Charles C., *Nationalism: Historical Prelude*, Washington, a separate from *International Law and Relations*, Vol. IV, 1935.

Taylor, Thomas G., *Environment and Nation*, Chicago, U. of Chicago Press, 1936.

Tharaud, Jerome and Jean, *La vie et la mort de Déroulède*, Paris, Émile-Paul, 1914.

Thompson, James Westfall, with collaboration of Bernard J. Holm, *A History of Historical Writing*, 2 vols., New York, Macmillan, 1942.

Tims, R. W., *Germanizing the Prussian Poles: The H-K-T Society of the Eastern Marches, 1894-1914*, New York, Columbia U. Press, 1941.

Tolstoi, *The Complete Works of Lyof N. Tolstoi*, New York, Crowell ed., 1898-1899, Vol. XXI contains the essay on "Patriotism and Christianity."

Tourville, Henri de, *The Growth of Modern Nations*, tr. by M. G. Loch, New York, Longmans, Green, 1907.

Treitschke, Henrich G. von, *Politics*, tr. by Blanche Dugdale and Torben de Bille, London, Constable, 1916.

Trevelyan, George M., *History of England*, London, Longmans, Green, 1926.

UNESCO, *The Race Concept, Results of an Inquiry*, Paris, 1952, one of a series by Morant, Klineberg, and others.

Van Deusen, Glyndon G., *Sieyès, His Life and His Nationalism*, New York, Columbia U. Press, 1932.

Vanel, Marguerite, *Histoire de la nationalité française d'origine; évolution historique de français d'origine du XVIᵉ siècle au Code Civil*, Paris, Ancienne Imprimerie de la Cour d'Appel, 1945.

Van Gennep, Arnold, *Traité comparatif des nationalités*, Vol. I, Paris, Payot, 1922.

Van Tyne, C. H., *The War of Independence: American Phase*, Boston, Houghton Mifflin, 1929.

Vaussard, Maurice, *Enquête sur le nationalisme*, Paris, Editions Spes, 1924.

*Veblen, Thorstein, *An Inquiry into the Nature of Peace and the Terms of Its Perpetuation*, New York, Huebsch, 1919.

Virtanen, Reino, "Nietzsche and the Action Française," *Journal of Modern History*, Vol. XI, 1950, pp. 191-214.

Voltaire, "Patrie," in *Dictionnaire philosophique, Oeuvres complètes*, Vol. XLII, Paris, La Société Littéraire-Typographique, 1785.

Vossler, Otto, *Der Nationalgedanke von Rousseau bis Ranke*, Munich, Oldenbourg, 1937.

Waldstein, Charles, *Patriotism, National and International: An Essay*, New York, Longmans, Green, 1917.

Walek-Czernecki, M. T., "Le rôle de la nationalité dans l'histoire de l'Antiquité," *Bulletin of the International Committee of Historical Sciences*, Vol. II, pt. 2, 1929, pp. 303-20.

Walworth, Arthur, *School Histories at War*, Cambridge, Harvard U. Press, 1938.

Ward, A. W.; Prothero, G. W.; and Leathes, Stanley, eds., *Cambridge Modern History*, London, Macmillan, 1902-12, esp. Vol. VII, *The Growth of Nationalities*.

Warfel, Harry R., *Noah Webster, Schoolmaster to America*, New York, Macmillan, 1936.

Wecter, Dixon, *The Hero in America. A Chronicle of Hero-Worship*, New York, Scribner, 1941.

*Weill, Georges J., *L'Europe du XIXᵉ siècle et l'idée de nationalité*, Paris, Albin Michel, 1938.

———, *L'éveil des nationalités et le mouvement libéral (1815-1848)*, Paris, Presses universitaires, 1930 (Halphen and Sagnac, eds., *Peuples et civilisations*, Vol. XV).

Weill, Georges J., *Race et nation,* Paris, Albin Michel, 1939.

*Weinberg, Albert K., *Manifest Destiny: A Study of Nationalist Expansionism in American History,* Baltimore, Johns Hopkins Press, 1935.

Weinstein, Harold, *Jean Jaurès: A Study of Patriotism in the French Socialist Movement,* New York, Columbia U. Press, 1936.

Wertheimer, Mildred S., *The Pan-German League, 1890-1914,* New York, Columbia U. Press, 1924.

White, Leonard, *The Federalists: A Study in Administrative History,* New York, Macmillan, 1948.

Whittlesey, Derwent S., *Environmental Foundations of European History,* New York, Appleton-Century-Crofts, 1949.

Wingfield-Stratford, Esmé, *The Foundations of British Patriotism,* London, Routledge and Sons, 1939.

——, *The History of English Patriotism,* London, Lane, 1913.

Winslow, E. M., *The Pattern of Imperialism: A Study in the Theories of Power,* New York, Columbia U. Press, 1948.

Wirth, Louis, "Types of Nationalism," *American Journal of Sociology,* Vol. XLI, 1936, pp. 723-37.

Wolf, John, *The Emergence of the Great Powers, 1685-1715,* New York, Harper, 1951.

Wuorinen, John H., *Nationalism in Modern Finland,* New York, Columbia U. Press, 1931.

Zangwill, Israel, *The Principle of Nationalities,* New York, Macmillan, 1917.

*Zernatto, Guido, "Nation: The History of a Word," *Review of Politics,* Vol. VI, 1944, pp. 351-66.

Ziegler, Heinz O., *Die Moderne Nation: Ein Beitrag zur politischen Soziologie,* Tübingen, Mohr (Paul Siebeck), 1931.

Ziemer, Gregor, *Education for Death: The Making of a Nazi,* New York, Oxford, 1941.

Zimmern, Alfred, *Nationality and Government and Other War-Time Essays,* London, Chatto and Windus, 1918.

*Znaniecki, Florjan, *Modern Nationalities: A Sociological Study,* Urbana, U. of Illinois Press, 1952.

INDEX

Chateaubriand, François René de, 158
Chaucer, Geoffrey, 78
Chenier, Marie-Joseph, 142
Childe, V. Gordon, 233
Childhood training, 40, 182
"Chosen people," 20, 84
Church, 82 ff., 120
Citizen, 111, 113 ff., 138, 197
Civil War (U. S.), 163
Clark, G. N., 73
Clay, Henry, 170
Clemenceau, Georges, 183
Clergy, 71, 103-04, 114, 141, 158
Climate, 29-32, 220
Clutton-Brock, Arthur, 180
Colardeau, Charles Pierre, 108
Comenius, 221
Commager, Henry Steele, 184
Common people, 86-87, 107, 159, 171, 173-74, 197
Communications, 10, 168 ff.
Communism. *See* Economic determinism; Marxism
Cosmopolitanism, 98, 132, 227, 235
Courts, 69, 72, 145
Coyer, Abbé, 108, 110, 146
Cromwell, Oliver, 84
Culture, 40 ff., 97, 166, 212
Customs Union. *See* Zollverein
Czechoslovakia, 164, 176, 205

Dante Alighieri, 90
Darwin, Charles, 35
Delaisi, Francis, 33, 205
Democracy, 109, 115, 163, 179
Denmark, 180
Deschamps, Eustache, 90
Dictatorship, 198, 204
Diderot, Denis, 111
Disraeli, Benjamin, 9
Divine inspiration, 18, 19
Documents inédits sur l'histoire de France, 187
Dryden, John, 100

Economic determinism, 41, 43, 168
Economic nationalism, 74 ff., 168 ff.
Education, 74, 121 ff., 135, 183 ff.
Edward I, 70
Edward III, 70, 74
Elizabethan Society of Antiquaries, 94

English nationalism. *See* British nationalism
Enlightenment, 104
Estienne, Henri, 79
Étatism, 68, 129

Family, 50, 111, 182-83
Fear, 136, 202
Federalism, 162
Federalist papers, 118
Fénelon, Bishop, 109, 113
Ferry, Jules, 184
Feudalism, 62, 65, 73, 88
Fichte, Johann Gottlieb, 19, 23, 34, 84, 123, 138, 141, 142
Fielding, Henry, 108
Fiske, John, 35
Folklore, 128, 189
Food, 40, 191
Foreigners, dislike of, 88
Frank, Lawrence K., 236
Frankfurt Assembly, 162
Frederick II, 74
Frederick William I, 74
Frederick William I, Elector, 73
French National Convention, 114, 120, 126
French nationalism, 63 ff., 94, 106, 112, 121 ff., 155-56, 210
Freneau, Philip, 108
Frustration, 136, 141, 175-77

Gaguin, Robert, 89
Gallicanism, 72-73, 85
Genes, 37-38, 225
Geography, 30 ff., 220
Germany, 137 ff., 158, 162-63, 184-86, 205, 210
Gibbons, Herbert Adams, 20
Gneisenau, August von, 138
Gobineau, Count Joseph Arthur de, 35, 229
Goldsmith, Oliver, 231
Görres, Joseph von, 23, 34
Government employment, 200
Grant, Madison, 223
Greece, 140, 161, 176
Green, J. R., 55
Green, T. H., 51
Gregariousness, 46, 50, 52, 220
Grégoire, Henri, 123, 124
Grimm, Melchior von, 110
Grotius, Hugo, 73